DNA
Did Not Anticipate

How one man's search for his roots changed his past, future, and definition of family

J Steven Osborne

Becky Brower Osborne

Black Sheep Library, llc

Ordering Information
Quantity sales: Special discounts are available on quantity purchases by corporations, associations, and others. For details, contact the publisher at the address below.
Hello@BlackSheepLibrary.com

Publisher's Cataloging-in-Publication Data
J Steven Osborne and Becky Brower Osborne
DNA - Did Not Anticipate: How One Man's Search for his Roots Changed His Past, Future, and Definition of Family

Cover design by Kara Rubinstein Deyerin.
Photographs courtesy of the authors.
Photograph of authors: @Kelly Production Group.

ISBN 978-0-9828336-9-8 (Hardback)
ISBN 978-0-9828336-7-4 (Paperback)
ISBN 978-0-9828336-8-1 (eBook)

Copyright © 2025
Black Sheep Library, LLC
PO Box 86
Maple Valley, WA 98038
USA

PRAISE FOR DNA - DID NOT ANTICIPATE

"DNA - Did Not Anticipate tells the unflinching, no-holds-barred tale of the roller coaster journey that Steve went on after a DNA test revealed that his biological father was not the man whose name was on his birth certificate. **It's an unputdownable, compulsively readable masterpiece.**

This is a brutally honest, emotional, and raw book. It's a riveting and important book: **the best of its genre that I've read.** As a fellow NPE/DNA Orphan it resonated with me in a 'me too' way again and again. I can't recommend it highly enough." - **Jo Lloyd, Somerset, UK**

"DNA – Did Not Anticipate takes you on a wild ride as the author discovers the surprise his DNA test reveals and how he ultimately comes to terms with the reality that his beloved father is not his biological father. Osborne's candor and humor make situations that are truly tragic, interesting, and palatable for the reader.

I felt equal parts sympathy, awe, admiration and envy (yes, envy!) for Steve. He has overcome much and found his family - if not of origin, then of choosing and his making.

I read it practically in one sitting - eager to learn how it all unfolded. It's a riveting story of acceptance, growth, messy relationships, and love. The reader enjoys getting to know the writer's personality, humor, strengths and weaknesses along the way. **Long after you finish, it will make you ponder the power of genetics, fate, love and what really makes a family.**" - Helen Fox

"This is a powerful, humorous, and thought-provoking memoir that captures the unexpected consequences of modern genetic testing. **It is an essential read for those interested in genealogy, DNA surprises, and the complex dynamics of family identity.** The book stands as both a cautionary tale and an inspiring journey of self-discovery. Highly recommended for readers who enjoy personal stories of resilience, humor, and truth-seeking."

- **Laura Olmsted, Executive Director & Founder, *DNAngels***

"DNA - Did Not Anticipate takes readers on an emotional journey through the shocking discovery of Steve's misattributed parentage. **Blending moments of gut-wrenching grief with laugh-out-loud observations, Osborne's storytelling makes this an unputdownable read.** His unique voice captures the raw, universal challenges of identity, belonging, and the redefinition of family after a DNA surprise.

Osborne's journey of learning he is a "DNA orphan" is both heartbreaking and eye-opening, shedding light on the profound loss of genetic continuity and the struggle to reconcile a new identity. **What sets this book apart is the inclusion of his wife Becky's perspective, offering a rare and invaluable look into the role of a significant other in navigating such a life-altering discovery.** Together, they weave his personal narrative with larger themes of self-discovery and resilience, making DNA - Did Not Anticipate relatable to anyone who has ever questioned their roots.

This memoir reminds us that family is not just about DNA, but about the people who stand with us—no matter when or how they come into our lives."

- Kara Rubinstein Deyerin, CEO & Founder, *Right to Know*

"Reading this memoir, I was immediately struck by the authenticity of the voice. This isn't a ghost or paperback writer or a workshopped vanity project. This is the author's authentic voice with all the bravado, wit, heart, bitterness, and armored anxiety you'd experience if you met him in person. This does not make the narrative any less jarring - it makes the puzzling maze intimate and significantly personal to the final page.

Neither is this book a simple monologue - the repeated motifs of gravity, particles, transport, and cultural references both frame and give it depth. **Steve and Becky use science, faith, optimism, frustrated aspirations and, in the end, an unlikely quiet confidence to reconcile how he came to be with who he is.** In the process they teach us that the definition of family can be fragile, often painful, but ultimately it is a choice that gives us voice."

- Eric Hansen, City Manager, *City of Mason, OH*

"DNA: Did Not Anticipate is obviously a work meant to process a deep emotional wound. It's at times raw and other times a bit self-conscious. But this is largely because it's genuine and authentic, and **written by a man who's had his entire life flipped on its edge, and then found a way to flip it back upright.** I have no doubt that others who've experienced similar upheavals in their lives would see themselves in this story and perhaps find hope that there's a road to the other side."

- **Carolyn Stoll, Director of Online Instruction, *University of Cincinnati***

"**I couldn't put this book down!** Shocking and astonishing life-changing events! I could practically hear the author telling his story to me, the reader, as if I was his best friend. Steve shares the story with so much detail that it pulls you right in to feel like you were there with him the entire time. I was able to imagine (and experience) the full range of emotions he must have felt—betrayal, anger, frustration, confusion, loneliness, relief, closure, happiness, and love. His perseverance and his unconditional love for his dads and family are a true testament of love!

I found myself tearing up or smiling in nearly every chapter. Steve's tenacity in overcoming the challenges life threw at him is truly remarkable."

- **Robin Throckmorton, Author, Entrepreneur, HR Thought Leader**

Author J Steven Osborne and I could be the same person. We're obviously not. My misattributed story is very different. But we share the same entrepreneurial spirit and irreverence for rules and regulations. We have also experienced the emotional upheaval and grief from identity disruption generated by the late discovery that our dads were not our biological dads. Eventually, we both found a deeper definition of family (including that our dads were still our dads).

Steve weaves a compelling story about navigating his trauma to come out feeling whole. First, he acknowledges the trauma. You can't fix what you can't see. So, he seeks all the information he can gather. And he gets help where he can. (His wife and co-author, Becky, is a gift.) Then he embraces forgiveness . . . for himself, his mother, and others in his life. And finally, he shares his story with us, which is healing in itself.

This book will help others heal from similar trauma—or better understand the impact of misattributed trauma felt by others.

- **Peter J. Boni, Author of *Uprooted: Family Trauma, Unknown Origins, and the Secretive History of Artificial Insemination***

To my four fathers, Jack Osborne, Jerry Condo,
Peter Holmes, and Fred Brower, whose
contributions made me the man I am today.
To my wife Becky, and our daughters
Sammie and Jackie, whose love, grace, and kindness
make me strive to be a better man tomorrow.

Steve

To the Brower and Hugh clans, I am grateful
to know that I unequivocally belong to you.
And to our daughters who maintained a rock solid
foundation for their parents when each new development
set off another aftershock.
We are so fortunate to have you as our own.

Becky

CONTENTS

PART FOUR
THE ROAD TO REDEMPTION

PART FIVE
MOVING FORWARD

DNA - Did Not Anticipate

The Forces Which Affect Us

Hell isn't merely paved with good intentions; it's walled and roofed with them. Yes, and furnished too.
— Aldous Huxley

Life and Fate are strangely intertwined partners, much like matter and gravity. Matter is the physical—easy to touch, feel, see. All things are made of matter: planets, stars, you, and me. Gravity, on the other hand, is an unseen force drawing all things closer. Sometimes, this attraction is imperceptible, but as the distance between matter decreases, gravity's pull strengthens. The speed of objects moving toward one another increases. Eventually, matter merges with matter. Its mass increases until it becomes something significant. Ultimately it reaches critical mass and sets off a reaction known as nuclear fusion, the process that fires our sun.

Life's events can seem completely unrelated, random, and disconnected. Moments, words, glances, and events—all appear scattered. Some actions, no matter how random, insignificant, or inane, can cascade into disaster, like pulling at a loose thread on a sweater only to watch the whole thing unravel. Or carefully selecting an item from a shelf only to have the adjacent items fall, beginning a chain reaction of uncontrollable chaos.

Yet, Fate acts as an unseen force drawing these particles of life closer to one another. Gradually, their relevance grows, and they begin to coalesce. They continue until they collide, compressing themselves into a dense and significant collection. When this happens, the once hidden image becomes clear, and everything changes in that one instant.

My innocent, almost frivolous efforts to locate my Native American heritage would unwittingly lead me down a path into my past, my family's collective past, and change my history, or at least our history as it had been told to us. It would bring to light events that would not only change what we understood about who we were, but it would alter our perception of the most foundational members of our family, specifically, our parents. For me personally, it would not only change our family, but it would also change me. It would change me at my core. In the end, it would trigger an epiphany within me that would force me to evaluate how the word 'family' is ultimately defined.

This is the story of a DNA Orphan.

Such is my life.

Such is *Fate*.

PART ONE
Family as We Know It

CHAPTER 1

Shootout at the Not-So-O.K. Corral

People like to say that the conflict is between good and evil. The real conflict is between truth and lies.
— Don Miguel Ruiz

I knew there was a high likelihood that the impending interaction with my mother wasn't going to end well. Primarily because I didn't want it to. If I had learned anything throughout my years as a professional negotiator, it would be how to turn almost any situation into an emotional and intellectual briar patch for my adversaries. I was prepared to do so in this instance if I experienced an unreasonable level of resistance from her. I must admit I was anxious. Partly because I was loaded for bear and ready for a fight. Partly because I was going to confront my mother, who even at eighty-plus years old, was no pushover. And partly because I had no idea where the next thirty minutes might take me.

Would this be a moment of reconciliation for a decades-long, damaged mother-son relationship? Would I get the answers I was seeking? The answers I felt I deserved? Or would it be a Waterloo-esque shit show where we leave more damaged than before the meeting began?

With my well-documented "level of intensity," as some would call it, this whole thing could go south in a heartbeat. It was also not beyond my mother to call the police and spin a tale of physical abuse or other heinous and arrestable offense. I'd witnessed her Oscar-worthy performances multiple times in the past. I had seen her do it to my dad.

It was partly why I had such a negative opinion of her. Her mistreatment of my dad was one of the reasons our relationship had deteriorated over the years. She was truly the devil I knew.

I knew I would likely need some protection. I opened an audio recording app on my phone to capture the ensuing conversation "for posterity"—and as potential evidence for the defense. I placed my phone upside down in the pocket of my sport coat, as one might place a pocket square, with the bottom of the phone and its microphone extending innocuously out of my jacket. Not quite James Bond, but it would get the job done. I knew I might be too emotionally charged to remember everything that was said, therefore, a digital recording would help. Surely, knowing I was recording the event would be enough to keep my own emotions and words in check, right?

Yeah, I know, no one else is buying into it either.

Walking through the door of my childhood home was akin to crossing the river Styx. I held no fond memories of it. My home, from the age of nine until I left at seventeen, doubled as a temporary foster home to hundreds of troubled youths. It was far from a welcoming place and it held no positive energy for me.

I entered the family room where I found my mother, Barb, and my sister, Carrie, awaiting my arrival. Carrie was the only one of Barb's five children who had any consistent contact with her at this point. I was the first to separate myself from her sphere of influence, with my other three siblings somewhere between extremely reluctant to visit her and full-on estrangement. Barb and I hadn't had any meaningful communication in almost two decades. But now, I was back. Yeah, this couldn't be good.

"Hello," I said stoically. Barb barely turned her head to acknowledge me. Carrie looked at me and responded with a similar quasi-non-salutation. "Carrie, I'd like to speak to your mother privately." I referred to her as 'her mother' as she had lost the right to be called my mother a long time ago.

I was sure my tone was more than direct enough for her to understand the time had come for her to exit the room.

"I'd like to stay," was her monotone and unemotional response.

Either I wasn't clear in my intent, or she wasn't that bright. I'm going to bet on the latter.

"I'd like for you to leave. It's a private matter. This doesn't involve you." My patience with her was razor thin at this point. A wise person would get up and leave before my blood pressure rose another milligram, but I had to remember who I was talking to.

"I don't know why I can't stay," she said, testing me. That was unwise.

Both my volume and tone jumped to a 'let's make everyone in the room uncomfortable' level. "I said this is a private conversation. Do you not understand the word 'private'? Get out." If words could have a physical edge, mine would have stuck in the wall behind her head like a knife. They held an intentionally brutal, hostile resonance.

She reluctantly got up and left. It was obvious she was hovering just around the corner to listen to everything that might be said. Maybe she stayed close to try to keep her mom safe even though her mother would never be in any physical danger from me. Maybe she was just being as nosy as ever. I sat down on the edge of the couch opposite my mother, a small coffee table between us.

"Why are you here?" Barb asked calmly and in an almost detached manner. She was never one to show any weakness in any situation that might resemble a negotiation or conflict. She tried to mask her trepidation, but even our prolonged separation wasn't enough to dull my ability to sense it behind her blind. She was fearful of the pending interaction whatever it might be. It was easy for me to detect. My first clue was my sister's reluctance to leave the room. It was obvious Carrie's presence and resistance to leave were discussed before my arrival. Barb wanted a witness should things go sideways. Ironically, with their notorious and well-documented ability to alter the truth to suit their desired narrative, Carrie's actual presence was unnecessary. She and her mother were going to make up whatever they wanted anyway. Again, this was one of the primary reasons I was recording everything.

"As I said on the phone," I opened my portfolio and reached for the pictures within, "I have something I think belongs to you." I slid a picture across the table of a man who looked strikingly similar to me when I was in my late twenties.

My opening salvo was, "You got anything you want to tell me?" I asked the question sharply to communicate the fact that I knew who was in the photo. I was fighting back the anger within me. At the same time, it crushed me knowing what that picture meant. We had arrived at the moment of truth, the moment where she might possibly tell me the truth, the moment when we might be able to have something that resembles a relationship again.

She picked up the picture and scanned it for less than four seconds. Her eyes moved between my face and the photo quickly, multiple times. Then she dropped the photo on the coffee table as if it were flaming pornography. Her next words were said in rapid fire succession.

"I don't know who that person is. Who is that supposed to be, your father?" she said dismissively.

Wow! She certainly went there quickly. I thought we might have a gentle prelude of semi-truths and subtle evasiveness before the full-on lying began.

"Is that my father?" I fired back in an incredulous tone. "Really? Of all the questions you could possibly ask about that picture, you ask, 'Is that my father?' Why would you ask that question? That's a stupid question. Of course that's not my father. My father is Jack Osborne, right, Barb? I mean, isn't he?" The tone of my mock inquiry was hateful and slathered in heavy sarcasm. Yeah, I was right, this wasn't going to go well.

* * *

THE STORIES WE WERE TOLD

To make sense of my DNA Orphan story, I suppose I should take us back to the genesis—the beginning, if you will. Not of our family, but of a story that our mother used to tell her children. An innocent, entertaining story that my siblings and I heard over and over. We believed it, we embraced it—and why shouldn't we? It was told to us by the most trustworthy person in our life, a loving Pentecostal woman of God, whose words were law to us. Throughout the years, the story she told would set into motion a series of random thoughts, casual comments, insignificant actions, and seemingly inconsequential decisions that in the end would change me, us, and our family's relationships forever.

When we were young, our mother, Barbara Condo, would tell me and my four siblings a story. What you'll discover, dear reader, is these siblings were only four of the fourteen total siblings I had in some way, shape, or form. More on that later. The story my mother would tell us was a fun story, an exciting story. It was a story that centered around the fact that we were descendants of two Native American tribes, Blackfoot and Cherokee. Not only were we genetically part Native American, but we descended from the tribal chieftain or princess.

For a seven-year-old like me, this was quite an intoxicating story. I'm not sure that any of the five of us ever really believed the chieftain/princess part—it seemed a bit too over the top to me. But the general concept of being part Native American was easy to accept and ultimately internalize. It became part of who we were. After all, most of my siblings have a markedly dark complexion. Most of us have very dark, if not black, hair. In fact, my oldest sister looked like she could be Cher's sister, and we believed that Cher was part Native American. We know now she's not; she's Armenian.

Likely the most convincing aspect was that my dad, Jack Osborne, looked very Native American. He had a dark complexion with a strong reddish tinge. His face was broad, and he boasted a full head of hair until the day of his death. Physically, he made an almost undeniable case for me having a Native American genetic component. My mother also had the physical characteristics of someone who was Native American, with dark skin and long black hair. In fact, whenever the occasion presented itself, like Halloween, Barb would dress up as an 'Indian' with braided and beaded hair.

I emphasize the "genetic" element of being Native American because we certainly weren't culturally Native American. Any Native American culture I had experienced was what Hollywood had put on my TV or movie screen (and we all know how accurate that was).

No, we were lower-middle class, white suburban Americans. We were a mix of God-knows-what European genetic material. And in the 1960s, '70s, and '80s, it really was "God-knows-what," as home DNA test kits weren't available. There was no easily available DNA analysis or way to truly discern biological lineage other than what we were told and perhaps what we could find in limited public records.

So, as it was, my ragtag collection of siblings and I strode through life without giving much thought to our tribal origins, other than simply believing that we had a good amount of it. Whenever anyone posed the question, "What is your background?" I would answer, "German and English with some Native American mixed in there somewhere." I was not sure how much was Native American. I didn't know if I was a quarter, an eighth, a sixteenth, or what. I just knew we had some . . . because my mom told us so.

The story stuck with us so well and for so long that after a while, it became a part of who we were. It became how others often viewed us, so much so that my in-laws gave me the nickname "Chief." I could never tell if that was an acknowledgment or a joke. I'm guessing it was a little of both.

CHAPTER 2

Family as Defined

You don't choose your family. They are God's gift to you, as you are to them. —Desmond Tutu

You don't choose your family. They are God's gift to you, as you are to them. All sales are final.
No Exchanges. No Returns.
— Someone who is not named Desmond Tutu

Family has multiple definitions. I know because I googled it. Here are some of the formal definitions:

Family (n):
1. *a group of one or more parents and their children living together as a unit;*
2. *a group of people related either by consanguinity (by recognized birth) or affinity (by marriage or other relationship);*
3. *all the descendants of a common ancestor, a clan;*
4. *a group, or collection of related things or items with similar properties.*

In comparison to the definitions above, my family was more akin to a collection or a clan than a classical 'Mom, Dad, two kids, a dog, cat, and a goldfish' kind of family. I guess a dated term might be the Ozzie and Harriet family (*The Adventures of Ozzie and Harriet*). Or you could advance a few decades on your TV and come up with the Cunninghams (*Happy Days*), the Huxtables (*The Cosby Show*), or the Keatons (*Family Ties*), all of whom we were not.

If I had to nail it down, I'd say we were more a mashup of the *Brady Bunch* and the *Addams Family*. Siblings with different parents, joining full siblings, half-siblings, and stepsiblings into a creepy and somewhat kooky clan, with wackiness occurring on a regularly scheduled weekly basis. Our family structure was akin to a small ranch house which grew into a two-story bi-level through a series of additions and renovations, each one made without recognition of the original plan, or any consideration for what might come next. It was assembled much like Frankenstein's monster, without the instant horror typically experienced upon first sight.

THE FAMILY TREE SPROUTS

Our family started when our mother, Barbara Melton, met and married Ed Sayre. During their marriage, they welcomed into the world my two older half-sisters, Kathy and Carrie. Their marriage lasted approximately four years. I use the word 'approximately' because we can find no record of their marriage. Alas, some things were not built to last, and Barb's marriage to Ed was one of those things. They divorced and Kathy and Carrie were placed in Barb's custody.

As they grew up, Kathy and Carrie would have very limited or practically no contact with Ed. With two small children in tow, Barb Melton-Sayre set out to find the next Mr. Right (if not Mr. Right Now), and by chance, she would meet my dad, Jack Osborne (I'm going to refer to him as Dad1). They were married three weeks after the ink dried on Barb's divorce from Ed. Jack entered Kathy and Carrie's lives at such an early age, Kathy would later state she was convinced Jack was her biological father, not her stepfather as was reality, until she found out differently at age twelve.

My sister Laura and I were born during Barbara Melton-Sayre-Osborne's six- year marriage to Jack. I was born in late 1963 and Laura about eighteen months later. Add in the two preexisting half-sisters, and that's the way we became the Jack Osborne Clan of the mid-1960s.

As it goes, some things aren't meant to last. Barb and Jack's marriage is on that list, too. Barb had become involved with her third soon-to-be-

Left to right – back row: Barbara, Carrie, Kathy, Jack.
Front row: Steve (me) and Laura. Circa 1967.
Of note: Laura and Jack have a very strong resemblance.
Why am I the only one looking at the camera?

husband, Jerry Condo. He and Barbara Melton-Sayre-Osborne-Condo were married in August of 1968. Our stepdad, Jerry (I'll refer to him as Dad2), had two daughters from a previous marriage, Tonja and Renee. They were just a few years older than me and about a year or so younger than Carrie, so the age progression worked astonishingly well.

In 1970 Barb gave birth to their only joint child, Adam. If anyone is keeping count, that totals seven children. In age order: Kathy, Carrie, Tonja, Renee, Steve, Laura, and Adam. I know it seems like a lot of siblings, but we are only about halfway through the list. Hang with me.

THE OTHER FAMILY TREE

To add to the sibling strangeness, Laura, my only full biological sister, and I (Jack's children) were members of not one, but two blended families. The one previously detailed above I refer to as the Barb and

Left to right – back row: Carrie, Kathy, Tonja, Renee.
Front/bottom: Jerry, Adam, Barb, Laura, Steve (me). Circa 1970.

Jerry Condo House, and the other I call the Jack and Mary Ann Osborne
House.

After his divorce from Barb, my "Dad1" Jack married the woman
who would become our stepmom, Mary Ann Osborne. She was one of
the warmest, most considerate and pleasant people I would ever meet
in my life. She treated our father like a king; therefore, Laura and I
loved her. We are also very fond of the stepbrothers and stepsisters that
came with Dad1's new marriage. Mary Ann had eight children of her
own: Arlene, Darlene, Charlene, Francene, Danny, Johnny, Gary, and
Jerry. I kid you not! Go back and read those names out loud. It's quite
funny, especially if done with a little Kentucky drawl.

Oh, and these other eight children were not only our stepsiblings,
but they were also our second cousins. That is correct. Second. Cousins.
But don't worry, we're from Kentucky—no one bats an eye at that sort
of thing. No one has ever asked a single question about it. When it
comes up, everyone simply moves on to the next topic. Honestly, it's
not as incestuous as it sounds. Mary Ann Osborne was a widow when
she married Jack. Her first husband was Jack's first cousin, Charles

Osborne. Jack married Mary Ann after Charles died. That's how my second cousins became my stepsiblings. The 'cousin' part of the relationship between Jack and Mary Ann was a marriage relation, not a blood relation. Therefore, it was a perfectly legitimate arrangement, no matter what state you live in.

Years ago, I asked Jack and Mary Ann how they met. Mary Ann said that she had known Jack through her husband Charles—she had seen Jack at weddings and other family functions. After Charles passed, Jack eventually asked Mary Ann out for a cup of coffee. They quickly became a matched set and were subsequently married in 1972.

"Oh, that sounds lovely. That's a little romantic and quaint . . . coffee for a first date," I remarked. "And how long after Charles had passed did you guys finally go out?" I inquired.

"Shortly after the service. Your dad asked me out for coffee at the funeral," my stepmom replied. "I left the funeral home and drove home. He followed me, but somehow, I lost him. He called me a few days later when he finally tracked down my phone number. That's when we met for coffee."

Are you fricking kidding me? Dad asked my future stepmom out on a date at her first husband's funeral!? Is it me, or does that seem just a little too soon? I mean, c'mon, Dad, Chuck wasn't in the ground yet! But I guess it makes sense. Where else could he find a woman who has eight kids who already has his last name? He couldn't pass that up! I guess I can understand his sense of urgency.

The only element of their story that matters to me is that they were devoted to each other. Mary Ann treated our dad as well as any woman can treat a husband. As a result, Laura

Dad1 and stepmom,
Jack and Mary Ann Osborne

Jack and Mary Ann Osborne House

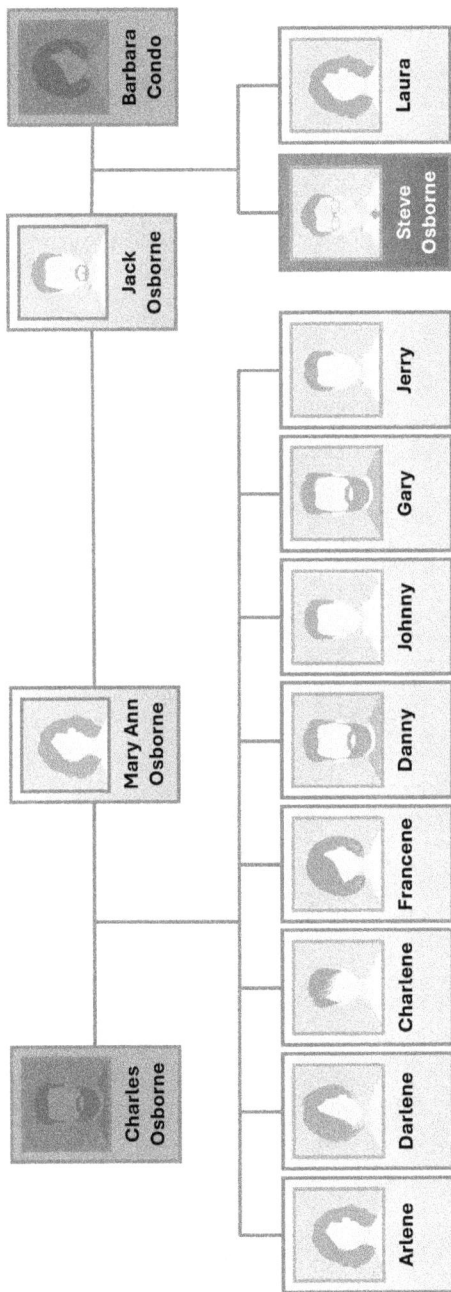

Barbara Condo

Jack Osborne

Mary Ann Osborne

Charles Osborne

Laura

Steve Osborne

Jerry

Gary

Johnny

Danny

Francene

Charlene

Darlene

Arlene

Jack Osborne divorced Barbara Melton-Sayre-Osborne. He married his cousin's widow, Mary Ann Osborne. Her eight children are the stepsiblings AND second cousins of Steve and Laura Osborne.

Jerry and Barbara Condo House

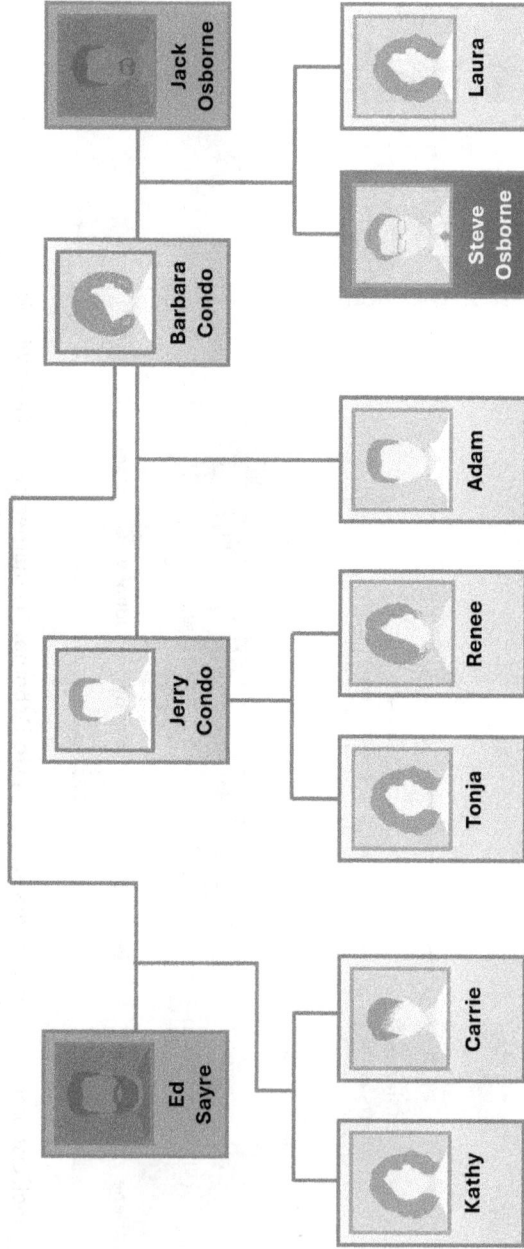

Barbara Melton married Ed Sayre and had daughters Kathy and Carrie. She divorced Ed, married Jack Osborne and had Steve and Laura. She divorced Jack, married Jerry Condo. He had two daughters from a previous marriage, Tonja and Renee. Barbara and Jerry had a son, Adam. There were seven children total being full, half, and step-siblings.

and I are eternally grateful to her. We love her dearly.

For five days a week we would live with our mom, Barbara Condo, and our stepdad, Jerry Condo (Dad2) in the "Condo House." On most weekends, Laura and I would go stay with Jack (Dad1) Osborne and our stepmom, Mary Ann Osborne, in the "Osborne House." It's not an uncommon arrangement, but it's also not optimal. It was strange, but we didn't know any better. Nor would our opinion have mattered anyway. The holidays were fraught with the "who is going to spend which holiday with whom" battles, which were horribly stressful and traumatic for both Laura and me. We both knew it wasn't really a question of "Who are you going to spend the holiday with," but more like a test of, "Who do you love more?"

Clearly, my family "configuration", as it were, is a bit messy. It's not a family tree. I'd call it more of a family vine. But it does fit one of the many definitions of family. Two sets of parents, a total of fifteen siblings, six in one household, eight in the other, sired by (at least) four different men. Only Laura and I belonged to both family houses and were connected in some way, shape, or form to everyone in both the Osborne and Condo family trees. As stated before, my family was more like a clan, not normal, but not horrible.

CHAPTER 3

I'm Just an Ordinary Guy Who Happens to Be an Alien

I'm exceptional at being ordinary.
— Some guy at the local coffee shop

I am and have always been an average guy. Growing up in Southwest Ohio, I loved all the things that a kid from Cincinnati would love: the Cincinnati Reds and the Big Red Machine of the 1970s. I dreamt of being an MLB shortstop someday, but I lacked the athletic ability to be so much as an MLB batboy. I couldn't even make the high school team. I loved the outdoors, playing touch football in the street, splashing in the local creek, catching crawdads, trekking through the woods, and building stuff out of scraps of whatever I could find.

I also loved planes and anything aviation-related. When I was five, I asked my mom for things I could do around the house to earn money. I had been to the local Ben Franklin Five & Dime store and had seen a toy fighter jet. It was a simple little toy, a red plastic injection-molded model of a B-58 Hustler. I was fixated on it. My mom gave me a list of things to do. If I completed them all, she would give me a quarter. Twenty-five cents would be far more than I needed to purchase the toy plane. In fact, with a quarter, I could buy two planes, which I did. The second was a P-51 Mustang. I loved building model airplanes. When I was thirteen, my major Christmas gift was a B-17 Flying Fortress model from Revell. Having hundreds of pieces to assemble, it was a generational leap beyond my first, solid red plastic toy. I was in aviation model heaven.

As I grew older, I maintained a tall and skinny build. Now I am 6'1", which is slightly above the average male height of 5'9". I have an average build and weigh about a buck-eighty. That's about ten pounds over the "you look decent" indicator on my scale.

Danny, Jerry, Steve (me), Johnny

In contrast, most of my stepbrothers/second cousins are all 5'6" or shorter. Now mind you, they are only second cousins, so some variation in physical traits between us is expected. But in any family picture, someone stands above the rest. That someone is me. I have a recent photo of me with three of my stepbrothers/second cousins that looks like something out of a J.R.R. Tolkien Middle Earth novel. It looks like three Hobbits and a Woodland Elf. Honestly, it's laughable and we all have a good chuckle every time we see it.

Other than me, all the Osborne males are stout, barrel-chested, with thick facial hair. To get a five o'clock shadow takes me two weeks. In high school I was 6'1", 125 pounds, and thin as a rail. My oldest sister Kathy even called me "Stevik"—a combination of Steve and stick. I was so thin, if I wasn't wearing a shirt a person could count my ribs from across the room. Kathy refused to let me sit at the dinner table without a shirt. Her objection was not because she was enforcing some social grace—Kentucky hillbillies don't care about that—but because she couldn't stand to watch my heart beat within my chest.

Growing up, I felt like an alien. I was so different from my siblings no matter whether they were full, half, or step. Hell, I was different from my entire family, and it was painfully clear. This feeling of uneasiness never left me, even in my adult years. There were multiple times in my life, during emotionally dark evenings, when I would sit on the couch and lament the churning turmoil within me. I could never quite put my finger on the problem. The only thing I could identify was my inability to connect with and relate to my siblings. I was completely unique within my family and at the same time, completely ordinary as a person. As ordinary as I might have been, I did have the distinction of being part Native American, which I always thought was cool.

JACK'S HEART CONDITION & MY GENETIC PREDISPOSITION

Besides passing along his presumed Native American genetic material and a full head of hair, Dad also passed along a history of heart issues. His arteries had narrowed due to smoking cigarettes in his younger days and the amount of bacon he consumed throughout his life. The walls of his heart had thinned due to lack of exercise. Knowing that heart disease has a strong genetic element to it, this condition was always a concern of mine. It would eventually take his life, and I was worried that someday it would do the same to me. Well, as of this writing, with the help of some corrective surgery, so far so good. But before any of that would occur, I would have to get through my youth and the craziness it would conjure up.

ONE OF THESE THINGS IS NOT LIKE THE OTHERS

Regardless of the amount of genetic material we shared, during my early years, the differences between myself and my siblings would grate on me. As an adult, I felt this disconnect when I was in their presence. I felt even worse afterwards, almost like a bad hangover.

I want to be clear: my family was nothing but loving to me. They are good people. We weren't mean to each other, at least not any more than typical brothers and sisters. The source of my discomfort wasn't my siblings nor their actions. It was my awareness of how similar they were to each other and how dissimilar I was when I compared myself to that group. There was a grinding, an irritation, just below my active and conscious thoughts. It was like a deep din or hum of road noise, a noise I'd notice only when I focused on it. It created an ever-present level of cognitive dissonance, the feeling that something was wrong but I couldn't quite put my finger on it.

Sometimes those thoughts would breach the surface of my foreground thoughts. I would doubt myself and question why I was so strange, such a misfit, or so different. Inside the Condo House with five sisters, I often chalked it up to gender, if not to the age differences. I didn't have a solution. But as preteen kids and teenagers do when they are growing up, they deal with the issues of the day. We were preoccupied with what to eat, grades, puberty, friends, the confusion of the teenage world, and trying to survive the daily challenges. Teens accept the things they experience and believe that this is the way things are supposed to be, even when something inside them says it is not.

As time passed, the incongruency gnawed at me slowly, month after month, year after year. The obvious difference between us made me question my self-worth and my sense of belonging. I remember watching *Sesame Street* on PBS and seeing the skit where they sing, "One of these things is not like the others . . . one of these things doesn't belong," and I knew which one it was. IT WAS ME. I was the odd man out. There were six shoes in the room and I was a spoon. I was that far off. I wasn't a boot; I was a spoon.

Genetic mirroring is the technical term used to describe the ability to see elements of ourselves in our relatives due to shared DNA. It is a critical component contributing to a person feeling like they belong to a group, a family. It is one of the most fundamental human needs. When an individual is unable to see themselves in the other members of their family, it creates a disconnect, a rub, referred to as monachopsis, the subtle but persistent feeling of being out of place. I like to also use the term cognitive dissonance. It is the feeling that "something isn't right here, but I can't put my finger on what it is." The cognitive dissonance begins to gnaw at one's sense of self-worth, as it did with me.

In my other home, the Osborne House, the differences were even more pronounced but not as consistently center stage. My Osborne stepsiblings/second cousins were much older than Laura and me, some by more than fifteen years. I rarely got to visit with most of them. But Jerry Osborne, my youngest stepbrother, was the closest in age and the one who I related to the most.

The Osborne stepsiblings/second cousins had a more country way about them. They spoke with a slight southern drawl. Not a deep southern drawl but a Kentucky-southern drawl. It's amazing what three miles and the Ohio river can do to create a cultural difference between people, but there it was. I was a child of two homes spanning two states, but never feeling completely at home in either one.

I didn't think like my siblings. I didn't look like them. I didn't hold the same values, which is very weird because I was raised in the same house, the same environment, by basically the same parents. I couldn't understand their approach to so many things, including life in general. Their reasoning felt foreign to me. Their choices befuddled me. Their values seem a half-bubble off-center to me. But they were all similar to each other. I was the one who was different. I felt like an alien and the source of that difference had no discernible explanation, no clear origin.

I didn't like it and I didn't like them. I didn't like me and the way the situation made me feel. Again, my siblings are not at fault one bit. They were always generally kind and loving to me. I was the one with the problem. There were times when I wished I was not related to these people. At times I wished I was an only child.

Foolishly I whisper. Fate bends an ear.

CHAPTER 4

The Education of a Rebellious Spirit

There is a rebel lying deep in my soul.
— Clint Eastwood

MY "EARLY GRADUATION" FROM HIGH SCHOOL

I would call the members of my family mostly "conservative." By that, I mean risk-averse, middle-of-the-road kind of people. I would say we were lower-middle class; that's just an uneducated guess. But as for personalities, none fell too far outside the box, with one major exception—me.

Dad1 was a bus driver and my stepdad, Jerry, Dad2, was a truck driver—honest, hard-working, proud union members. I, however, never developed an affinity for unions and became an entrepreneur instead. "Rules were made to be followed" was a common phrase that I heard in my home. I believed that "rules were made to be followed—by other people," not necessarily by me. Rules were made to keep other people in line. Rules were—and to this day, are—more like guidelines . . . broad guidelines . . . with blurry lines . . . and not much guidance.

Another popular phrase in my household was "don't stick your head up or it will get shot at." My thought was to shoot first and pin the other guys down. It seems like a stronger position and better strategy to me.

If it hasn't been obvious so far, I possess a natural aggression that has driven me my entire life. I assume far more risk than anyone in my family would be comfortable with or even believe was sensible. I can also be a contrarian. If 100 people are in a room and are asked a question to which 99 of them answer "black," I will answer "white." Then I'll ask what the question was. I've never had the desire to be grouped with everyone else. I've always been a rogue. I've always been a maverick. I am a non-conformist. It seems I'm that way by design, not by choice.

As a student, I was a comedian and a class clown. I learned early on that I could get away with so much more BS if I was funny when doing it. That dynamic became my calling card. Turning a phrase, playing innocent, even leveraging my misfit/mischievous reputation became a tool (What? Who? Me?). For all my devious ways, I was never destructive. My actions were never criminal. I was never truly "bad." I was just a pain in the ass for anyone who got sideways with me. Need proof? Check with my high school teachers.

While I wouldn't call myself a "problem child," I would certainly call myself a problem to some. In high school, my quasi-rebel, non-conformist characteristics put down roots and grew like bamboo shoots. I attended, or uh, was sent to, a small private Christian school associated with the Pentecostal church my parents took us to each Sunday. At our devoutly Christian school, there were fewer than 350 students in grades K-12, fewer than thirty-five in my senior class, and five of them were expelled before the end of the year for their less-than-Christian activities. The curriculum was marginal and some of the teachers even less so. Their inadequacies and weaknesses were not lost on me. Nor was their lack of ability to control a small group of juvenile delinquents in training.

I knew what true juvenile delinquency looked like through my experience living in the Condo House. My mother and stepdad ran a temporary foster home. There was a never-ending, constant contingent of troubled youth parading through our house and sleeping in my bedroom. I had seen it all when it came to disruptive behavior. However, I was wise enough not to make it blatantly obvious that I was the culprit of the day's disruption. That's the difference between subversion and rebellion. Rebellion gets a person hanged (expelled). Subversion will get a person glares, suspicion, and ongoing simmering resentment—

but not expulsion.

A typical day during high school might find me being sent to the administrative office for making some smart-ass comment or snide remark. I knew the routine well.

One of the reasons I got away with what I did was I had skills in areas of technology which the adults running the asylum didn't possess. Technology always seemed to come naturally to me. Computers were just making their way into the school offices. They were strange and complex. The audio/visual devices were often in need of someone who understood them. I would frequently get called out of my class to go assist a teacher with the AV devices in a different class. I suspect that was one of reasons that administration was reluctant to get too heavy-handed with me.

One time I was sent to the principal's office with a note from the teacher, Ms. Zeckler. She had written on it, "He's doing it again!" That was it; nothing more. Good God! I wish I had saved her note. It would be framed and hanging on my wall. That's something to be proud of. "He's doing it again;" there is so much to deconstruct in that note. Clearly, Ms. Zeckler and the principal, Mr. Wagnor, had previous conversations on the topic. The situation and aggravation must had gotten so bad with Ms. Zeckler that she and the principal had discussed . . . ME in exclusivity! But my subversion was so subtle and well camouflaged that she couldn't say exactly what I was doing. She could only say that it bugged her and use words or phrases like "generally disruptive," or "he was doing . . . you know . . . that thing he does." When pressed for specifics, there wasn't much administration could do. Mr. Wagnor set out to appeal to my sense of empathy and our mutual respect (or at least my respect of him).

"Steve, look, I have a very, very busy week ahead. I don't have the time to have Ms. Zeckler here, in my office, crying about YOU for two hours. Can you please do me a favor and not be a thorn in her side for just a few more days this week?"

"Look," I responded, "that woman has a problem. She's not qualified to teach. She cries at everything. She's incompetent and now this has somehow become my problem? She can't teach and I'm the bad guy?" I feigned injustice within the question.

Mr. Wagnor dropped his chin to his chest and looked over his glasses to communicate his complete rejection of my high-road position. It was followed by a short dismissive shake of his head. He skipped the anticipated mock debate which might have occurred between us and jumped directly to the bottom line.

"Her qualifications are not for you to assess, not to mention your assessments are inaccurate. Also, I said 'please.' The word 'please' should elicit the response, 'Yes, sir, Mr. Wagnor.'" His tone communicated that he was not going to spend more than ninety seconds on this endeavor and that I better get on board the bus or get run over by it.

"Yes, sir, Mr. Wagnor, because you asked, I will try not to trigger her volatile and unstable emotional state," I acquiesced.

He rolled his eyes as he shook his head in frustration. "I do not expect to see you again anytime soon." He attempted to speak his wishes into existence.

"If you do see me, it won't be my fault," I shot back as if the entire situation was an inconvenience to me. That statement had a 93.5% chance of being a complete and total lie.

Incidents like this played themselves out repeatedly throughout my three years of high school. I only attended three years. I skipped my junior year and jumped directly to my senior year. Some people might think, "Gee, Steve must be smart," but it must be put in perspective. I didn't graduate early as much as I was asked to leave the school once I had enough credits to get my diploma. At the time, I was dating a girl who was two years older than me, so I wanted to get out of high school as soon as I could. Combine that with the frequent trips to the administrative offices and eventually, the solution became clear to Wagnor. During one of my many "counseling sessions" late in my sophomore year, Mr. Wagnor pulled a form from his desk.

"Take this form home and have your parents sign it. Bring it back tomorrow," he directed as if I had no other options.

"What is it?" I asked.

"It is a form that says they will grant you permission to graduate next year, a year early. You need nine credit hours to get your diploma.

There are only eight bells [class periods]. You would normally have two study halls each day, so that would only be six classes. You need nine. What you will do is take eight classes each day, no study halls. No time off. You will take an additional class either at night or in summer school, I really don't care which. That should reduce your ability to create trouble." (An incorrect assumption, might I add.) "You will take a fully-loaded course schedule. You will pass, or you will fail. Either way, next year will be your last year at this school."

I guess some situations (read: students) are not worth the tuition exchanged. I was that child.

At the end of my senior year, the faculty at my high school voted me "Most Likely to Succeed, Criminal or Otherwise." Not really. They didn't have that award. But if they did, I'm sure I would have been a finalist. Who are we kidding? Winning that would have been a perp—I mean cake—walk.

UNCLE SAM WANTS YOU! (BUT HE DIDN'T WANT ME)

During my senior year of high school, I considered joining the US military. I desperately wanted to learn to fly but didn't have the money to attend a flight school such as Embry-Riddle. Part of my motivation was both of my dads, Jack and Jerry, instilled in me a strong sense of patriotism. Jack served in the Army during the Korean War. Jerry served in the US Coast Guard between the Korean and Vietnam wars. I held the belief that I could serve my country for some period of time and possibly become a pilot in the Air Force or the Navy.

After discussing the possibilities with two close high school friends, Kevin and Doug, we all agreed to see our local recruiting officer and enlist. Doug went first and came back to proudly announce he was joining the Navy and would eventually deploy as a submariner. The next week Kevin slapped down his paperwork showing he was headed into the 82nd Airborne unit of the US Army. Then came my turn. I went to see a recruiter and told him that I wanted to join a branch that would afford me the opportunity of flight training and the ability to become a pilot. Fighters would be the preferred assignment, but flight in general was my focus. I said these things looking through my ridiculously thick glasses. I was nearsighted to the point I needed glasses as thick as the bottom of a Coca Cola bottle. I also felt compelled to disclose that I was colorblind.

It was 1980. Jimmy Carter was still president and the military was at one of its lowest states of readiness in decades. There was an anti-war/anti-military sentiment held by much of the country. The current administration had cut military funding to the point where the military was forcing people out and recruiting was selective. I was not, shall we say, an A1 prime recruit.

I said to the buff, granite-jawed recruiter, "I want to join, but I'm concerned that my eyesight might keep me out of pilot school. I'm afraid I won't be able to fly."

"Son, I'm not worried about you flying," he said in a droning southern voice, "I'm worried about you getting hit by a bus on the way home. You're damned near blind. Your next prescription should be a seeing-eye dog. Fighter pilots need to have perfect vision. You should go home and think about joining the Army or Marines where your eyesight doesn't matter as much."

A crushing statement to hear for sure, but he was correct. The military wanted their pilots to have 20/20 uncorrected vision. My vision was closer to 20/400. To put that into real world perspective, it means what I could see at 20 feet, the average person could see at 400 feet. Yeah, I was damned near blind without my glasses.

I left the recruiting office and drove home. I did think about what the recruiter said to me. I decided if I wasn't going to get the opportunity to fly, I didn't want to spend four years of my life in the military. Instead, I would attend college and get a business degree. I was good with technology. At fifteen years old, I could already program a computer in BASIC and Fortran, both of which are now long-dead programing languages. But in 1979, knowing how to use them was no small accomplishment. Since flying wasn't an option and physical labor sounded difficult, I decided I would head to the realm of higher learning. I targeted Miami University in Oxford, Ohio, as my school of choice.

As ironic as life can be, my eyesight had gotten so bad by my late twenties that I decided I would opt for Lasik surgery to correct my nearsightedness. To my surprise, my eye surgeon informed me that due to the shape of my eye socket and the configuration of my eye tissue, the procedure would likely produce a result much better than the average person experienced. From pre-surgery to post-surgery, my vision changed from a horrific 20/400 to 20/5. I went from being unable to read the clock on my bedstand (it had 4" tall numbers) to seeing objects in the distance most other people couldn't even detect. Things a normal person can see at five feet, I could see at 20 feet.

The ironies continued with my educational path. A decade later, the nation's premier aviation university, Embry-Riddle, would open a branch campus in Cincinnati. I was able to overcome my previous inability to fund my education by leveraging my employer's tuition reimbursement program. I had previously graduated Miami University with an associate degree of applied science (systems technology). I would gain my bachelor of business administration degree from Embry-Riddle in airline and airport management. It was a degree from a flight school, but not one that secured for me a pilot's license or even any true pilot training.

Even my entrance to Miami University was fraught with challenges, which we will explore later. But for now, let's skip to my work life and the meeting of the future Mrs. Osborne.

CHAPTER 5

Building Things that Make Other Things Fly

Doubt is the origin of wisdom [or of truth].
— Rene Descartes

GEAE, EEO, AND E-I-E-I-O

My rebellious high school days gave way to my rebellious college days. College hijinks surrendered to the need to eat, have shelter, pay bills— therefore, a job was necessary. I found employment in the technology sector (NEC, Computerland, Radio Shack) and with other companies that leveraged technology, like General Electric.

It was at GE Aircraft Engines, the division that makes commercial and military jet engines, that I met my wife, Becky. She and I worked for managers who each worked for the same next-level manager. Hey, it was like I married my work cousin! Not that anyone in my family would do something like that . . . marry a cousin . . .

While working for GE Aircraft Engines, I supported the executive level management team and higher-level human resource managers for all their computing needs. It was a great job. I got exposure to skilled professionals with high-level positions. One of those individuals was a delightful gentleman by the name of Clarence Keller. Mr. Keller was the head of GE Minority Relations. At some point over the two-plus years when I had visited his office to address his computer problems, the topic of my Native American heritage came up. Mr. Keller held high interest in the topic because GE, being a defense contractor, had certain objectives for hiring different minority classes. Unfortunately, in Cincinnati, Ohio, the Native American population was a little difficult to come by.

"Steve, would you consider changing your EEO code?" Mr. Keller inquired. EEO stood for Equal Employment Opportunity. In other words, would I consider checking the box next to "Native American" (along with Caucasian)?

While I hadn't hesitated to share the childhood story told by my mother for many years, this might have been the first time I had ever paused in confirming the story. Being asked to commit that concept to paper, on a form for some governmental agency to make note of, was enough to make me seriously question this story for the first time.

"Mr. Keller, I really have no idea how much Native American I have in me. It could be an eighth. It could be less than a sixteenth. I just don't know for sure." Considering the concerns I had about the validity of my mother's story, I certainly didn't want to do anything fraudulent.

Clarence enlightened me. "The percentage of your heritage is not the question. The question is do you believe, that you believe, that you are Native American, and do you hold yourself out to be so?" He always had an interesting way of putting things.

"I do believe I am, and I do talk about it, but I have no proof. I wasn't raised on a reservation or anything close to that."

Early in our friendship and over lunch, I shared with Becky what was transpiring in the conversations I had with Mr. Keller and my EEO concerns.

"If you believe it's true, why wouldn't you make the change?" she urged.

"I don't want to be promoted because I checked a box. I want them to hire me because they want me, the person that I am," I responded. I hated the idea of advancement on anything other than merit. Growing up middle-to-low class in a small Ohio town instills a few key values; earning your way by merit was one of them. A more compelling but unspoken reason was the seriousness of the doubts I held about the story being true.

"I don't know; I can see how you could be Native American. I think you have the look of someone who has some Native American heritage. Your mom told you that you are. I don't know how you tell either way," Becky mused.

In the weeks following, I seriously considered changing my code. I was in the GE Management Development Program for high potential managerial candidates. I knew that being "a minority," especially Native American, would be very helpful in advancement, but I had a nagging concern that kept me from making that move.

About a year later, I applied for a promotion within GE. It was a major advancement—two levels higher than my current position. But during the interview, I was asked to change my EEO code again. Why? It would be helpful in the consideration of my potential selection for the promotion.

That is when I truly railed against the idea. My rebellious spirit was coming out of me again. I wanted to be hired because I was the best candidate for the job, not for my EEO code. I told the manager to make the hiring decision first. I'd make the EEO decision after that. Surely that would be the noble way to approach the situation. Unfortunately, I didn't get the job.

More seemingly unrelated particles of my life are drawn inexplicably toward each other.

* * *

Shortly after leaving GE, I started the first of a half-dozen companies. They would become the majority of my life's work. These companies would provide income, excitement, enrichment, difficulties, and near unmeasurable stress. I often wonder if our lives would have been better if I had stayed in the corporate world. When I voice this concept to my friends, most of them cannot contain their laughter. "You are not fit for captivity," and "You wouldn't last ninety days in a corporate setting before you walked out," are the two most common responses. So, I guess I made the best choice. I'm still not sure, but I can't see an alternative.

Little did either of us know that within three years of those friendly lunches, Becky and I would be married. Nor did we foresee the role that the Future Mrs. Osborne would play in deconstructing my mother's story about my Native American heritage. Looking forward to the present day (some twenty-five-plus years), Becky and I have two wonderful daughters. We have a home in a nice suburban area in Northern Cincinnati. We have had our struggles and our successes. We have worked hard to survive them both.

As our girls became older and more self-sufficient, Becky took up a hobby—genealogy. She loves the detective aspect of it. She loves the human story aspect of it. She not only loves it, but candidly, she has become a recognized expert at it. She is the family historian for her own family and for other families as well. What started for her as a curiosity turned into a hobby, then a skill, and now a revenue stream. She has become so skilled that she does it professionally, part-time, for a few law firms who are seeking to settle estate/trust distributions and need to find descendants and heirs. Again, I'm a firm believer in earning everything, based on merit—compliments included. I don't just say these things because she is my wife, but because it's the truth.

The best evidence I can provide of her advanced ability came to us on a trip to Utah. We were in Salt Lake City visiting my sister Laura and her husband. At Becky's request, we carved an afternoon out of our itinerary to visit the FamilySearch Library world headquarters (FSL).

During our time on their research floor, Becky looked for a specific person who had proven to be elusive even to her. The few records she had uncovered about this person were often contradictory. Becky asked for assistance and was introduced to a member of the FamilySearch Library staff who was the expert for that specific geography and population. They worked together for almost three hours. At the end of the session, they had not found one item that Becky had not already known about or found from her laptop in our home. Finally, the FamilySearch Library expert surrendered with an exasperated sigh: "I can't find anything that you haven't already found. That almost never happens." I am of the firm belief that if Becky can't find it, it isn't there.

Don't believe me? Let's hear it from her.

CHAPTER 6

Searching for Hiawatha

People Seek and ye shall find.
— Mathew 7:7 Bible KJV

GENEALOGICAL SLEUTHING PART I

Becky...

When Steve and I met at GE, we quickly became good friends for a number of reasons. First and foremost, I found him to be the funniest person I had ever met. Once when we were driving together to an off-site meeting, he had me in stitches with his impersonations. He introduced me to the joy of Bobcat Goldthwait before I even knew who Bobcat Goldthwait was. And once I saw Bobcat perform, I was disappointed: he wasn't nearly as funny as Steve's impersonation of him.

Working in similar positions gave us many opportunities to hang out with each other. Because I didn't have Steve's strong technical aptitude and experience, I often relied on his assistance when trying to solve technical problems. I was constantly paging him for help. (This was in 1990 and paging was the closest thing we had to texting before mobile phones.) When he moved up to a different job in the company, I applied for and got his old position but didn't get to see him as often. Fortunately, before leaving for his new job, he trained me in the nuances of his client group and we got to know each other better.

During our work hours together, I became privy to the fact that our managers' boss was encouraging him to change his EEOC status.

It was obvious to me that Steve had Native American blood in him. He had told me about his oldest sister, Kathy, who looked like Cher. I saw a strong resemblance between him and his other older sister, Carrie, and she definitely had the dark coloring of a Native American. Steve himself had almost black hair at the time, and whenever he was outside in the summer sun, his skin turned red. Not the red that a pale person gets when sunburned, but a deep brown, blood-red associated with Native Americans. What further proof did anyone need?

As I got to know Steve and his family better, I wasn't so convinced about the veracity of the story his mother had fed the kids, the one where two of their four great-grandmothers were the daughters of Native American tribal chiefs. That seemed a little far-fetched. But I definitely believed that there was Native American blood running through his veins.

In time, I also came to know Clarence Keller in his role as Head of Minority Relations at GE. He was definitely a force to be reckoned with, and not someone I wanted to disappoint. Whenever Clarence called me with a computer problem, my knees would knock a little as I walked to his office. I couldn't understand why Steve would not acquiesce to Clarence's encouragement about changing his EEO code. It made sense to me.

GENEALOGY AND BECKY—A PERFECT FIT

Becky...

I was thirty years old when Steve and I met and had never been married. I would say I was a late bloomer. We got married when I was thirty-three and our first daughter arrived just before my thirty-sixth birthday. I was pushing forty when we decided our family was finished with the arrival of our second daughter. I was equally late in finding a hobby, but when Ancestry.com arrived on the scene, I was hooked.

In a perfect example of how adversity shapes the person we become, I fell in love with genealogy research because of my hearing loss. At the age of seventeen months, I contracted spinal meningitis and spent a month in Children's Hospital in Cincinnati. In the months following my release, my mother noticed that I wasn't responding to sound the same way that I did before my illness. Sure enough, a doctor confirmed that I had suffered a significant loss of hearing. Naturally, this impacted the rest of my life in profound ways. Out of necessity I learned to find ways of filling in information I may not have heard. Resources like telephone books, class lists, and newspapers became my go-to sources. If I didn't hear someone's name, address, phone number, teacher's name—whatever—I would go to a printed document to fill in the blanks. This trick worked for me in school and I learned how to find the necessary resources to make it work for me in the professional world as well.

By the time an Ancestry.com advertisement caught my eye, I was well-versed in how to use printed and online materials to help me capture the information I might have missed. And I found I loved to read almost anything printed, i.e., books, newspapers, magazines, cereal boxes, instructional manuals, recipes, you name it. It got to the point where I enjoyed eating with a book propped open in front of me more than eating with other people.

All this to say that Ancestry.com looked to me like something I would enjoy immensely due to the historical value and variety of its many resources. It involved plotting family lines and solving mysteries through the perusal of written records. Each genealogical relationship typically has a plethora of records to tie two people together. With Ancestry.com, finding those records for anyone's parents and grandparents was akin to picking low-hanging fruit off the tree—simple and extremely rewarding. However, as the relationships retreated in time, it became harder to find ancestors or to understand how people were related. It could turn into a puzzle, a mystery, a knotted-up ball of yarn that I loved unraveling. I had already become the de facto family historian over the last decade, collecting family photos and keeping everyone in my extended family abreast of each other's birthdays, contact information, new family members, and the like. Ancestry.com seemed like it was tailor made for the person I had become, the girl who couldn't hear but who loved reading and learning about people's stories.

The first genealogical mystery I solved featured my cousin, Terri. Ironically, it contained the saddest ending of the many genealogical mysteries I have resolved over the years.

Terri's father was my mother's much older brother, Bob, making Terri and I first cousins. Uncle Bob had been married once before and fathered four children with his first wife. Unfortunately, their marriage fell apart when he went out of state for a job. Upon his return home for a visit, his wife and children were gone. At least that is what our side of the family heard. I'm sure his ex-wife had a somewhat different take on those events, but no matter how it's perceived, those four children lost all contact with their father. My uncle got on with his life, taking another wife in his new home state, with Terri as the sole product of his second marriage. Bob died in 1976 when Terri was only twelve.

In 2012, Terri and her teenage son traveled cross country to reconnect with her father's family in Ohio. They stayed in our home for part of the visit, and one night we began talking about the four older half-siblings that Terri had never met. She knew their first names but nothing else. After her departure, I began searching for them on Ancestry.com. My mother recalled that during her brother's first marriage, the family had been based in Long Beach, California. She still had photos from the trip she and my grandmother took in the 1940s to visit Bob and meet his wife and new baby. During their visit, it became clear that the baby could not see or hear, and soon the parents discovered that he had lost these senses as a result of his mother contracting German measles during her pregnancy. Sadly, he died in an institution before reaching adulthood. This is the only child that my mother met. The three children who were born later were simply names to our family, and no one knew what happened to them.

This family saga occurred long enough ago that I was able to find federal census records which led me to the elderly brother of my uncle's first wife. When I reached him on the telephone, he was gracious enough to relay his deceased sister's side of the story and pass along a phone number for his niece—Terri's half-sister, Marianne. When I reached Marianne on the phone, she was not so happy to hear from me, even less so when I answered her one and only question:

"Is my father still living?" she asked.

"No," I replied, "he died in 1976 after a brief visit to Ohio. That was the only time I remember meeting him."

Our conversation continued but I could sense she wasn't interested in connecting. I let her know about her father's subsequent marriage—and about Terri. I gave her Terri's contact information and they eventually connected, but a lasting relationship was not to be. Terri felt that Marianne had lived too long with the myth that their shared father was a monster who had deserted his family. For her part, Terri had always heard that Marianne's mother had hid the children. Whatever the truth, it hung between these half-sisters to the point that they remained strangers to each other. Marianne was kind enough to put me in touch with her two brothers. The photos she sent me of the three of them just blew me away with the resemblance to their parents. One of the brothers was the spitting image of our shared grandfather, but when I sent him a photo of this ancestor he so closely resembled, he showed no interest. He didn't care to learn about the family; he did not really want to talk to me.

Terri eventually reached out to her brothers and even made plans to visit one of them while on vacation in California. But on the day of their meeting he begged off due to severe back pain. Sadly, both this brother and Marianne have since passed away. Their remaining sibling did not honor my request for their obituaries. Despite our efforts, Terri never met any of her half-siblings.

One would have thought such a sad and empty ending would have discouraged me from digging around old records in search of people who want nothing to do with me, but it only served to whet my appetite. I'm happy to say the majority of cases I've solved have ended successfully with long lost family members getting back in touch with each other.

But nothing has come close to being as chaotic and secretive as the research of Steve's family tree.

* * *

Becky's love for genealogy has always been a bit puzzling to me. It's a damned difficult hobby to say the least. Honestly, I live in the present with my eyes looking forward. I'm not much into family history. I don't know these dead people and they didn't leave me any instructions. I've watched Becky as she has done her research for our family and professionally for her clients. It's confusing as hell to me. Many of the records she finds are hand-written, incomplete, and contradictory. At best it's like assembling a jigsaw puzzle with missing and duplicate pieces, some of which need to be trimmed to go into their correct spot.

I recall sitting on the couch with Becky as she watched shows like "Who Do You Think You Are" and "Long Lost Family." I saw the lies and secrets that played out in the lives of those people. I said many times, "Those poor pathetic bastards. I can't imagine what it would be like to lose a parent in that manner." Those situations are like a slow-motion train wreck.

GENEALOGY IS ARCHEOLOGY, DIGGING THROUGH DOCUMENTS

Becky...

Ancestry.com and the other genealogical research sites are fantastic, but sometimes a person just needs to visit the courthouse or office where the actual records are kept. And like archeology, it can get dirty digging through those papers, photos, and records. Which is how Steve and I ended up in Owenton, Kentucky, searching for Hiawatha.

At this point in our married life, Steve was still deeply entrenched with work and our daughters were still living at home. Getting away during the week to go searching for dusty records was not something we really had time for. But on our wedding anniversary, we did what we always do and traveled to Lexington, Kentucky, to stay at the location of our first honeymoon. Owenton was the Osborne ancestral home for many years and it wasn't far out of our way on the journey to Lexington.

We quickly located the records office in the center of this tiny town before they closed for the weekend.

We discovered so many records about the Osbornes of Owenton and quickly found the ones that pertained to Steve's great-grandfather, Greenberry Osburn, and his progeny. It turned out that Steve's grandfather, Clarence, was quite the marrying man. Steve's aunt had told me that her father Clarence had remarried a prior wife. But nobody knew about Clarence's first wife, a fifteen-year-old girl in Owen County, Kentucky. Digging through that dark and dusty records office, we found not only their marriage license, but also a scrap of paper on which the young bride's father scribbled his written approval for the marriage. Not surprisingly, this youthful marriage didn't last long, and Clarence soon moved north to get a job in Cincinnati where he would wed his next wife, Edith. Less than a decade later, Clarence appeared in the 1930 Census with yet a different spouse, this one named Opal, who would become Steve's grandmother. When Opal died of multiple sclerosis many years later, Clarence remarried Edith and is now buried next to her. Wow, who knew? These records would serve as a foreshadowing of my husband's twisted family roots.

I felt certain that this visit to the record repository in Owenton would turn up some evidence of Greenberry Osburn's Native American history, but we didn't find any. However, our trip solidified my commitment to continue looking for Steve's Native American roots, because certainly his mother wouldn't lie about such a thing. Just to be sure, I suggested Steve take a DNA test which would provide clarity regarding his ethnicity.

CHAPTER 7

"Why Don't You Take a DNA Test?"

Never ask questions that you don't want to know the answers to. — Tom Krause

By the winter of 2020, Becky had been building my family tree, off and on, for more than a year. She had collected hundreds of individual records, forms, images, and pictures. The tree was extensive and looked back seven generations with over 800 individuals identified. But there was still a nagging problem. If Hiawatha was hiding in the branches, he was hiding extremely well. As much and as hard as Becky searched, nothing screamed—or even whispered—Native American heritage. But surely my mom wouldn't make up such a story, would she?

"Sweetie, your Native American heritage is proving extremely very difficult to find," Becky said. "I see records of Osbornes who are Native American that lived in the same areas of your people, but I can't make a genealogical connection to any of them."

While she was finding plenty of relatives from both sides of my family, Becky was coming up just short of our goal, which was to find formal documentation that tied me to anyone who we could positively identify as Native American. Anything would do: birth records, census records, baptismal records, wall carvings, smoke signals.

Becky asked me questions like, "What can you tell me about so and so . . ." or something similar. It didn't matter what she asked, I had so very little information about the Osborne clan that I couldn't provide any substantial answers. I knew about Dad1, his three siblings, and their kids, my cousins. Other than that, I was all but useless.

To be honest, our family's oral history was more akin to a drunken, slurred, off-color joke than an orated soliloquy performed by Charlton Heston. That is the way it is with much of the Appalachian population in the region, a population we were squarely ensconced within. We were so well rooted in the population that more than one person in my family lineage signed their legal documents with an "X," and this was long before Twitter changed its name. How forward thinking of them.

Don't get me wrong, I don't want to present our family as non-diverse. It is very diverse. My family has a broad range of social strata: lower-middle class, hillbillies, white trash, rednecks, and felons. We do not discriminate. We embrace everyone!

Despite the issues she was encountering, Becky soldiered on in her efforts until one day she approached me and asked if I would take a DNA test.

"It will connect us to any of your ancestors that might be Native American, and it will show you your genetic makeup. You'll be able to see what percentage of your genes come from what genetic groups."

That certainly sounded reasonable. "Let's do it," I said, "we've got nothing to lose." Looking back, perhaps I should have given it just a millisecond more thought.

I pull at a thread in my sweater. Fate tugs back.

J STEVEN OSBORNE'S DNA TEST RESULTS

Becky ordered the test kit from Ancestry.com. It came in a nice, brightly-colored box about the size of two decks of cards sitting side-by-side. The instructions were simple: Go online and register the kit for tracking and reporting purposes. Wash my hands, spit in the tube. Spit in the tube again. Spit some more, because the tube must be filled to the "Okay, we've got enough saliva" line. Seal it up. Send it off. Wait a few weeks. I did as I was instructed. Candidly, I didn't think conjuring up that much saliva would be an issue, but it was.

Five to six weeks passed when Becky got notification that my results were in. Because of her intense interest in genealogy, I was happy to have her manage my Ancestry.com and DNA information within her account. It would be one less login ID and password I would have to track. Becky excitedly told me my DNA results were in. She couldn't wait to go through them together. Huddled around our morning coffee, we opened the Ancestry website, found the link to my results, and bypassed everything else in favor of the DNA Ethnicity Report.

Here is what we found: I am . . .

- 60% English and Northwestern European
- 15% Irish
- 12% German
- 6% Norwegian
- 6% Welsh
- 2% Eastern European or Russian and . . .
- 0.00% Native American!

Zero point zero, zero percent Native American! Not a chief. Not a tribal leader. Not Blackfoot. Not Cherokee. Nothing. If the results were accurate, then the whole anthology of Native American stories that our mother had told us was a lie. Those stories would be complete fabrications. I mean not even a fraction of a percent real.

It was sad and funny at the same time. If the results were right, it also wouldn't be completely shocking considering my mother's very casual relationship with the truth. But it was also a bit embarrassing. Wouldn't it make me out to be some kind of a fraud? I had lived five and a half DECADES telling people I was some part Native American. I truly believed that fabricated bucket of BS. Or at least I believed my mother. How could we be that far off?

My mother's fabrications were as heavy as granite.
Gravity dropped them on my head.

PART TWO

Discovery &
Disconnection

CHAPTER 8

Heading to Chicago

*It's 106 miles to Chicago, we got a full tank of gas,
half a pack of cigarettes, it's dark and we're wearing
sunglasses . . . hit it! — Jake Blues*

In July of 2021, our eldest daughter was engaged to be married to a young man she had met in college. He was from Hinsdale, Illinois, which is a lovely suburb outside of Chicago. My daughter's fiancé's family was throwing a wedding shower in the Chicago area (the likes of which I ain't never seen before in all my hillbilly raisin'). The trip from our Cincinnati suburban home to their Chicago suburban home was a 350-mile drive, about five and a half hours in duration. I've always liked going to Chicago. For five months out of the year, it is by far and away my favorite major city. I've loved it since I saw *The Blues Brothers*.

We were packing our bags for the trip when Becky received an email notification from Ancestry.com stating they had identified a new "Close Relationship Match" for my DNA profile. The email was sent to Becky because she manages my Ancestry.com account. Her interest in genealogy far exceeds mine. Her genealogical skills and understanding of the science behind it make me look, by comparison, like a chimpanzee randomly banging my hands on the keyboard. I was about to experience that difference again.

"Hey, did you see this?" Becky asked, pointing at her phone screen.

"See what?" I responded. I had limited interest in genealogy because I was busy packing my bags for Chicago Wedding Stuff. So there isn't any misunderstanding or misrepresentation, let's be clear: guys hate weddings. Guys really hate driving five and a half hours to go do

Wedding Stuff. Weddings are for the bride and the mother of the bride. I would not have attended my own if it wasn't absolutely necessary.

"You have a new close relative that popped up on Ancestry," said Becky.

The words registered, but not the potential gravity of their meaning. "What does that mean, 'close relative'? You mean like a third cousin or like a half-brother?" Honestly, at that point, I was less than half-interested in this conversation.

"It says here that it is most likely a first cousin," Becky replied as she wandered out of the room, gathering items for her own bag. I knew all my first cousins—there were nine of them. My first thought was, *I wonder which one of my Osborne cousins did the DNA test thing?*

"It says that your cousin is from Montreal, Quebec in Canada," Becky reported from the other room.

Hold the damn phone. I stopped packing for a brief second. That's not possible. ALL my cousins are in Southwest Ohio and Northern Kentucky. They are all within a fifty-mile radius. They are sure as hell not in Canada. Most of my cousins don't even know where Canada is. They couldn't pick Canada out on a color-coded map of North America. Some of them couldn't spell Canada if they were spotted the "Can-" and the "-da". I was convinced that this had to be a mistake.

"Who is this person?" I shot back. I was a bit annoyed by the inconvenience of the whole thing. Couldn't this Canadian cousin pick a better time to expose himself? (Pardon the vernacular.)

"His name is John Watson," Becky responded.

"John Watson?" I responded with an incredulous query.

"Yes, like Dr. John Watson, from Sherlock Holmes."

"Is he a doctor?" I inquired with a bit of sarcasm.

"No, I don't think so, but it's not definitive," Becky replied adding her own more subtle style of a jab.

"There's no possible way that is correct," I said, my terse staccato accentuating my disbelief. "Gotta be a mistake," I continued. Unimpressed and uninterested, I returned to packing for my Bataan Death March to Chicago for Wedding Stuff. Maybe I could catch COVID and stay home. *Let's see . . . killer flu or weekend full of Wedding Stuff?*

Hmmm, tough choice. I think I'll risk my life with the virus. Becky said I chose wrong, and my attendance was mandatory. I continued to pack.

As my daughter Sammie has pointed out, "Wedding Stuff" for me meant golfing with Sammie's future in-laws and standing for a few pictures at the bridal shower, along with a very enjoyable evening out for dinner with the groom's parents. Admittedly, it wasn't exactly a Bataan Death March.

* * *

NEW RELATIONS FROM ALL DIRECTIONS

Becky...

What Steve didn't know was that I had seen this DNA match from Montreal a few weeks earlier, but had blown past it because, well, it didn't fit the preferred narrative. Eventually it dawned on me how important this match was; first cousins are a strong and close relationship in the DNA world. I owed it to Steve to investigate this one.

Ancestry makes it so easy to reach out to matches without revealing much about personal identity. I took full advantage of their private messaging function to contact Mr. DNA Match in Canada.

> Hello,
>
> I manage my husband's DNA results, and they show that you are his first cousin. We are baffled by this close DNA relationship as we live in the Cincinnati, Ohio, area and you are in Canada. We think we know all his first cousins. Is it possible that you are adopted or one of your parents isn't your biological parent? I apologize for asking these questions; we just can't make any sense of this without considering those options.
>
> We should also be asking if your biological father spent any time in Cincinnati in Feb. 1963?
>
> May I ask what year you were born? My husband, Steve Osborne, was born in Cincinnati in 1963. His parents were born in 1933 and

1937—similar to when your parents were born.

Forgive me if this message gives you any offense. We would love to know if Ancestry's DNA is truly accurate. Steve was always told he has Native American ancestors yet his DNA results showed no Native American lineage, which is why we have some doubts about his test results.

We hope to hear your thoughts on how the two of you could be related.

Many thanks,

Becky Brower Osborne

Read 07:59 PM

The man who received my message took a hard pass—he didn't respond. I assumed that meant it didn't make any sense to him either.

Finally, I realized it couldn't be ignored any longer, which is when I brought it up to Steve. I'll never forget how simple and harmless this conversation seemed as we packed for our trip to Chicago. But it became an issue that would soon blow us out of the water.

I was not about to let this go. So, eleven days after my first message, I wrote to Mr. DNA Match again as we headed north to Chicagoland. At the bridal shower, I got all caught up in the festivities. It was easy to forget the DNA mystery with forty lovely women of all ages making a fuss over my daughter at a swanky country club. That is, until my phone pinged with an Ancestry message.

12:41 PM.

Hi there. Nice to meet you [began the message from Mr. DNA Mystery Match],

I am not offended. Lol. As far as I know, I was not adopted. As far as I know, my father, Allan John Watson, made a few work-related visits to Chicago, IL in the '50s, but never heard of him going to Cincinnati, Ohio. I was born in Montreal, Qc, Canada, in Sept 1961. My father was born in Montreal, also in 1934. I regret not asking more questions when my parents were alive. Wish I could be more helpful. Take care and God bless.

— J. Watson

02:49 PM.

Hello Becky. I made a mistake. My father did visit Cincinnati not Chicago, but I am unable to tell you when. This is weird.

03:31 PM.

I apologize for making things more confusing. I jumped the gun in my first message. Cincinnati yes, late '50s I was guessing. It could have very well been in the early sixties; I can't be sure. Sorry, I'm not going to be much help to you. I am trying to remember brief conversations with my dad from when I was a kid. My head is spinning right now trying to recall.

Suddenly the party came to a screeching halt—in my mind anyway. I devoured the message and quickly tapped back a reply. Ironically, after looking forward to the shower for so long, I suddenly couldn't wait for it to be over. I desperately wanted to tell my husband about this incredible development. Fortunately, Steve soon arrived at the party with the future groom and his father, fresh off the golf course. I slid up to him, gave his sweaty face a quick kiss, and whispered sotto voce into his ear, "He wrote back!"

Steve's initial facial expression communicated his lack of understanding who I was referring to. It quickly changed to surprise and amazement when he put the concepts together.

Later that evening as we were out for dinner with the groom's parents, my phone pinged with another response from Mr. DNA Match. This time I could not keep the news to myself.

"Hey, a funny thing happened today at the bridal shower," I said to the groom's parents. "Did we tell you guys that Steve took a DNA test?" I briefly took them through the basic details and we had a lively discussion about it. In many ways, it was a good introduction to the crazy family their son was about to marry into. And it served to quickly solidify our rapport with our future son-in-law's parents. Kind of like, "Hey, now that we're going to be family, here's one of our many dysfunctions . . ." Our dinner partners gave the topic their full attention and asked thoughtful questions. This conversation marked the first of many we would share about our respective families.

But bottom line, after a few back-and-forths, Mr. DNA Match and I were no closer to solving the mystery of how he and Steve were first cousins. All we knew was that Steve and John Watson shared a set of grandparents.

CHAPTER 9

Elementary, My Dear Watson

Come along, Watson. The game is afoot!
— Sherlock Holmes

There were so many questions on my mind. The primary one centered around the fact that I knew all my cousins, and John Watson was not on that list. I knew all my parents' siblings, again, no Watsons anywhere. The big issue is that my family is concentrated in the greater Cincinnati, Ohio, area with a heavy emphasis across the river in Northern Kentucky. John Watson was from Montreal, Quebec, The Great White North, about 800 miles as the crow flies. How the hell do we connect those dots? I've been told that sex requires relatively close proximity in order to complete the process. Its requisite distances are measured in inches, not miles (as so many things are). None of this made sense to me. It had to be a mistake.

I proceeded to step through the same process that anyone would who receives highly questionable results from a DNA test. The first and obvious thought is the test is flawed. There has to be some error in the collection, labeling, transportation, processing, assignment, or communication of the results. I began to research "flawed DNA tests" on the Internet to gain an understanding of the process and science behind the technology. I learned that the chance of a DNA sample mix-up is almost nil. DNA sample processing errors are equally rare, as the process has its own built-in cross check and verification steps. If collected and handled correctly, DNA tests are 99.99% accurate. Maybe this John Watson guy did something wrong, because I, of course, could not have. I sent the kit in with my email address and barcode, so communication couldn't be the issue. That all but eliminated 'error' except for in our imagination.

The second thought was to explore the science of DNA matching. In a nutshell, the DNA tests are looking for a number of segments that the person taking the test and any other person have in common. The segments are known as centimorgans (cM). The higher the count, the closer the relationship. Each type of relationship has a range determined by a common distribution of tests collected. For example, a parent/child relationship would have a range of 2,376 to 3,720 matching cMs with an average of 3,485. Full siblings would have a matching range from 1,613 to 3,488 cMs with an average being 2,613. First cousins would have 396 to 1,397 with an average being 866. John Watson and I shared 743 cMs, fairly close to the center of the range for a first cousin. The other potential relationships that match the cM range made no sense due to our closeness in age or generation so I won't detail them here.

So there we were, unlikely to be an error and very likely to be first cousins. If the centimorgans are correct, someone's parent is NOT their parent. Knowing my family situation, I'm thinking it's got to be John's problem.

Proceeding with some Holmesian deductive logic, I came up with these four possibilities:

1.   **I was adopted.** This had its possibilities. I had suspected it from time to time. The differences between me and my siblings would certainly support that. When I was eleven years old, I'd even asked my mother if I was adopted. Her response was, "You weren't adopted. I had you. I was there." I had quizzed my mom and older sisters about it and they all assured me that it was not the case. Mom said she gave birth to me and brought me home from the hospital. My sisters remember Mom being pregnant and then bringing me home in my swaddling clothes. They could be lying, but I trusted my oldest sister Kathy to shoot me straight. Not only that, but Dad1 would have told me at some point. I was told that to question anything else was absurd.

2.   **John's mom or my mom was not our respective mom.**
This is highly unlikely. The missing link would most likely be
a man. It almost always is. It would be extremely difficult to
hide a pregnancy for nine months and then have the mom and
baby leave the country and not have anyone figure it out and
not have it be part of family oral history. It's not impossible, just
significantly more feasible for the father of either John or I to
not be our respective father. Not to mention that this scenario
didn't fit either our family stories or other dates and information
that we had.

3.   **John's father could likely be my Uncle Harold**. I only
have one known Osborne uncle, Harold, Jack's brother. This had
possibilities. I found this one the most likely because frankly, it
was the most palatable. It generated the "Harold's Me Uncle"
theory we will explore later.

4.   **The worst of all possible outcomes.** My biological father
would have to be one of John's uncles. At this point we didn't
know how many uncles he had, if any. But this theory was hard
to believe. Dad1 and I shared a signature dimpled/cleft chin.
My sister Laura has it too. It was the only thing we seemed to
share, but it was solid and as plain as the, well, nose and chin
on my face. Only 25% of the population has this feature, but
ours was prominent and therefore a stronger argument for our
genetic connection. The possibility of Jack Osborne not being
my father would be the worst of all possible outcomes due to the
closeness I shared with him. Such a large part of my person was
invested in, and rested upon, being his son. He was more than
just my dad. He was elemental to my construction. I considered
this outcome unlikely and distasteful, therefore, I dismissed
this option practically out of hand. Frankly, it was upsetting just
to think about.

But as I stated above, there was a solution that was easy to
understand, easy to believe, and made sense quicker than you can say,
"Harold's Me Uncle."

CHAPTER 10

Occam's Razor and DNA Issues

For every complex problem there is an answer. One that is clear, simple, and wrong.
— H. L. Mencken

There is a somewhat well-known problem-solving principle known as Occam's Razor, which emphasizes that the most likely correct answer to any problem is the one with the fewest possible elements or variables. Some people might oversimplify Occam's Razor and state it as the simplest answer is most likely the correct one. While that's not a completely accurate summation of Occam's Razor, let's go with that definition and apply it to the problem of "How might John Watson and Steve Osborne be first cousins?"

With little to no other information, some creative thinking, and a bit of bourbon, Becky and I (she says it was just me and the bourbon) came up with a construct which was somewhat feasible, somewhat believable, and solved all the outstanding issues we were currently facing. In other words, we assembled a story that would fit the few facts we had and would lead us to our desired solution. We referred to it as the "Quicker than you can say 'Harold's Me Uncle Theorem.'" It goes like this:

Moving forward on the premise that John Watson's late father was not his biological father (sorry about that, John and Allan), and the fact that we are first cousins, then Jack Osborne's only brother would be the genealogical culprit. We knew Harold was in the US Army in the late 1950s and early '60s. He would have been single, so that works nicely. He was stationed in upstate New York, just ninety miles from Montreal, Canada, which is where the Watsons lived at that time. It's very easy to conjecture that, with a long weekend pass, a short drive to Canada, and a little international intrigue, happenstance would generate the outcome we were seeking. In short, Harold is the biological father of John Watson. That would make John and I first cousins, just like the DNA test results show. That would explain the 800-mile distance between Cincinnati and Montreal and therefore resolve the issue of geography and the limited proximity required for sex. We had absolutely no idea if this was true, but it was the best working theory we had, and we began to pursue it and its viability. I think we somehow convinced ourselves to explore this angle because the alternative (that one of John Watson's uncles was MY biological father) was too painful to consider and therefore not possible.

Fate is causing undeniable and accelerated effects
upon the particles of my life. Like Gravity, Fate is
drawing them ever closer.

If our theorem was correct, then proving it via a couple of DNA tests would be simple. It's a bit complicated and confusing to explain without graphics and a family tree, so here's the simple version. We needed my sister, Laura, and Harold's daughter, Sandy, (my first cousin) to take DNA tests. Their results and how they related to John Watson would eliminate all other possibilities. As the saying goes: "There can be only one!" The expected solution would be that John Watson is also Laura's first cousin and Sandy is his half-sister. That one's a little tougher on the digestive system for Sandy and her mother. But the results from these DNA tests would present a solution neatly resolved through the power of deductive reasoning; they would be scientifically substantiated and provide us with the answer to the question: Who did who at the zoo? The resolution would become elementary, my dear Watson.

Getting my sister Laura to take a DNA test became our primary focus. Despite the fact that Laura and her husband were living in Utah, it was easy to broach the subject because we were in regular contact.

More accurately, my wife Becky and Laura were in regular contact. Sandy was a different issue. She and I had not spoken since her father's funeral more than a decade ago. Asking Sandy to take a DNA test out of the blue would require a great deal more explanation and would have seemed well outside the norm. So, we started with Laura by making a quick phone call.

"Hey, Sis, I've got something I want to ask you to do for me," I began the conversation. "Remember that DNA kit we sent you from Ancestry. com a few years ago? Do you think you could take that test and send it in?"

"Yeah, I guess so," her voice was strained and her words elongated. There was a definite hesitation in her response. I wasn't sure what I was hearing. Was the reluctance because she was running a mental search trying to locate the test? Was I hearing a reluctance to take the test for some other reason? Was she trying to determine my motive? Did she know something that I didn't? Should I be worried here? It wasn't easy to decipher.

"Why do you want me to take the test?" she fired back.

"Well, I recently took the test and my results came back showing I have a close relative living in Montreal, Quebec. His name is John Watson. We can't figure out how we're related—it says we're first cousins, but that can't possibly be right. I'd like you to take the test to see if he shows up on your test results or if this whole thing is a mistake. I don't think he's truly my cousin. If he is, he'll show up on your results too." I had erroneously oversimplified the permutations of lineage in my mind and therefore in my conversation with my sister. I knew there were other options, but frankly, I didn't want to go into that level of detail with her, or I didn't want to peek into that dark box of possibilities, or both. There was a monster in that box. The less I thought of it, the less likely that potential outcome could be the truth. Yes, I am aware my thought process of today cannot change elements and actions of the past.

"Sure. Let me find it. I'm not sure where it is. You gave it to me a few years ago, and we've moved twice since then. It might be packed in a box somewhere."

Ok, lost, that's the hesitation, I thought. As it would turn out, Laura could not locate the test kit. Becky contacted Ancestry and explained what had happened; they were kind enough to send a second test to Laura's new home at no additional cost. Thank you, kind people at Ancestry.

I called Laura back. "There is a new test on the way. Can you do that thing when you get it? I'd like to get some quick turnaround. This mystery is kinda bugging me."

"I'll do it as soon as I get it, I promise." That was good enough for me. About a week later I got a text, "I did the test and sent it off. Let's see what happens. Love you!"

"Thx. Love you back," I replied. And now we sit and wait. Well, not really. We didn't sit and wait. In fact, we went about our lives not giving the test much thought.

About five weeks later, we had another trip planned, this one to Hilton Head Island, SC. There was no Wedding Stuff there, only sun, beach, food, alcohol, and some close friends—the five basic requirements for a good vacation. We headed to HHI, unconcerned as to when the DNA test results might return. The test was a hobby, a curiosity, a lark which became an afterthought. What could possibly come of this other than some spicy tale of someone's salacious behavior from somewhere deep in their past? Something that would be interesting, but distant from my life in both time and lineage. A good ten minutes of gossip, I would estimate. I was still focused on the Harold's Me Uncle Theorem and was convinced I would be telling my Aunt June that her husband had a child in Canada. Won't that be a laugh? Well, maybe not for Aunt June, but I sure will think it's funny. It's all fun and games until someone loses a parent, right?

Gravity has entangled the fragments of my life and pulls
at them hard. They accelerate. Their trajectories now
place them on a collision course.

CHAPTER 11

Tell Me About Your Dad

It doesn't matter who my father was; it matters who I remember he was. — Anne Sexton

All this DNA talk had me thinking about Dad1, Jack Osborne. "Tell me about your dad," is a request I love to hear. I love to talk about my dad. I'm named after him. J Steven Osborne, the 'J' stands for Jack, of course. I wear that association with pride. I think he's the greatest. Maybe that's because he's my dad . . . or maybe he's just great. Whichever it is, he's my hero.

The most effective way of describing my dad is to draw the comparison between him and Ralph Kramden, the character played by Jackie Gleason in *The Honeymooners*. *The Honeymooners* is a comedy TV show that originally aired in 1955–56. Ralph Kramden was a city bus driver, a blue-collar kind of guy. So was my dad. Ralph wore a uniform with a tie and a cap with a patent leather brim, just like my dad. He was big and round and loud, just like my dad. Ralph had a goofy friend named Norton. My dad's goofy friend was named Chuck, but he was just as goofy. Ralph and Norton and their wives would get themselves into trouble, often due to Ralph's questionable judgment. Jack and Chuck did the exact same thing and put their wives through hell at times. But just like Ralph, Jack was hard not to love. The primary reason that he was easy to love is that he was full of love himself. Behind the growling, snarling, deep voice was a big softie who would do almost anything for his friends and absolutely anything for Laura and me.

The Honeymooners was in syndication originally on the BBC, and as of the date of this printing, it shows on ME-TV. The Honeymooners is definitely worth a watch. It will showcase a somewhat exaggerated glimpse of my dad. In lieu of *The Honeymooners*, which is usually found as black-and-white TV reruns, let's move ahead a few decades and amp up the color. A newer and more vibrant version of my dad was Fred Flintstone of *The Flintstones*. This animated TV show was an unabashed, total rip-off of *The Honeymooners* (my opinion only). Fred would be Dad's animated avatar.

The reason I like the Jackie Gleason comparison is because it fits Jack in more ways than one. He was not only the character Ralph Kramden from *The Honeymooners*, but Gleason also played another iconic role in *The Hustler*, the 1961 Paul Newman movie in which Gleason portrayed Minnesota Fats, the renowned pool shark. My dad was also extremely good at shooting pool. Gleason received a nomination for Best Supporting Actor for his portrayal in the 1961 movie.

Dad loved to go boating. His boat was nothing special, just an old sixteen-foot outboard. Dad loved to fish. Only when I began to take my daughter Jackie fishing did I realize how much Dad had taught me: bass, bluegill, crappie, how to bait, how to tie a leader and hook, how to cast with accuracy. Some of the best days of my youth were fishing with Dad. My daughter Jackie has said the same to me about our time as anglers.

Dad loved to gamble. He loved to play poker. He played most weekends with his friends, his brother Harold, and their cousin Woody. Dad would take us over to Harold's house. Laura and I would play with our cousins Sandy and Tommy until I could weasel my way into his lap and watch the big boys play poker. The logic and math were almost as fascinating as the language I heard. By seven years old, I knew the ranking of poker hands. I knew a full house beats a flush. I learned that my dad was a "check-raising, sandbagging son of a bitch," (according to Cousin Woody). My dad would cuss when he got beat by what he referred to as bad cards. I remember Harold calling my dad a bad loser, to which Dad responded with "That's only because I don't get much practice." Yeah, that's my old man.

He really loved to shoot pool and he was damned good at it. With his large size and pool shooting acumen, the Minnesota Fats moniker was

Cousin Woody (left) and Jack (right),
playing poker on a Friday night.

used to refer to him frequently. Jack would pick me up from my mom
and stepdad's house (the Condo House) on Friday evening or early
Saturday morning for his bi-weekly visitation. If it was Friday night, we
would sometimes end up at a bar that had a pool table. Frequently, that
was the Eighth & State Bar and Pool Hall on the west side of Cincinnati.
It was not the high rent part of town, but I didn't fear being there. I
probably should have, but I was young and didn't know any better. This
was the scene of one of my most vivid memories of the legendary Jack
Osborne.

One Friday evening, Dad picked me up from my mom's house. For
some reason, Laura was not with us that weekend. We were in the bar
at Eighth & State and Dad was playing pool for cash as he did so often.
While driving a city bus was honest and steady work, it wasn't the best
paying job. Dad struggled to make ends meet and that fact was not lost
on me. At nine years old, there were times that I thought I had more
disposable income than he did. This was one of those times.

I watched the action from my perch on a bar stool, which I had
pulled across the floor and placed up against the wall near the pool

table, but not in the way of anyone who might be taking a shot. Dad was playing whoever would come to the table with the requisite amount of cash, typically $10 per game. That was a lot of money in 1972.

A strapping young lad approached the pool table. He seemed very old to me. I would guess he was in his late twenties. He wore a plaid work shirt and beat-up jeans and sported a scruffy beard. He had a head full of cockiness, topped with a Redman Chewing Tobacco ball cap. He would have been the typical high-quality patron at the Eighth & State, if the patron wasn't a biker. He challenged my dad to play. I remember thinking he would look like a lumberjack if he could get that beard to cooperate and fill in the blank areas of his face. I noticed I had never seen him before. He wasn't from around here. I recognized the regulars, which made me a regular myself, which I guess is not a great thing at only nine years old.

I watched as they played multiple games. The games went back and forth for about an hour plus; dad winning some, dad losing some and swearing loudly when he lost. I got to get a bag of Fritos and a Coke. I was loving the show despite the cloud of cigarette smoke that could obscure the view of the table from time to time and the smell of last week's beer coming up from the floor. I had designs on playing the pinball machine if Dad won some money, which he did when Mr. Lumberjack Wannabe Man scratched on the eight ball. For those who don't play pool or haven't spent hundreds of youthful hours watching their old man do it, that means the white ball (aka the cue ball) went in a pocket when Lumberjack was shooting at the eight ball. The eight ball was the last ball he needed to sink to win the game. Instead, the white cue ball went into a pocket, causing him to lose the game.

"Damn it!" exclaimed Mr. Lumberjack Wannabe Man. As he was putting quarters into the table for the next game, he suggested, "What do you say we up the stakes a bit?" This is a strange thing to do when you have just lost a game . . . unless a person is setting a trap for their opponent. I had an unsettling feeling he was trying to trick my dad.

"What are you thinking?" Dad asked.

"Let's do $100 per game," came the response. My dad's eyebrows rose and his head cocked back and to the side a bit, indicating his incredulous surprise. Even at nine years old, I knew $100 was a shipload of money. I also knew that my dad couldn't afford it. For reference, $100 in 1972 is like $746 in 2024. Imagine playing pool for close to $750 per game! I certainly could not. That was nearly half his monthly wage. I was not going to let this guy take my dad's money that we needed for gas and groceries. I quickly jumped off the bar stool and tried to inconspicuously tug on my dad's sleeve as I whispered.

"Dad, you can't do that. You don't have that kind of money," I pleaded quietly while keeping a wary eye on his opponent.

"Go sit down, boy," he said without eye contact, an ounce of compassion, or affection. He said to his target, "Do you have that kind of cash?"

Mr. Lumberjack Wannabe Guy nodded in the affirmative and pulled a large number of bills from his front pocket and fanned them out a bit.

Dad nodded and said sharply, "Rack 'em up."

In an instant, the room changed from a Friday night entertainment parlor into a gladiator coliseum. Patrons who knew my dad began to watch. All humor, casualness, and emotion left my dad's persona as he transformed into total hunter/killer mode. He broke the rack and it sounded like a crack of thunder. I jumped in my seat. It was like nothing I had heard earlier that evening. Multiple balls ran across the felt and fell into their pockets. Dad moved quickly around the table as if he was double-parked at the curb. But when he came to focus on a shot, he grew still like he was made of concrete. I watched the cue ball do things I didn't think physics would allow. I saw it dance like it was on a string. I saw it roll in one direction and then completely reverse course 180 degrees. If someone said there was a ghost moving the ball, I would have agreed. I saw it move in an arc around other balls. Most of all, I saw it strike whatever my dad aimed at. The target ball would scurry its way to the corner or side pocket and then the cue ball would come to a stop perfectly aligned for his next shot.

Dad ran the table three times straight. That means he won three games and his opponent never got the chance to shoot, not once. The young buck walked to the table, threw down the third payment—clearly the last of his money—and then got in my dad's face.

"You hustled me, you [expletive]. You know it. You didn't play anything like that until we raised the stakes," he said in a loud and angry voice. Now everyone in the bar was watching. I thought for sure he was going to hit Dad, which scared me more than anything. There was no way I could protect him.

Without blinking an eye, Jack said, "You raised the stakes, not me, [expletive]. And at $10 a game, you didn't have my full attention." His tone was completely dismissive. Those words hung in the air the way they still hang in my mind.

"You didn't have my full attention."

That was just another way of saying, "Your fault, not mine. Make sure you know where you're swimming. There could be sharks in the water." This kid tried to hustle my dad. Instead, Dad hustled him, and I was, unwittingly, part of the con. I was part of the setup. An old man and his son in a bar on a Friday night. That's not what a pool shark looks like. As we have learned from watching nature shows, some sharks are camouflaged.

That night I played multiple games of pinball and then we ate at Frisch's Big Boy Restaurant. The next night we ate at Ponderosa Steak House. I got a chocolate shake both nights. Life was awesome. So was my dad. I loved him so much. He was a god to me.

Jack Osborne left this Earth on March 11, 1999. He died that morning of a heart attack. We were hundreds of miles away from each other. He was in Texas for the winter; I was on a flight to Boston for business. It was the saddest day of my life. For all his faults, for all his shortcomings, for all the lack of social graces he may have displayed, Jack Osborne was perfect in my eyes.

CHAPTER 12

Fate Calling and the Worst of All Possible Worlds

There is an hour, a minute—you will remember it forever—when you know instinctively on the basis of the most inconsequential evidence, that something is wrong. You don't know—can't know—that it is the first of a series of "wrongful" events that will culminate in the utter devastation of your life as you have known it.
— Joyce Carol Oates

In September 2021, our long-awaited vacation in Hilton Head had come to an end. We had just boarded the plane in Savannah for the return flight back to Cincinnati with a stop in Atlanta. Becky and I were sitting across the aisle from our friends, John and Robin, waiting for the flight to take off. Sun-kissed from our week at the pool and beach, each of us was relaxed with a drink in our hand. In the final moments before the door of the plane closed, my phone rang. It was a call from Laura. Six weeks had passed since my request for her to take a DNA test.

"Hey, sis, what's up?" I answered in my typical greeting to her.

"Stevie, I wanted to let you know I got my DNA test results back," she reported.

"That's great. Did you see anything interesting?" I quizzed.

"I see a lot of people I know on my list of DNA matches, but some of this information doesn't make any sense to me."

"Well, those reports have a ton of information and I think some of it can be a little confusing. It took me a while to digest all of it. What's the issue?"

"Under the DNA Matches heading it shows a bunch of people. A lot of them are Meltons from Mom's side." This was no surprise to me. I also saw Meltons on my list of DNA matches. She continued, "And I'm seeing Steve and Dave and Peggy from Dad's side." This was chilling news to me. She was seeing members of the Osborne clan, none of whom were on my DNA report. Why would they be on her report and not mine? I knew the answer already. My stomach began to knot and my chest began to tighten—not a great feeling for a former coronary bypass patient.

Laura continued, "Stevie, I don't see John Watson listed anywhere on my report. And it says here that I have a half-brother, J.O. Who is J.O.?"

I responded with the words that had been buried deep within my head since this ordeal began, before we left for Chicago for Wedding Stuff. Before I spit in the tube. Before I had spoken of John Watson. Before the search and subsequent request to Laura to help us piece this puzzle together. The words I hoped I would never say, but always knew might be the case no matter how I tried to deny their possibility.

Long before this call, I had already worked through all the possible DNA relationship permutations. Laura not seeing John Watson was a critical data element that could occur in only one instance—the worst possible outcome. I also knew who J.O. was, and the answer was excruciating. I paused to confirm my own thoughts and to work up the courage to say the words I knew to be true—the words that would change our lives, our relationship, and destroy my own world.

"Sis, J.O. stands for J Steven Osborne. I'm J.O. I'm your half-brother," my voice quivered. "J.O. is how I identified myself on Ancestry." Those words packed a plane full of ramifications. I bit my lip to keep from breaking down into tears.

Laura shot back in denial, "That can't be! Mom is our mom and Dad is our dad."

"No, Love. What you just told me from your report is that Mom is our mom . . . but Dad . . . well, Dad is your dad. What you've just told me is that Jack Osborne is not my biological father." I continued the unspoken thought, "And my life and lineage are lies."

"That can't be. There has to be something wrong here."

"No, Sis, something tells me it's right."

Over the PA came the flight attendant as she continued her announcements. We were instructed to end our calls and put our phones into airplane mode. "Laura, I've got to go, we're taking off. I'll call you later, okay?"

"Yeah, sure. Are you . . . are you okay?" She knew the answer. Anyone would know the answer.

"No . . . no, I'm not." I paused and then continued, "Love you. We'll talk later. Bye." I ended the call. I closed my eyes. I was thrust out of the physical world I was in. I found myself disassociated and lost. I was out of time and place and dimension. I was floating in the ether of disbelief, panic, and loss.

Becky had been listening to the entire conversation. She was seated to my left so I had held the phone up to my left ear so she could listen with her right. She was fully aware of what had just transpired. She knew I had just taken a full salvo broadside and was listing hard to port. I felt her hand squeeze my thigh and then move to my hand. She held it tight. Fight them as I might, I knew the tears were coming. There was nothing I could do to stop them. Becky squeezed my hand again. Screw it. I didn't care. Let the tears come. Go ahead and cry.

Our friend John was sitting across the aisle from me. He was puzzled as to what could be happening. He and Robin talked quietly.

Becky said quietly in my ear, "I've got you. It's okay, Sweetie. It's going to be okay. I've got you." She consoled me as only she can. As wonderful as her loving voice was, it wasn't going to change what I had just heard. It wasn't going to change the reality of the situation.

My entire life, I had always heard a voice in my head, like a whisper. Now the voice screamed into a megaphone, inches from my mind's ear, "Your family is not your family. Your dad is not your dad. You are an alien." Then it hit me. I was right all along. From the age of nine I had been right. I was different and separate and now I knew why.

I had lost my father for the third time in my life. The first time was when I was four years old and he came into my room to tell me he and my mom were getting divorced. I lost him again in 1999 when he died of a heart attack. I was on a plane that morning he died. This third time, once again on a plane, I lost my biological connection to him.

The official term for what I just discovered is called NPE, or Non-Parental Event. It is where someone learns that their parent is not their parent. I think 'DNA Orphan' is more to the point and makes more sense. I became a person who has lost a parent to the cruelty of science and the uncaring light of a DNA test.

My dad was the one and only person in my life who had consistently shown me true and unconditional love. He was the man who traveled eighty miles round trip, twice every other weekend, just to see me. He was the man who was the source of my drive and my focus. It was my goal to make him proud. This was the person to whom I attributed so many of my positive characteristics, for whom I named both my daughter and even the bar in my office building. Suddenly, my connection was lost— severed. I was beyond devastated.

I was still sitting on the plane but now my heart was shattered, my soul was crushed. Panic rushed over me. My brain told me to get up out of my seat. I needed to get off the plane. Just as I unclicked my seat belt and stood up, the lead flight attendant announced over the PA system, "Ladies and gentlemen, we will be pushing back from the gate in just a few moments. As we are preparing for takeoff, everyone, please take your seats."

Damn it. I sat down and closed my eyes.

I spent the flight trying to rationalize what had been presented to me. It couldn't be true. The primary reason it couldn't was because I didn't want it to be. My mind raced through the events of my life with Dad. The memories were numerous and emotional. They were elemental to my being. They were the underlying structure to who I was. Were all those times, all those experiences, somehow fraudulent? Did Dad know about this? My mom surely had to know. What the hell was going on?

We landed in Atlanta for a short layover. I quickly exited the plane with Becky, John, and Robin behind me. As a well-worn traveler (about two million miles on Delta alone), I always try to gather my people and keep them together when traveling, much like a herding breed of dog. Not this time. I walked away from them all. I didn't want to talk or make eye contact. I wanted to be alone, which would prove almost impossible in the world's busiest airport. Without a word between us, Becky knew how to handle the situation and communicated with John and Robin.

I don't remember much after boarding the flight to Cincinnati. I know I kept my eyes closed for most of the flight as I pondered the irony: Me—the man who once claimed to have fourteen siblings—is in fact an only child. At this point a child who has no clue who his father is. I lost my connection with Jack Osborne . . . and with Arlene, Darlene, Charlene, Francene, and the whole hee-haw gang—GONE!

I knew we landed in Cincinnati. I knew we said goodbye to John and Robin. During the drive home from the airport, I remember staring out the windshield, unable to muster any semblance of conversation. When I'm that upset, silence is the only language I speak. Becky and I uttered only standard navigational phrases. She would occasionally reach over and rub my shoulder or hold my hand. Normally her touch has the power to heal whatever ails me, but in this situation, I was beyond such help.

Someone once said to me when they heard this part of my story that my whole life must have felt like a lie. I think more accurately I felt as if I had a part of my core stolen from me. Being the biological son of Jack Osborne was one of my most critical and central tenets. I now knew that tenent was a lie. I've been asked throughout my life where my competitive drive comes from. Where did this intense fire for achievement, both personal and business, originate? My belief has always been that it had its nexus in one core value. That value centered around making my dad proud. Nothing gave me a greater sense of accomplishment, of completeness, of satisfaction, than to hear Jack Osborne say, "That's my boy."

In a cold instant, a scientific document fractured that pillar of my person. I had built my belief system around an illusion. As with most illusions, there was someone who knew the truth. Someone whose intentional sleight of hand was meant to deceive me for their benefit. That person gave little or no thought to the collateral damage this deception could cause. I had been betrayed by someone I was always told I could trust more than any other person: my mother.

In that moment, in a single fateful phone call, Gravity and Fate had forced the elements of my life into an unstable critical mass. Under the crushing pressure of scientific DNA evidence, my past, my life, everything about my person went supernova. My life, my history, and much of what I knew about myself was hurled into space and scattered to the cosmos.

HE NEEDS HIS SPACE

Becky...

Immediately following Steve's call with his sister, it became clear to me that he was experiencing an internal meltdown. I recognized the far off look on his face that indicated deep internal stress and a desire to escape. Unfortunately, our aircraft was the last place he would find any privacy. Once we got inside the Atlanta airport, I suggested that Steve stay with our bags near the gate of our next flight, while John, Robin, and I went in search of something to eat.

The three of us pushed our way through the throngs of people coming towards us. As usual, the airport was chaos. We came to the corner of an intersection where we huddled to form some kind of strategy for finding food that everyone liked. But there was a bit of confusion on Robin's face.

"What's wrong with Steve?" she asked. I looked at her somewhat incredulously, wondering how she could not understand why he was about to implode. But that wasn't fair—no one could possibly know how the seemingly innocent conversation with his sister had just blown the roof off his sanity. Our friends were aware of the existence of a mysterious first cousin in Canada, but that was the extent of their knowledge.

"He just found out his dad is not his dad," I said.

"What?" replied Robin. Her confused expression remained.

"His sister just told him that she's only his half-sister. That means his biological father is someone else."

Robin is a smart chick; she absorbed that information and didn't ask any more questions. The three of us quickly found some decent food options among the airport culinary choices and made our way back to Steve. He was right where we left him, leaning against a wall with our luggage. I suspect he had lost all awareness of his surroundings and was deep inside the whirlpool of chaos that had engulfed his brain. He was most certainly trying to make sense of this news.

It was a long, quiet flight back to Cincinnati. Inwardly, I was antsy to start researching who might possibly be Steve's biological father. To be honest, I was actually very excited about the challenge ahead. But my devastated husband was in deep, silent pain. The more troubled he is, the quieter and less responsive he becomes. At this point I expected almost nothing from him. I knew I needed to channel my energy toward supporting him and making sure he didn't mentally implode from the shock. The research could wait.

THE WISH I WISH I HADN'T WISHED

For a good portion of my life I had wished that I was not related to my siblings. In an instant that wish came true. As I sat on the couch after arriving home, with my eyes closed but welling up, I trembled with fear, doubt, and loss. The thoughts and questions flashed in my mind so quickly I didn't have time to process them before the next life-altering realization crashed my train of thought. I tried desperately to control my emotions and manage my panicked state, but I knew that at any second the tears would begin to stream down my face again. At least now I was in the privacy and familiarity of my home.

I realized the couch was shaking due to the convulsions caused by my body as I silently sobbed. I had lost my dad. In my world, God had died. I had lost my rag-tag group of misfit siblings. I had lost my sense of belonging even if that sense had always been an uneasy one. There was nothing I wanted more desperately than to have my family back, the whole dysfunctional group. Goddammit! I had gotten exactly what I had always secretly wished for. Now I realized just how effing stupid that wish was. I realized how ignorant, arrogant, and shortsighted I had been.

So many people say, "You don't know what you got 'til it's gone." I finally realized what I had and what I had just lost. In some way, I felt I had wished this state of chaos into existence, and now regret sat heavily like an elephant upon my chest. It was soul-crushing. I was in complete shock. How the hell did I get here? What could possibly come next? Where do I go from here? Is it possible to un-ring this bell? I was lost in an impenetrable fog of grief and confusion. Completely lost. I was lost without my lighthouse, my Dad, to help me find my way.

Fate, like Gravity, is uncaring, unforgiving, and unrelenting.
My wellbeing is not its concern.
My demise is inconsequential and irrelevant.

PART THREE
The Descent

CHAPTER 13

The Morning After

Secrets tear you apart. — Mitch Albom

The next morning was a warm and comfortable Sunday in mid-September. My head was still spinning and my stomach was in knots. I was sitting outside on our screened-in porch. I leaned forward with my elbows on my knees and my face in my hands, a common position for me when I'm stressed or upset.

SCHRÖDINGER'S CAT'S DNA TEST RESULTS

I was struggling with a torrential emotional cycle that would hold me captive for many months to come, much like a never-ending hangover. The cycle began with utter shock, combined with disbelief, wrapped in the soul-crushing reality that this situation wasn't going to change. This was my new reality. My dad was not my dad. It's still difficult to type those words. How could that be? With all that we shared and all that he meant (and still means) to me, how could that be? What did that mean for us? Not to mention, now I had no idea who my biological father was. Major elements of my life and belief system were lies. I had parts of me stolen. It was horrifically unsettling.

If I had been made from Legos, it would have been as if someone had dropped me onto a hardwood floor and the impact violently disassembled me. No two bricks would be connected to one another. I was scattered across the room and I would swear I could hear a vacuum cleaner in the next room coming my way.

Then came the logical thoughts: *Wait, if you think about it for just a minute, I am who I am. I am where I am, and that hasn't changed. In fact, considering this new knowledge, if one were to look back at my life, what part of my fifty-seven years would have changed? Maybe nothing. Has anything really changed? Is this a big deal?* Maybe I was overthinking this. Maybe I was okay. Sure, I was okay. And then the bottom would drop out of my stomach and I would be back to soul-crushing shock and disbelief. This cycle would repeat itself about every ten minutes whenever I wasn't preoccupied with the task in front of me.

The mental and emotional cycle I just described was not unlike the unsolvable quantum physics thought exercise known as Schrödinger's Cat. In the realm of quantum mechanics, particles can be considered to exist in multiple states at the same time. To illustrate this concept, the theoretic physicist Erwin Schrödinger proposed a sealed box and within said box was a hypothetical cat and a vile of poison. Under certain conditions, the poison would be released and the cat would be killed. But as long as the box was not opened, no one could know the true state of the cat. One could theorize that the cat was both alive and dead at the same time—two completely different outcomes sharing the same space. Only by opening the box and inspecting the contents could one determine the cat's true state. A dizzying thought exercise indeed.

I found myself in a similar conundrum with the "state" of Dad. I had lost him, but not lost him at the same time. My test results told me that he wasn't my biological father and everything we had based our relationship on was a lie. My heart and logic told me that nothing in my past had changed, though everything had. Dad1 was both everything he always was, but nothing that he was. I was living Schrödinger's Cat's DNA Test, but I had no physical box to open to resolve the conflict. If I had a box, I'm not sure I would have wanted to open it.

There is nothing that I can write that can force someone into that place or cause someone to experience that feeling. I suspect it would be impossible to get there unless someone has experienced it firsthand themselves.

Notwithstanding that previous statement, I have a couple of friends who began to cry as they listened to the story of my loss. I believe they, too, have a close relationship with their dad and could somehow put themselves at least in the same area code. I can only suppose that a close relationship with their dad makes understanding this type of loss easier and more acute. Or perhaps my friends who cried didn't really feel the loss of their father but could see the grief within me. Perhaps the tears were tears of empathy for my pain. Either way, I appreciate the fact that they understood the gravity of the situation.

Becky came out of the house with a fresh cup of coffee for each of us. "How are you doing, Sweetie?" She knew the answer to the question, but she asked it anyway.

"Bec, I'm really struggling with all of this. I'm lost and I'm in pieces. I've lost Dad all over again." When my dad passed in 1999, the loss was so acute that there were times when I felt as if I was missing a limb, as if something had been amputated. My mind told me that I had more than one problem. Not only had I lost Dad1—again—but I was now some form of an orphan. I had lost my dad and then realized I was also missing a biological father (dad3).

"And hell, I have no idea who my real father is." If I were to have any chance of moving beyond this disaster, finding the identity of my biological father would be a big step forward. "Bec, do you think you can find him for me? Can you find my biological father?"

Her eyes lit up. I'm quite sure she had been dying for me to ask that question, and I might have caught her off guard by asking so soon. "The only information I have is that he's somehow related to John Watson." While it was not much, it was at least something. My expectations were tempered. I knew enough to know that parental (especially paternal) searches can take months or years and even then, not come up with any definitive results. But I also knew that if anyone could possibly find him, it would be my wife.

The Epidemic of Misattributed Parentage

Becoming a DNA orphan, or experiencing misattributed parentage, comes in multiple flavors. The three most common are:

- **Late Discovery Adoptee (LDA)** — Someone learns that they were adopted but were never told about it.
- **Late Discovery Donor Conceived Person (LDDCP)** — One or both raising parents typically had fertility issues and were only able to conceive using an egg or sperm donor or donated embryo and they don't tell their child about it.
- **Non-Paternal (or Non-Paternity) Event (NPE)** — Someone (like me) who discovers, typically via a DNA test, that dad is not their biological father as a result of an affair, sexual assault, or other event.

Misattributed parentage was originally estimated at 3% of the population, but now with the tsunami of discoveries being produced from home-based DNA tests, that estimate has continued to rise. In 2020, it had been adjusted to 5 to 7%. It was recently adjusted again to be as high as 8 to 10%. Not one in thirty, but now, one in ten. The condition has become so common that, whenever I tell my story, almost without exception, the listener tells me of their friend or acquaintance who has experienced a similar discovery.

CHAPTER 14

Becky Gets to Work

Finding a needle in a haystack is easy.
Just bring a magnet. — Keith DeCandido

BECKY'S GENEALOGICAL SLEUTHING PART II

Becky...

Steve was right, I was chomping at the bit to begin searching for his biological father. But first I needed to get him off to work so I could focus. When Monday morning arrived, I encouraged him to eat breakfast and take a shower. It would help just to get him moving. I knew once he did, his own work ethic would send him to the office. This would be the best place for him, at least for now. The demands of the day would distract him from this situation and the immense pain he was in. It would also allow me to focus on the detective duties given to me by Fate and my husband. I was excited by the challenge but felt the weight of its importance. This would be the most important genealogical research I would ever undertake, and time was of the essence.

I don't know how other hobby genealogists perform their research but when faced with a challenge, I like to inundate myself with records and feel my way through them with part of my brain disconnected. It has something to do with using one's intuition rather than sharp analytical skills. To be sure, I'm trying to match up what few clues I have with the records I am wading through. But mainly, I'm waiting for something to go "*DING*," kind of like a burglar slowly turning the dial of a safe, listening for the tumblers to go *"CLICK."*

All day Monday I tried a variety of searches to find someone in John Watson's family who could possibly be Steve's biological father. John and I had been in communication about the few facts he knew regarding his family tree. I started with his father's family to see if there were any brothers who might have traveled to the States. I found that John had an uncle, Danny, who had died about fifteen years ago. When I shared this information with John, he admitted that he wasn't aware of Danny's death, that in fact, he had lost touch with all surviving members of his family other than his sister. With so little information from Steve's mystery cousin, this was going to be harder than I thought.

Despite my infamous frugality, I did not hesitate to pony up the extra dollars required for the World Edition of Ancestry so that I could access records outside the United States. After all, this was my husband's father I was looking for, and the grandfather of our two daughters. Having exhausted John's paternal family, I began thinking about John's mother's family. We'd been so focused on his father that I hadn't thought much about whether his mother had any brothers. John shared the names of his maternal grandparents with me, and I began to research the records for them in Montreal.

I was easily able to find one, two, and then three brothers of John's mother. Wow, this was a fresh new field to forage. The oldest brother had died in his forties, the next brother had died in his fifties, and the third brother proved to be elusive, but at least I had his full name.

I widened my search to all of North America in the hopes of finding him in the States. After all, whoever Steve's biological father was, he had been in close proximity to Steve's mother in Cincinnati in 1963. I quickly came across an obituary for someone by the exact same name of the third brother, but this gentleman had died in Palm Beach, FL. Nope, our guy had to be in Cincinnati. I continued wading through the plethora of records belonging to men with similar but slightly different names. Finally, I circled back to the man from Florida, and began to read his obituary:

> **HOLMES, Peter E.**, age 57. Passed away October 19, 1982, in West Palm Beach, Florida. Residence [local address]. Formerly of Mariemont.

Tick-tick-tick . . . *CLICK.*

Mariemont is a suburb of Cincinnati, and upon further examination I discovered the obituary had appeared in *The Cincinnati Enquirer.* While some genealogists would howl in protest that this alone was not enough information to prove the identity of Steve's father (and they would be right), I knew in my gut that this was our man.

I texted Steve: "BINGO."

THE NEEDLE AND THE GENEALOGICAL HAYSTACK

It was Monday, the 20th of September. The Monday following my DNA surprise, which occurred the previous Saturday. We returned from vacation to the typical backlog of items needing to be addressed, having worked at only a minimal level while in Hilton Head. Monday was hectic at the office. I was aware that Becky had begun the search for my biological father but was unaware of how far she had progressed or if she had made any progress at all. Work was difficult due to my inability to concentrate on any single task for more than a few minutes. My primal emotions would surge through the mental breakwater I had erected. Prior to this day, compartmentalizing had never been a problem for me, but I was failing miserably at it now. The emotions came from a place far too deep within me to ignore, the pain was too acute. I soldiered through the day and the required tasks.

By mid-afternoon I had heard nothing from Becky. And then I got a text with a single word: "BINGO." I know that it is obvious now, but at the time, I read my phone and thought, *What the hell is BINGO?* I'm typically much more on top of it than to miss a flare shot into the air like "BINGO." I brushed the text aside to complete whatever urgent demand-of-the-minute was pressing me. By the time I left the office early, I was at the limit of my operational capacity.

My three-minute drive home didn't allow enough time for me to review Becky's communications and decipher her text. I walked in the door and there she sat at our kitchen table with a look of expectation and excitement on her face. My thought process was still five steps behind hers.

"Did you see my text?" She was trying to cap her excitement.

"Which one?" My response did NOT meet her expectations. I think I moved her from excited to disappointed, maybe even frustrated.

"BINGO! The text that said BINGO!" Her mouth didn't come close to saying, "*WTF?*" but her eyes were quite vocal.

"Yeah, what's that mean?" Clearly my brain was completely disengaged. We had been talking for two days about the search for my biological father and I couldn't connect that with the Bingo text. Two plus two was not equaling four to me.

"I found him. I found your biological father. His name is Peter Edgar Holmes. He's John Watson's uncle, on his mother's side," Becky said proudly. She had every reason to be proud. She had found Peter Holmes, my biological father and confirmed his connection in less than six applied hours, an achievement some people might never be able to accomplish. She had solved the puzzle of my paternity in less than a day, complete with documentation. FLAT OUT AMAZING!

"Are you kidding me? How did you do that so quickly?" So, there's my defense. I didn't make the "Bingo" connection because in my mind, there was no possible way she could have found my bio dad in less than a day. Not possible, therefore, no Bingo. She had been building my family tree for over a year. It's not my fault she's mind-blowingly good at genealogy stuff.

Becky began to detail the steps of familial exploration and mapping, analysis of the data captured, process of elimination, narrowing the target field, document search and collection, dates and location, and the final assembly of the puzzle. Admittedly she did have a single solid starting point (John Watson) and a required relationship match (an uncle of John's). Even so, finding and researching John's grandparents, parents and uncles, culling them down to possible suspects, and then chasing them through documents and records, literally around the world, should take months if not years. She killed it in hours.

I was astonished that Becky was so incredibly proficient in the field. It is a true superpower. Once I got over her accomplishment, I began to internalize the work product of that accomplishment: the information regarding my biological father, Peter Edgar Holmes. For the first time in my life, I was able to say the name of the man who gave me 50% of my genetic material. It was a moment of relief. I was at the headwaters of a new chapter of my life. It was some amount of salve on my wound. But it also rubbed salt in another still open wound. It would cause fatal damage to my genetic relationship with Jack. We had come full circle. We then knew the truth. It was an uncomfortable one.

A FAMILIAR FACE

Although Becky had discovered who Peter Holmes was, there was still so much we did not know. Becky would not stop her research at this point. She was back at it the next day. When I arrived home, she said, "I have something to show you." She slid her phone across the table to me. Displayed on the phone was a picture I had never seen before. It was in a perfectly square format, black and white, denoting it was from the pre-1960s era. In it stood a tall, slender man with a head of thick, dark hair. He was in a double-breasted suit with wide lapels.

"Do you recognize that person at all?" Becky asked expectantly. I picked it up and examined it. Although I was seeing it for the first time, the man in the picture looked strangely familiar. He seemed like a ghost of someone I knew. There was something about his eyes, his lips, his forehead, and the overall shape of his head, yes, his odd-shaped head. It was like a big lightbulb. Yes! I had seen this person before. It was me, thirty years ago! But, of course, it wasn't me, it was my biological father.

"Holy Batshit, Batman!" I exclaimed.

"Yes, you're right. That's Peter. That's your biological father," Becky explained the painfully obvious. She was giddy. "John, God bless him, rooted through a box of old pictures and found this one of Peter. He's twenty-six in this photo." That is why he looked like a ghost. It was me from my past, damned near dead-on. At one time I had even owned the same double-breasted suit with wide lapels.

I always thought I shared my dimpled chin with my dad, Jack. The concept is correct. I just had the wrong man. I shared it with Peter, my bio dad. By chance, they both had this specific facial feature. Only about 25% of the population has it, which makes the chance that all three of us share it around 8%.

Seeing the resemblance of one individual in a picture to that of a second person is an interesting experiment. We have shown the picture to dozens of our family and friends. The responses have ranged from a few, "I don't really see it," to the majority who say, "Oh, my God! You don't need a DNA test to tell that man is your father." Yet apparently, I did.

Peter Holmes, my biological father, at age 26.
This is the first image I had ever seen of him.

CHAPTER 15

Peter Holmes

*The more original a discovery, the more obvious
it seems afterwards.* — Arthur Koestler

In an inconceivably short amount of time, Becky had discovered many details about my biological dad. His name: Peter Edgar Holmes. He was John Watson's uncle on his mother's side. The discovery answered the mystery of how my newfound Canadian cousin and I were connected. John's father, Allan Watson, had married Evelyn Holmes, the sister of Peter. In this story, NOT written by Arthur Conan Doyle, Holmes and Watson had a child who became the critical clue to solving my DNA mystery. It became elementary, thanks to my dear (John) Watson, a wonderful, God-fearing man now living in Prince Edward Island, Canada. This previously unknown relative is now a permanent and valued part of our lives.

PETER'S EARLY YEARS

We learned that Peter Holmes was born in Montreal in 1925, the third child of Sydney Harry Holmes and Evelyn Holley. While still in his teens, this ambitious young man left his home in Montreal, possibly to escape his volatile father and unhappy home life. By the time he was seventeen, he was serving as a purser's clerk on the passenger ship RMS Tamaroa. The Tamaroa would become a troop transport during WWII.

'Tamaroa'. Dickie, John, 1869-1942: Collection of postcards, prints and negatives. Ref: 1/4-010149-F. Alexander Turnbull Library, Wellington, New Zealand. The ship my biological father, Peter Holmes, served on as a purser's clerk at the age of 17.

COMING TO AMERICA

In 1951, Peter emigrated to New York City where he worked as an accountant. There he met Helen Smith, an educated and refined young woman from an excellent family in Quincy, Massachusetts. Helen was working for a wealthy woman as a companion and continued living with her employer even after she married Peter in 1953. At some point, Peter became a sales executive for BOAC—British Overseas Airways Company. He took on the role of training the airline's sales representatives and reservation specialists. By February of 1960, Peter was living in Mariemont, a planned community in Cincinnati just thirteen miles from Jack and Barbara Osborne's house in Groesbeck. How Peter and Barbara closed the gap on those thirteen miles is not known, but three years later, I was conceived in February of 1963 while Barb was still married to Jack. My sister, Laura, was born eighteen months after that.

At the time of my birth, Peter, Helen, and their two adopted children had settled in Anderson Township, a suburb on the East side of Cincinnati. From all available records, it does not appear that any biological children were born into this marriage. Peter later became a financial advisor for an investment firm called MONY. We discovered multiple stories in the Cincinnati newspapers that would suggest he was an accomplished speaker. We know he spoke frequently for the aviation/airline and financial/investment industries. We even found a few advertisements showing pictures of him. One photo was particularly unflattering. Peter looked mad, as if someone had just stepped on his toes.

It's hard to know just when Peter and Helen separated, but their divorce was finalized on June 23, 1977. Less than a month later, Peter resurfaced in North Palm Beach, Florida, where he married a woman named Kathleen Smith on July 15. One would assume that Peter's marriage to Helen was already long over by the time their divorce was finalized. One would also assume his relationship with Kathleen started sometime before his divorce.

Peter's new wife was originally a resident of the UK and had two children from a previous marriage. She was also fourteen years older than him. How did they meet? One possibility is that Peter and Kathleen met in the UK when he traveled to London for BOAC. Or perhaps Peter helped Kathleen with her travel plans once she became a resident of Cincinnati. This latter theory is the one broached by Kathleen's son, Walter, who Becky found during her research of Kathleen's family. Walter was willing to talk to me about his stepfather, Peter. He had pleasant memories of Peter but admitted he didn't know him well, having only spent holidays together over the five years that Peter was married to Kathleen before his death in 1982.

According to Walter, Peter treated his mother very kindly and they had a good relationship. "He was always well-groomed and debonair, quite the dresser." Every day at 5:00 p.m., Peter would fix them both a single cocktail. Peter was kind and gracious to their family and devoted to Kathleen. But Walter said he did not know that Peter had been married before nor that he had two adopted children of his own back in Cincinnati.

However, Walter was able to provide a very important piece of information which no one we talked with had told us. On the day of his passing, October 19, 1982, Peter was giving the keynote speech at a luncheon. When he completed his speech he returned to his seat, placed his head down on the table, and died of a heart attack. He was fifty-seven. Coincidentally, on the day that I learned this fact, I too was fifty-seven. It was not a heartwarming feeling, no pun intended.

Unfortunately, other than Walter, and Peter's former son-in-law, Charles, everyone who had a relationship with Peter has passed away or was unwilling to talk to us. I must admit that this is a very disappointing but likely end to the trail. But through our research of records and conversations with family members, I came to see Peter as a bright young man who sought adventure in his early years. One would assume he had some element of charm and/or charisma and was a hard worker. He seemed to possess some daring and perhaps entrepreneurial traits. Yes, I could see myself in this man very clearly. As far as I know, Peter Holmes and I never met—or did we? There is only one person I know who knew the truth, and that person wasn't forthcoming.

THE MYSTERY THAT IS STEVE'S GRANDFATHER: SYDNEY HOLMES

Throughout Becky's research we uncovered numerous persons in my new lineage but none more colorful and mysterious than Peter's father, a man named Sydney Harry Holmes. Sydney arrived in Montreal, Canada, in 1901 or 1906 (more on that later) from Liverpool, England (or was that Scotland? —more on that later as well). That makes his son, Peter, a first generation Canadian and me, his grandson, a first generation American. So much for my being one of the Native American originals on the continent.

Sydney is somewhat of an enigma. We can't find any documentation on him until he joins the military in Canada at age twenty-one. We have since come to the realization that any record we have found about him was created with information provided *by* him. A perfect scenario for personal obfuscation.

What we do know about Sydney is this: a quality human being **he was not.** Through Becky's extensive genealogical research, combined with stories from the Holmes tribal lore, we found that Sydney was a man with many dimensions. In one census he was listed as an engineer. In his military record he was a sawyer and teamster. Making his way cutting lumber makes sense as tree harvesting and lumber shipping was a major industry in Quebec at that time.

Sydney also had dark elements about him. For starters, he was a bootlegger. In discovering this fact, I might infer that my periodic familiarity with alcohol is genetic. He was also associated with the Montreal organized crime syndicates. (Sorry, no further connections following that one.) He maintained close relationships with some of the less-than-ethical members of Montreal's law enforcement community by providing them with their adult (and illegal) beverages.

Sadly, it was also not uncommon for him to strike his wife Evelyn when he was angry. When in reference to Sydney, the term "wife-beater" held a more literal meaning than the oft-referenced white tank top t-shirt commonly worn by my relatives. Family stories of his violent nature and explosive temper are many, and we learned that he was loathed by most of the family, even his sons. We would come to learn how this animosity from the family played out when it came time to bury Sydney.

Sydney was also a philanderer. In the only photo we have of him, he is leaning against his wife, as if she was a wall, with his arms around another woman. How demeaning that must have been to Evelyn who reportedly had a heart of gold. Sydney was *in flagrante delicto* when his heart gave out. If your Latin is a little rusty, that means he was not exactly sleeping when he died in bed with his girlfriend.

In August of 2024, three years after my DNA surprise, we visited Montreal to continue Becky's genealogical research on my paternal lineage. Coincidentally we were there on what would have been Peter's 99th birthday. A few years prior we had all but struck out at the FamilySearch Library in Salt Lake City, and the suggestion was made that we might have better luck if we visited the city where the original records were kept, in this case, Montreal. We planned the visit with my new cousin John Watson and his wife Kathy. They made the twelve-hour drive from Prince Edward Island to Montreal. John coordinated dinner with more of my previously unmet paternal relatives, including his daughter and granddaughter. It was a pleasant additional piece to the closure wall.

As for the research, Becky and I spent an afternoon at the National Archives of Montréal researching the Holmes family. We focused almost exclusively on my mysterious grandfather, Sydney. After a couple of hours in this wonderful establishment, we had uncovered virtually nothing new. Becky, whose knowledge of French is more extensive than mine (which is none), inquired if there was anyone who might be more familiar with the records and perhaps could assist in the research. The very friendly staff at the archives graciously offered to assist. Becky provided them with the basic information we knew about Sydney Holmes: his birth and death dates and immigration information. It was close to noon and the archives would close for lunch so it was suggested that we return in a few hours and see what our expert in Montreal records could dig up.

Upon our return, our archivist was excited to report that she was able to find multiple documents on Sydney, including a family tree. As we scanned the information she provided, it looked extremely familiar. Becky asked where the information was found and the archivist replied it had come from Ancestry. Becky responded with the revelation that the family tree the archivist had found was the one Becky had created herself. Her name was on the document as the author. It appeared we had traveled internationally only to have the information Becky carefully researched at our kitchen table delivered back to her as the best result of the Montreal national archives. I submit this as Exhibit B in reference to Becky's genealogical research abilities.

I can honestly say that I was hoping for something a little more regal or perhaps even respectable from the efforts Becky had put in. But my family tree is what it is. I wonder if Ancestry would like to make a commercial about me and my roots. It would be a little different than the commercials we are seeing today, but I suspect my story is more common than what is currently being portrayed.

Becky...

Traveling to Montreal to find Peter's stomping grounds was pretty high on my bucket list, but I thought it would be years before we ventured there. However, in August of 2024 as I began brainstorming where to go in celebration of a major birthday of mine, Montreal seemed like the perfect location. It is an exotic city outside the US yet easy to get to from Cincinnati.

Finding online records of Peter and his family in Montreal had been an easy and rewarding exercise in research. The family was listed in several censuses, and John Watson had corroborated the names of the Holmes relatives I found which included the five children of Sydney Harry Holmes and Evelyn Holley.

When it came to tracing Peter's mother, the path into the past was equally easy to track. Knowing from the Canada censuses that she was born in Newfoundland, I traced her family back several generations. A passenger manifest tracked Evelyn's emigration from Newfoundland to Quebec. But I couldn't understand why she was considered an emigrant if she had simply traveled from one part of Canada to another? Cousin John explained to me that Newfoundland wasn't part of Canada until 1949. Evelyn arrived in Montreal as a domestic servant in 1916 when Newfoundland and Labrador was a separate country. She died the year cousin John was born.

When and where Evelyn Holley met Sydney Holmes is anyone's guess, but I found them early in their marriage with an infant son in 1921. Sydney was listed as having been born in England in 1896. His immigration year was listed differently in different documents. As I focused my search on Sydney, I began to hit roadblocks. There was no marriage record for him in Montreal, nor in Newfoundland, thus depriving me of his parents' names. Young Sydney and his family could not be found in the first census after his reported immigration year. And even the year of immigration was fuzzy: the 1931 Census listed it as 1901, the 1921 Census listed it as 1906. Once again, these bits of information came from Sydney himself. Did he not remember exactly when he emigrated? Or was he trying to cover the tracks of his early life?

A further search of Sydney turned up a Military Attestation record from 1917 when he joined the Canadian Expeditionary Force. The information he provided stated that Sydney Harry Holmes was born in "Suddinham," England, a town that I later determined doesn't exist. His mother was listed as Violet Holmes, a woman for whom I could not find any record of in that time and place. Suddenly I was looking at a very tall and wide brick wall. Despite many extensive searches, I could not find the elusive Sydney Harry Holmes in UK records, Canadian immigration records, or local Montreal records other than those two censuses. How does a person jump from one country to another without leaving a trace of themselves behind? Typically it is not difficult to find documents which detail the early life of a person, i.e., records regarding their birth, baptism, and residences over the years. But Sydney Holmes had none of those in England. I was baffled.

When I discussed this brick wall with John, he mentioned that his mother always reported her father as being from Scotland because that is what *he told her*. And sure enough, the 1931 Canada Census lists Sydney as being born in "Ecosse" (Scotland). But in the 1921 Census, his birthplace was listed as England. Maybe his parents hadn't been honest with him until later in life when he discovered the true country of his birth? A quick search of the esteemed Scotland's People database turned up nothing. And Steve's DNA showed very little Scottish heritage. When we visited the FamilySearch Library in Salt Lake City, the Canada records expert retraced my research efforts and was not able to find anything on Sydney in either England or Scotland.

Aha, someone might say, he must have changed his name. People did that all the time! I am inclined to believe that. But how could I search for someone if I don't know their name? And everything I do know was provided by the elusive and likely deceptive person themselves?

The answer lies in DNA.

CHAPTER 16

A Dissociative Loss

To lose your father is to lose the one whose guidance and help you seek, who supports you like a tree trunk supports its branches. — Yann Martel

The discovery of Peter Holmes and the entire situation with my DNA test discovery makes my heart grieve. On one hand, it answered so many of the questions that gnawed at my psyche throughout my life. It provided me with reason, answers to the puzzle, and validation. Everything finally made sense. But on the other hand, it also severed my biological connection to Jack Osborne. Let me be clear, I still hold Jack Osborne as Dad1. I am 1,000% in Camp Jack despite learning that Peter Holmes is my biological father (Dad3). Jerry Condo (Dad2) is my stepdad and a fine one at that. My DNA test results changed nothing between Jerry Condo and me. More than twenty-five years after Barb and Jerry's divorce, Jerry and I still maintain our stepfather/stepson relationship, and we will for the balance of our time on Earth. We still talk regularly, and he comes to visit from Florida every year. Jerry is still Dad2, with Jack being Dad1.

But with Jack, the DNA results had invalidated our biological relationship. We no longer shared blood. The realization had left me with a gaping hole in my psyche. I cannot fully explain the pain; it's not an unbearable or excruciating pain, it's more of a void, an emptiness. It's like reaching for a wall in the darkness of night to steady yourself, only to have that solid familiarity not be there. It is a feeling that is difficult to fully describe and nothing like anything I have experienced.

In some ways I'm happy that Jack isn't alive to experience this. I wouldn't want him to go through the shock and potential embarrassment this revelation might cause him. I wouldn't want him to worry that this would alter our relationship. And honestly, I don't think I could bear to see the pain on his face when I told him what I had learned. But I wish he was still here because I desperately need him. I need his warmth, his love, and his extended bear hugs. My stepmom, Mary Ann, has assured me that a simple DNA test would change nothing between Jack and me. Jack loved me unconditionally, period. I am still his boy. He is still my old man.

> *Dad, I love you so and still do. I hear your voice within me. Your granddaughters hear your voice when I tell them I love them, as you had always told me. Your strength and love flow through me to my girls and to everyone else we care for. Your love has touched hundreds or perhaps thousands of people connected through me. Your small daily actions, your giant decision to take the path of love, has changed our lives. I'm desperately praying that, if there is life after this one, the reality of this situation doesn't hurt you. I hold our bond unbreakable—DNA test results be damned. They are but a momentary footnote in a saga of decades.* **I will never surrender you, the thought of you, as my dad. I am, and always shall be, your son.** *I reject any and all other realities. I hope that you are still proud of me. I still live to make that happen. I love you. I'll see you soon.*

* * *

People often ask me if I believe Jack Osborne might have known, or at least suspected, I was not his biological son. I have two schools of thought on the topic:

The first is he didn't know and that makes him a good man and a great dad. He did everything a dad should do, even after a messy divorce.

The second is he was aware of Barb's infidelity and my origin. He knew I was not his biological son and at some point, he decided it made no difference to him. For over three decades, he completed his paternal duties no matter how difficult my mother made it for him, no matter how inconvenient life made it for him. No matter, any matter, it didn't matter. He chose to be my dad and he executed those duties without fail. If this second scenario is true, then that makes him a GREAT man and an unbelievable dad. Either way, it matters not. Jack Osborne is my true dad. He resides at the center of my being.

***

A LONG-DISTANCE CALL

I was asleep in our bed when the phone rang and jolted me awake. I reached for the handset while trying not to knock anything off the nightstand.

"Hello," I said, trying to force myself into a higher state of consciousness.

"Son, it's me. It's your dad," the voice on the other end said. My heart leaped. We had been separated for months. I had not heard from him. I was ecstatic that he was calling. It was an answer to my prayers.

"Dad, where are you? Are you okay?" The tone of my voice was desperate.

"I'm fine, Son, I'm fine. I don't want you to worry about me," my dad said. His tone was reassuring and comforting but within the pitch there was a bit of pleading as well.

"Dad, I do worry about you. I miss you. Where are you? Are you in heaven?"

"No, Son, it's not like that. But I'm fine. I know you worry, and I don't want you to worry about me. I'm okay." His voice was calm and he was trying to transfer that calmness to me.

"Dad, I want to see you. Where are you?" I was ready to go anywhere I needed to go.

"Boy, I've got to go. I've got to go. I love you." I heard the sorrow and sadness within him.

"I love you too . . . but, Dad, wait. I want to talk . . ." I pleaded.

"Goodbye, Son." The phone disconnected.

I shot up from my lying position, turned, spun my legs out, and sat on the edge of the bed. I tried again to force myself into a higher state of consciousness. This time I was awake. I glanced at the phone that had not been disturbed. The handset was in the cradle. The conversation, not the dream, but the conversation I just had with my dad took place in a state of consciousness, or a place, that I had never experienced before or since. I was not awake, but I was not asleep. It didn't happen in the waking, physical world but it wasn't in a dream. It was a state of being, an ether, in which I was fully submerged. A state that I do not have words to fully describe.

This was 1999 and my dad, Jack Osborne, had recently died of a heart attack. We had buried him eight weeks prior but my grieving would continue for another year or more. It's hard to say exactly how long. The grieving process doesn't simply turn off one day like a light switch. It subsides to the point that it's not interrupting your thoughts on an hourly basis. The loss of my dad was so intense that there were times I felt as if I had a limb amputated. I felt the loss physically as well as emotionally. It would alter me as a person.

As with many men, my dad was the most important male relationship I had in my life. When he died, I was thirty-five years old but my dad still referred to me as 'Boy,' a title I wore like a medal of honor. It was a word I wouldn't allow anyone else to utter in reference to me. Not because of its occasional derogatory nature, but because it was reserved for Jack Osborne and the unique bond between us.

"Sweetie, are you okay?" Becky had woken up. She saw me sitting on the edge of the bed. It was 1:40 a.m.

"Bec, Dad was on the phone. He called me. He was there, but it wasn't real. He's not here. I . . ." I said sobbing, my chest heaving as I was trying to regain a rhythm to my breathing. I told her word for word what had transpired, how incredibly real it seemed, and how devastated I was. I thought how cruel my subconscious was being to its weaker daytime cohort. Becky saw things differently.

"Baby, you weren't dreaming. That was your dad. He was reaching out to you." She had her arms around me, squeezing me, attempting to calm me. She continued, "He knows how badly you're hurting, and he doesn't want you to hurt like you do. He called you, on the phone, just like he would if he was still with us." Throughout our lives, most of our conversations had occurred over phone calls. Distance necessitated that condition. Becky continued, "He loved you so much and still does. Can you see that?"

Becky has always been the significantly more spiritual of the two of us. She sees and feels things I cannot see nor sense. But I trust her unquestionably in these situations. I still couldn't shake what had happened. The call's emotional impact would stay with me for weeks.

I never received another call from Dad or anything similar. I never again experienced that state of being, but the event has weighed upon me ever since. I thought I should talk to my sister Laura about it. At the time, we believed she was one of Jack's two biological children. Years later, my DNA test results would prove she was his only biological child. Just a few weeks after the "phone call," we were at Laura's home enjoying a summer cookout. As the flow of the day would have it, Laura and I had found a quiet moment alone in the midst of the family activities.

"Sis, do you miss Dad? Is he still on your mind as much as he is on mine? Do you think about him that often?" I asked.

"I do miss him and I think of him all the time. It's so hard to think about life without him." She took a few seconds in a thoughtful pause. She was weighing what to say next. Then she continued, "In fact, the strangest thing happened the other night. I had a dream, but I wouldn't call it a dream. It was weird. I don't know what to call it, but Dad called me on the phone. He called to tell me he was okay and told me not to worry about him."

I shook my head quickly from side to side, trying to clear the disbelief triggered by her words. "When did this happen?" I asked.

"A couple of weeks ago."

She confirmed my suspicion. We had the same experience, likely within days of each other, if not the same night. I cannot explain these events to the satisfaction of anyone who does not believe there is more to us than this physical plane of existence. It's hard to accept that it was a bizarre coincidence. Dad was worried about Laura and me and the grief we carried. He wanted to erase that burden.

MY SISTER, KATHY

My oldest sister, Kathy, is seven years older than me. (Okay, she is really my half-sister. Her dad was Ed and my dad was Jack—no, I mean Peter. But I've never considered her anything but my sister.) When a kid is growing up, seven years is a big gap. That gap has almost always been to my advantage. Kathy is a sweetheart of a person (to me). She is loving, giving, and protective of her little brother. However, she can be a bit rough-and-tumble. This chick is an iron-plated ass-kicker. She dated and eventually married a biker, Jimmy, who, if I remember correctly, was a member of the Iron Horsemen. She was no debutante herself. For all her loving sweetness, if someone crossed her, or made the mistake of picking on her little brother, they could plan on getting themselves in the deep end of trouble. She was a fearless hellraiser.

She not only raised hell, but she also raised me, which to some people, might be considered the same thing. Our mother, Barb, was consistently consumed with the troubled youth she brought to our home. As a result, Kathy became my surrogate mom. She was my protector and provider. She gave me money for gas and food when I needed it. When I would come home from any one of my jobs (I began working at the age of thirteen), she would offer to make me something hot to eat, so I wouldn't resort to my usual bowl of cereal she loathed to see me eat. She took me shopping for clothes, which was a real challenge because I was a real string bean. There were not many places we could find pants with a 28-inch waist and a 33-inch inseam.

In my teen years, I would get excruciatingly painful muscle tension headaches in my neck and at the base of my skull which would extend to my forehead. These headaches were the result of a car accident when I was eleven. I would writhe on the floor in pain, crying for relief. Kathy would find me, take me to the couch, place my head on a pillow in her lap, and rub my head until I fell asleep. It was my only source of relief other than a Darvocet if I could find one.

The age difference between us has been exceptionally valuable when Becky and I began to attempt to piece together the fragments of my youth. What happened to whom and when? Most of my life between the ages of three and seven years old is difficult to remember. But Kathy was between the ages of ten and fourteen at that time. The memories are much clearer and complete for her. Combining our two memory sets into a collection has been priceless in my search for the truth following my DNA test.

But we were at the beginning of that journey and it was time to make the first inquisitory and revealing phone call.

"Sissy, how are you?"

"Stiv! I'm great. How you are you, little brother?" Kathy still calls me her little brother, which is accurate by age, but I feel like I'm her older brother now. I have tried to take on the role of caregiver between us, though she frequently resists.

"I'm fine. Becky's great. The girls are great." Okay, the preliminaries are done. Now to the main event. "Hey, I've got something really weird to tell you, and I need your help."

"Whatcha need?"

"Well, you are not going to believe this, but I took a DNA test and the results came back and showed that Jack is not my dad." There was a long pause before any sound came out of the phone. I waited for Kathy to process the information.

"What? Did you just say that Jack Osborne is not your dad? Well, if not Jack, who the hell is? How did this happen?" Kathy was always quick to the point. No BS. No varnish. No pleasantries.

I proceeded to tell her about the extensive search for my Native American lineage, the DNA test, and Laura's bombshell. I told her about Becky finding my biological dad, a Canadian named Peter Holmes. But now I have questions that I'm hoping she can answer. I didn't know enough at that point to ask the right questions to jog the memories that would hit me months later. At this point I wanted to know anything that she knew, especially IF she knew about Jack, Barb, and Peter.

"Stevie, Mom never said a peep to me about this. But, sweetie, it does explain so much about you. You are different and we all see it.

Remember when Grandma Condo used to say, 'Stevie is the smart one and Laura is the pretty one'?" she said to support her claim of my difference. I needed no convincing.

"Yes, but that is not a compliment to either one of us. That means I'm not good looking and Laura's not smart," I answered. We know the latter is not accurate. Laura is smart. She has an above average IQ and her EQ is way above normal. She sees with her heart. Her physical good looks are immutable. She could be Cameron Diaz's twin sister. That's how I refer to her: my Cameron Diaz sister. That should have been the first clue to my misattributed paternity.

"I know, that's a bad way of saying that, but it's true. You are different. Stevie, I don't know anything about Barb and Jack's marital issues. You say your dad is some Canadian guy named Peter Holmes? That name is in my head for some reason but I'm not sure why." I think the memories were too far back in her dusty cerebral archives. It would take time, alcohol, and prodding to bring them forward.

"Here is what I do know. You and I never shared dads. Mom is our mom. Your dad has changed so we still have different dads. Nothing has changed between us. Nothing will. You know I love you. I always will. That ain't never changing. You will always be my little brother. I don't give a damn who says what about who and when." Kathy was adamant and no-nonsense. That certainly hadn't changed.

Her words were targeted and she hit the mark. Despite my effort to hide my pain, she knew it was there and it was intense. How could she not? She knew me and loved me to a level that made me completely transparent. Her only concern was for me. She was aware that my foundation had been fractured. She began the salvage and repair operations immediately, in earnest. She would continue them until this day. I love her dearly. How can I not?

CHAPTER 17

DNA Flows Downhill

The truth hurts because it's real. It hurts because
it mattered. And that's an important thing to
acknowledge to yourself. — John Green

It had been just over a week since my life flipped upside down when it became clear that I needed to discuss this issue with the other select Osbornes who were affected by the results of the collective DNA tests. Those Osbornes were our daughters, Sammie and Jackie. Knowing them as well as I do, I knew how each of them was likely to react.

Sammie, the older of the two, is very much like me. She is an analytical, critical, and logical thinker who, at times, can be uber pragmatic. She would see this event as more of a science project. But she does have a spiritual side to her. Coincidentally, Sammie's employers were the couple who were with me on the plane when I received Laura's DNA surprise phone call; Robin was actually Sammie's direct boss. Therefore, we were already keeping a secret from her in that very short period of time. I didn't want her to learn about her disassociated grandfather through an unintentional comment at work.

Jackie is much more like Becky. She is kind, sensitive, and feeling. Like her mother, she has an extremely high EQ. And like me, she was named after Jack. I knew this information was going to hit her much harder than Sammie, at least on the surface. Jackie took great pride in being named for her grandfather. This news would hit her almost as hard as it hit me. Both conversations could only occur in person. As their dad, I wanted to be there to assure them that Jack loved them no matter what and to catch their tears as they might flow. Sammie was out of town; therefore, the first conversation would be with Jackie. She came by the house often so the opportunity to have a conversation presented itself quickly. I took the first chance I got.

"Hey, Da," Jackie greeted me by my special name as she walked into the enclosed porch.

"Hey, Sweetpea. What's happening?" The small talk would continue for only seconds. I play a lot of poker, but when it came to the girls and news like this, I knew I would have my tells. The quicker I got to the point, the less time she would have to sense that something was wrong. As it was, it had already taken too long. She was on to me.

"Jackie, you remember when we were in Chicago and Mom was telling you about that Canadian cousin we found, John Watson?"

"Yeah . . ."

"Well, we had Aunt Laura take a DNA test so that we could confirm how John and I might be related to us. The test showed that John is only related to me, not Laura." Jackie had a puzzled look on her face which was the only thing she could have. No one could be expected

Three generations of Jacks: Jacqueline (Jackie), Jack,
and J(ack) Steven (me). Circa 1998.
We loved the phrase "Jacks or better to open."
It is a poker term that seemed to fit us.

to have gone through the variations and deciphered what the results meant. I continued, "Baby, the test also showed that your grandpa, Grandpa Jack, is not my biological dad." My delivery was somewhat sterile as I didn't want to add emotion into what I knew was going to be an emotional exchange. I was fighting my own feelings. This discussion happened early in the process and I was still devastated and reeling in my own right. I didn't want to show her those cards. I wanted Jackie to feel whatever she was going to feel based on her own position.

"He's not your dad?" I could already see her thought train speeding down the tracks.

"No, Love, he isn't," I said in a consoling voice.

"Are you okay?" she asked. What a wonderful question by a caring person.

"I'm working through it. It's tough." I thought there was no use in lying. She had to know I wasn't.

"So, he's not my grandpa either?" Her voice was strong but her eyes were quickly giving way to the tsunami of shock and sadness.

"That's right," I replied. "He's not . . . but he still is. He may not be biologically, but he loved you more than anything. He was over the moon when we named you after him. Nothing changes. Nothing. He is still your grandpa." I was saying words to her that I was still trying to ingest myself. Everyone whom I had spoken to had said similar words to me, but I still hadn't completely grabbed that life preserver. I was hoping Jackie could grab it quicker than I did.

Jackie broke down into a full sobbing cry. I held her and tried my best to reassure her that while this sounded big, it would change nothing for her and her namesake. It was ironic how disjointed this scenario was. I was trying to convince Jackie that nothing had changed using the same words that others had said to me. Words that I had not internalized nor completely believed. Was that hypocrisy or a father's love hoping to speak healing into a horrible situation? I'm still not sure. Jackie and I would have multiple conversations over the ensuing months. With each one, she became a little more settled with the new reality. It wasn't an ideal situation by any means, but it was one that became tolerable for her over time.

The conversation with Sammie was different but not unexpectedly so. Sammie is much more analytical, running things through her logic center first, then her emotional center. Sammie and her husband had just returned from a short jaunt somewhere. Becky called Sammie and arranged for us to come over to their house for a drink.

I delivered the news of the DNA test and its ramifications. I told her where I was emotionally. I also assured her that the change in parentage did not change the relationship. Jack was still her grandpa. In response, Sam was more curious. She was constantly apologizing for asking for more detailed information. She didn't want to seem uncaring, but she was fascinated by the twists and turns and the whole absurdity of it all. She didn't want her lack of tears or emotional upheaval to be perceived as callous, which it wasn't. I know her well. She is a younger female version of me. Everyone processed this information differently. As expected, Sammie dropped into intellectual/analytical mode. However, weeks, months and even years later, the emotional elements have caught her from time to time and she has experienced moments of angst, frustration, a sense of loss and the associated tears. There is no doubt that becoming a DNA orphan reaches farther and sticks around longer than one might imagine.

CHAPTER 18

Family Redefined: The Asterisk and The Family Tree

My family is my strength and my weakness.
— Aishwarya Rai Bachchan

As one might expect, my DNA test results brought massive, devastating changes to my family tree. From pre-test assumptions to post-test results, **61% of my immediate family changed status. With 56% of them, I lost all genetic connection between us. As for my extended family, I lost 72% of all my known relatives** (siblings and first cousins only—the total percentage is much higher). Only my two older half-sisters, two of my stepsisters, my youngest half-brother, and my mother remained unchanged. As they say, "Ouch, that's going to leave a mark."

One odd complication of the changes was how, going forward, we would refer to those members of my family whose status had changed. Our relationships had changed. Clarity became an issue. What is the protocol for referring to someone? Should we use our past connection or their new connection? A real example is: "My stepbrother/second cousin, who I'm not actually related to anymore." Anyone can see how arduously difficult it is to say (and read) those words. The gyrations and contortions become almost comical. It just goes to show that when we started with a family vine, not a family tree, and then tossed a live chainsaw into the vegetation, the results got pretty ugly.

Steve's Family Tree Pre-DNA Test

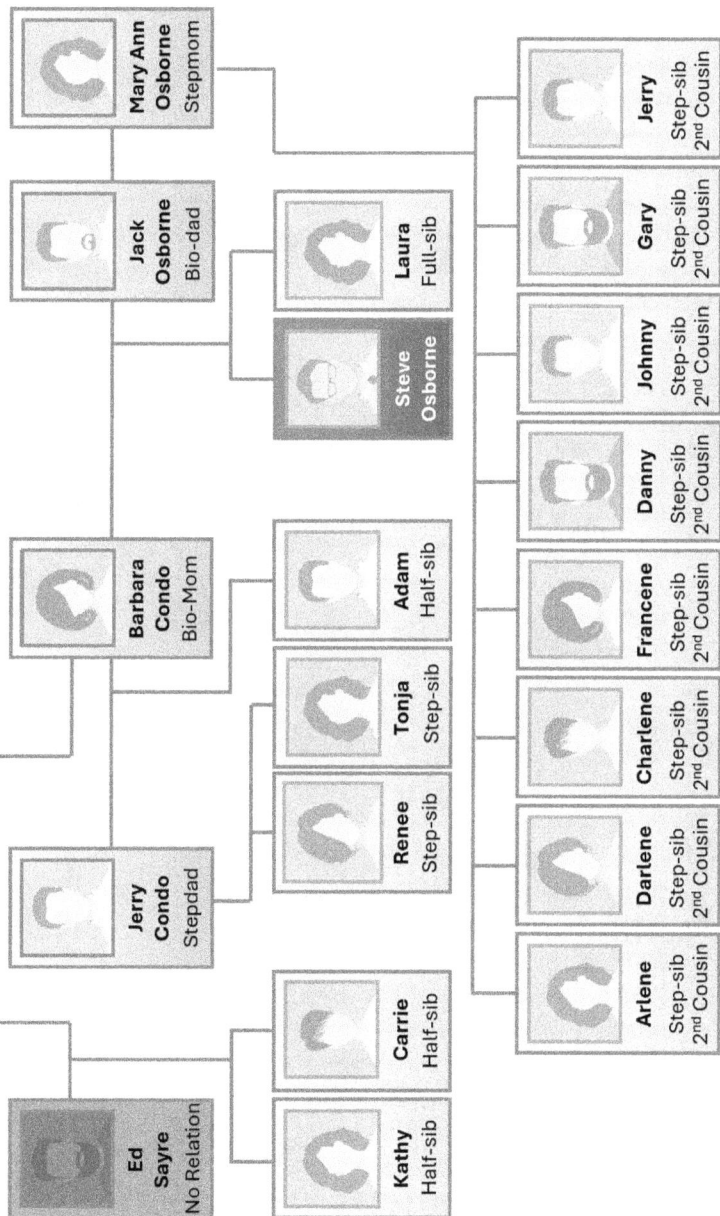

- **Mary Ann Osborne** — Stepmom
- **Jack Osborne** — Bio-dad
- **Barbara Condo** — Bio-Mom
- **Jerry Condo** — Stepdad
- **Ed Sayre** — No Relation
- **Laura** — Full-sib
- **Steve Osborne**
- **Adam** — Half-sib
- **Tonja** — Step-sib
- **Renee** — Step-sib
- **Carrie** — Half-sib
- **Kathy** — Half-sib
- **Jerry** — Step-sib / 2nd Cousin
- **Gary** — Step-sib / 2nd Cousin
- **Johnny** — Step-sib / 2nd Cousin
- **Danny** — Step-sib / 2nd Cousin
- **Francene** — Step-sib / 2nd Cousin
- **Charlene** — Step-sib / 2nd Cousin
- **Darlene** — Step-sib / 2nd Cousin
- **Arlene** — Step-sib / 2nd Cousin

Steve's Family Tree Post-DNA Test

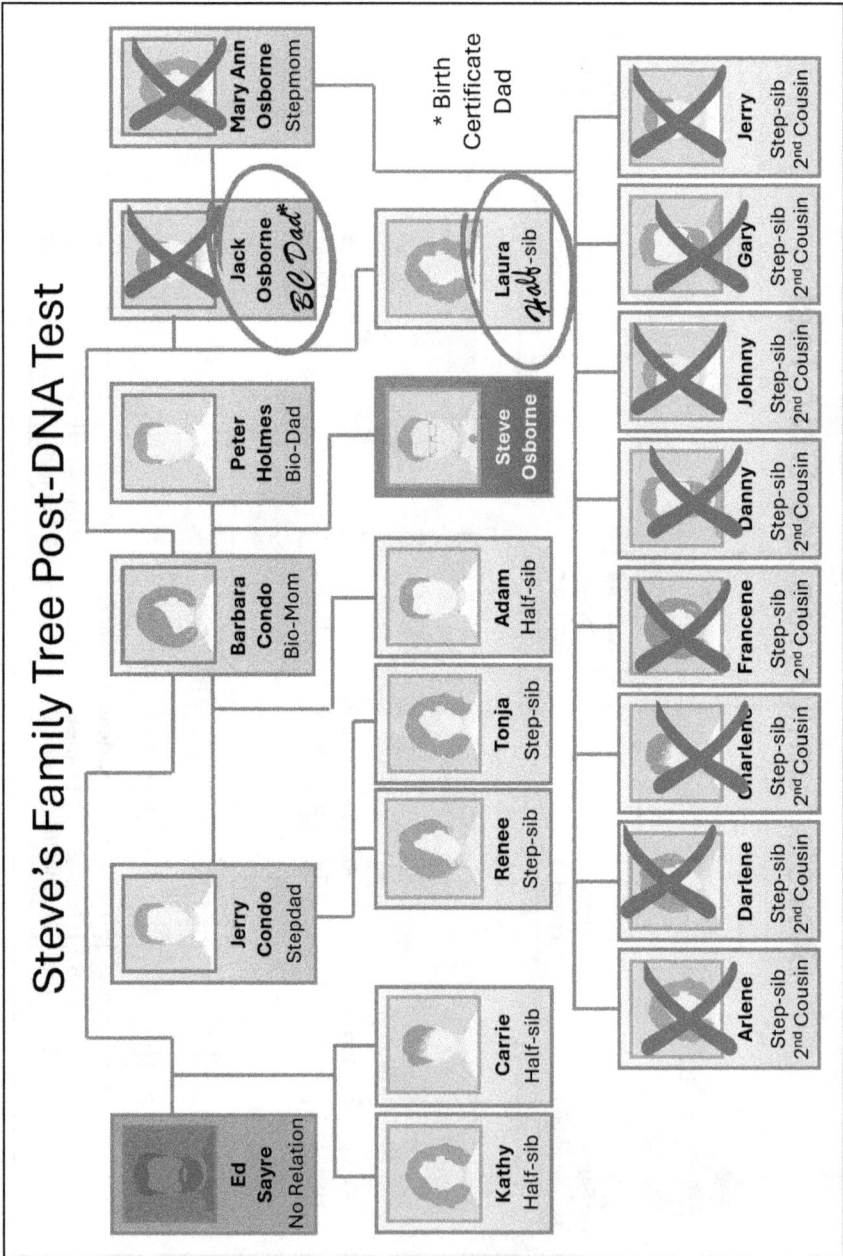

* Birth Certificate Dad

Mary Ann Osborne — Stepmom

Jack Osborne — BC Dad*

Laura — Half-sib

Jerry — Step-sib — 2nd Cousin

Gary — Step-sib — 2nd Cousin

Johnny — Step-sib — 2nd Cousin

Danny — Step-sib — 2nd Cousin

Francene — Step-sib — 2nd Cousin

Charlene — Step-sib — 2nd Cousin

Darlene — Step-sib — 2nd Cousin

Arlene — Step-sib — 2nd Cousin

Peter Holmes — Bio-Dad

Barbara Condo — Bio-Mom

Jerry Condo — Stepdad

Steve Osborne

Adam — Half-sib

Tonja — Step-sib

Renee — Step-sib

Carrie — Half-sib

Kathy — Half-sib

Ed Sayre — No Relation

We needed a better, more efficient method of reference. One evening we were discussing my DNA-related events and the relationship mutations said events had brought about. Someone suggested we use the original relationship moniker and simply append an asterisk. For example, Jerry Osborne, my stepbrother, is now my stepbrother*. The asterisk indicates we are no longer related by blood or marriage. Jerry and I are now brothers by choice. We made a joint decision to remain brothers—which is a much stronger bond than we previously had. It is more efficient and easier for everyone. There it was. We went with the asterisk convention.

The events of the month of October 2021 were akin to fifty vehicles trying to get through an intersection all at once. It was as if all the events of our lives, the secrets of our family's past, the strained and painful elements of our relationships, all came together in one simultaneous, chaotic, cataclysmic collision.

CHAPTER 19

The Imposter Syndrome

It is as easy to deceive ourselves without noticing as it is hard to deceive others without their noticing.
— François de La Rochefoucauld

MARY ANN OSBORNE'S BIRTHDAY PARTY

My DNA Discovery Date was September 18, 2021. On October 3, 2021, just two weeks later, my extended family held a surprise ninetieth birthday party for my stepmom, Mary Ann. She was ninety-one years old but COVID kept us from celebrating her life milestone prior to that. She was the wife of Jack Osborne, and the mother to eight of my stepsiblings (who used to be also my second cousins*). The DNA test had severed my genetic consanguineal (relation recognized by birth) connection with Jack Osborne, therefore by extension, severed my connection with Mary Ann Osborne and her eight children. But at this point, only Becky, our daughters, Jackie and Sammie, and my half-sisters, Laura and Kathy, were aware of the DNA deck shuffling.

The party was to be held outside under a park shelter near the Ohio River. The day was damp, gloomy, and depressing. The weather was a cloudy, rainy mess. My mental and emotional state mirrored the weather in every way. How could I possibly go to this party, with family members who are now genetic strangers, and pretend that everything is hunky-dory? How can I look them in the eye knowing what I know and not tell them the truth? My fear of rejection was in the forefront of my mind. I feared it like young kids fear Godzilla. It was terrifying, most likely because I wouldn't have control of the direction or outcomes. I feared the situation because it takes two to tango. Going forward, both parties would have to agree that we were going to continue our relationship—our broken relationship. I could easily imagine some of them opting out. If that happened, that would be on me. I was the outsider, and I had either subconsciously or consciously created distance between us for decades. I have always been on an elliptical outer orbit with this group. Months or years could go by without seeing some of them. The spouses, the new kids and their spouses, would have to be introduced or reintroduced to me. I was more of an alien than ever. And even worse—now I was a fraud as well.

"Bec, I'm not sure how to handle this. I'm not related to any of these people anymore. What do I say?" I bemoaned the impending discomfort as Becky and I drove to the park.

"You say nothing about it. This is not the time to tell them for many reasons, Babe," Becky counseled me. "Today is Mary Ann's birthday, and opening a can of DNA worms would shift the focus to your news and take away from her celebration. Let's not do that. Today is about her. Not only that, but we still have too many unanswered questions to get into this discussion. You still have so many questions you must answer for yourself. You haven't talked with Barb about this yet. Let's just sit on it and enjoy the day—her day. Make it all about her. We'll get through it."

I hate it when she is logical and mature. I wanted to wallow in this emotional pigsty for a while longer. Becky has always been selfless and thinks of others first. Maybe someday she'll rub off on me before her patience runs out.

We arrived a bit early for the cookout. After all, it's always better to get there before the guest of honor arrives and everyone yells "Surprise!" Unless, of course, we were trying to hide from everyone—even said guest of honor—which I was.

The one bright spot of the day? The food. My stepsiblings/second-cousins* know how to eat the best, most delicious, unhealthy food. All the typical favorites: hamburgers, hot dogs, bratwurst, mettwurst, beer, potato salad, coleslaw, baked beans, beer, chips, pork rinds, salami, cream cheese, fruit salad, beer, ice cream, cake, as well as ice cream cake (commas do matter), donuts, and of course, beer. Experience had taught me that with this group, some things disappear faster than others. With this in mind, I headed directly to the item I feared we would run out of first: beer.

Maybe I wasn't worried it would be gone as much as I was worried how I was going to get through the next three hours sober. I addressed that issue quickly. It was one of the few times in my life that I said, "I need a drink," and I meant it.

I walked over to the grill that was currently being manned by one of Mary Ann's four sons, Johnny.

"Hey, Johnny," I said.

"Steve! How you been, man? I haven't seen you in a month of Sundays." The statement was accurate and not unusual. John and I didn't cross paths very often, but it was always good to see him when we did. John is a good soul and we had always enjoyed a cordial relationship, but not an overly deep one. Our ties were between his mom, Mary Ann, and Jack. If it weren't for their marriage, we would have never met. Nevertheless, John was always pleasant and always put forth the effort to make me feel like one of the family. I desperately needed that. I guess that might be why I sought him out first.

His youngest brother, Jerry, whom I am closest to, had not arrived at the event yet. He was tasked with bringing Mary Ann to her surprise party. Their other brother, Danny, was also there. Most of the time, Danny and I struggled to be much more than connected strangers. There were never much more than pleasantries exchanged and Danny seemed distant, or perhaps I was. This was likely one of the many cases where my deep-seated discomfort with my own differences fostered unnecessary distance between me and other family members. Particularly this branch.

It's a shame because they are all nice people. But I felt more ill at ease than ever. In the past, we were blood relatives and related by marriage so they had to accept me. But now, I knew we were neither. This mask of false familial relations I wore weighed on me with each moment. It felt like a transgression against these kind and loving people, unrelated as we are now. I could feel my DNA secret hanging over my head like the sword of Damocles. At some point, that sword would be released; it would fall and dispense its justice upon me, whatever it might be. Jesus, can I get another beer?

My stepbrother*, Jerry arrived with my stepmom* in tow. Everyone yelled, "Surprise! Happy birthday!" Admittedly, it was a risk to surprise a great-great-grandmother over ninety years old, but it went without the need for CPR. As soon as I could, I got Jerry to the side to catch up. I handed him a beer, but he doesn't drink, so I drank it for him. We chatted briefly to get caught up on our lives and how our mom/stepmom* was doing

I couldn't get comfortable anywhere in that crowd. I made a plate of Kentucky's finest health foods and found a place where Becky could join me out of the rain and out of earshot from most everyone else. We quietly reconnoitered the party and conversations to date. While this pattern wasn't so different from other events with my family, it was the first time I found myself trapped in such a genetic iron maiden.

I asked Becky how soon is too soon for us to leave. She smiled and told me to smile and enjoy myself. She is far too kind to ever say, "Shut up, dumbass," so I'm guessing it was implied. I had no choice but to seek out the company of another beer. My relationship with beer hasn't changed since I learned about my DNA test results. If anything, we've gotten closer. I think, perhaps, beer is beginning to get a little jealous of the time I've been spending with another Kentucky staple, bourbon.

We successfully finished the day as imposter and co-conspirator. We smiled and hugged and wished everyone well. We headed back home to our northern suburb of Cincinnati. Night fell. Darkness descended. And that was the end of it. Because, really, when should a person tell someone something they know when they are still processing the event themselves and not ready to speak about it? How can they talk to someone about something they're unable to discuss? Unknowingly, I would face this situation much sooner than I thought.

Becky...

Heading south to meet up with Jack's family was never a comfortable experience for me. I always felt like an appendage to an appendage: Steve was a distant stepbrother to Mary Ann's children, and I was a step further than that. Lots of things kept us from feeling like true family. I know this is probably the norm for many, many people. But it wasn't for my family growing up, and I felt inauthentic within this group, even more so now. So here we were, headed toward what felt like Doomsday. I had packed a lot of numbing agents (adult beverages) for us in anticipation of the discomfort.

We were super early, and there were very few people present whom I recognized. COVID had prevented us from celebrating Mary Ann's true ninetieth birthday, thus increasing the time since we'd last been with the family. I approached someone I knew to be Mary Ann's younger sister. "Hi Sylvia! How are you?" I asked.

"I'm not Sylvia, that was my mom. She's been dead for several years."

An awkward silence followed. I attempted to recover from my mistake and inquired about her family. Damn it, where did Steve set down our cooler??

Throughout the day, I followed Steve's lead of never being without a drink in my hand. I wouldn't say we pounded down the alcohol, but we definitely kept it flowing at all times, which was unusual for us.

Also like Steve, I had never felt he was like this branch of the family. He did not look, act, or talk like his stepsiblings/second cousins*. Now that I knew why, it made their differences all the more apparent. I so wanted to tell them, "You know, we're not really related to you," but I bit my tongue . . . several times. We got through the drizzly gloom of the event and scurried back home to what felt like safe ground.

AUNT IRMA'S FUNERAL

About a week after Mary Ann's birthday party, we got the news that Jack's sister, Irma, had died. She was the last of his three siblings, which included Aunt Mary* and Uncle Harold* (yes, from the "Harold's Me Uncle" Theorem). I had not spoken with Irma in about five years, but Becky was in a family Facebook group and interacted with those relatives periodically. During Becky's efforts to construct Jack's family tree, she would reach out to Irma for more information but not hear anything back. And now Irma was gone, taking the last bit of Osborne family lore with her.

Funerals are generally uncomfortable events to begin with but having to drag this dead horse of genealogical embarrassment along with me made attending Irma's service even less desirable. But our motto is: Weddings are optional; they might have another one. Or in the case of the Osborne/Condo clans, there might be several more. But funerals are mandatory; they're not scheduling a second one. Therefore, we set our plans to attend.

Funerals are events where we see people we should recognize but don't. I'm not talking about just the deceased, but about my first cousins, whom I hadn't seen in decades. After the initial awkward realizations of who each other is, and getting past the thoughts of, *Gee, you got fat*, or, *God, you got old*, we can settle into polite and safe conversations, covering decades of life events in minutes. It seems to be a rushed sequence. I'm not sure why it is. It's not like the dearly departed is going anywhere soon. We've got time.

As it happened, and it always does, a member of the family approached and identified me despite the years and changes that time has etched on my face and body. Despite my prayers of anonymity, I was identified as a relative. Shirley, Jack's first cousin, came toward Becky and me with a knowing look on her face. She smiled as she got close.

"You're Stevie! You're Jack's son, aren't you?" Shirley inquired, surprised and somewhat giddy, with an accent known specifically to these parts.

"Yes, ma'am, I am," I said humbly but proudly at the same time. No matter the DNA results, I was proud and humbled to be Jack Osborne's son. I wasn't surrendering that position to anyone for any reason. Shirley's tone took a hard left turn and she added the inquisitory lilt as she continued.

"Well, you don't look anything like Jack. Who do you look like?" *Ouch!* That hurt. Becky and I often hold hands in public. Not unlike middle-schoolers. But now she was squeezing my hand, hard. The message was firm and as obvious as her grip, which was to say, "Down, Fido. Sit. Do not bite the nice lady. Again, this is not the time nor place." I said to myself, *Forgive them, Lord, for they know not what they do.*

"I think I do look like my father," I protested. It was a guise for sure. It was 100% accurate and completely misleading at the same time. There was no way for her to know the duplicity of my response. I, however, knew the confused look on her face. She was right, I looked nothing like Jack. I did look, not surprisingly, like Peter Holmes.

Several months later as my news became more public, Becky reached out to Shirley to explain and apologize. Shirley was a gem about it. She spoke kindly and graciously and dismissed the DNA test results. She claimed it changed nothing and I appreciated that. Shirley, thank you, Love.

Becky...

Dear Lord, how many more times are we going to have to play "Pretend Family"? I'm not sure how much longer we can continue lying by omission, but we have to get ourselves right with the facts before blasting it out to the family.

Irma's death was especially untimely coming so soon on the heels of Steve's DNA discovery. Over the last decade, I had reached out to her many times in an effort to glean more information about her parents and siblings. The first time I asked, she offered up lots of new revelations that we hadn't known. While some of her facts were confused or slightly off, the records I found on Ancestry corroborated or corrected them all. She shared that her father was actually buried with a woman other than her mother. Apparently, her father had remarried a former wife after Irma's mother died from MS. Irma also revealed that she had half-siblings, something Jack had never mentioned. There's probably not a family in existence that doesn't have skeletons in the closet, and we didn't make a big deal of it. But later I heard whisperings that Irma didn't like me "snooping" into the family history. After that, she went radio silent.

This was the first time I had ever encountered someone who was reluctant to talk about their family. Most people just love to prattle about even the most mundane and irrelevant details. For whatever reason, Irma was not that person. I was only too aware of the fact that she was the last living sibling of Jack's, and therefore the only person who could fill in some blanks and add color and dimension to the facts about her original family. She was the only person alive who could provide an oral history of the Osborne clan. But in light of the DNA surprise, maybe her reluctance had its origin in something she knew and we didn't, until now.

VISIT TO DR. CUNNINGHAM

Shortly after my aunt's* funeral, I had a regularly scheduled visit with my cardiologist. Previously, we had covered heredity multiple times. When my initial cardiac issues came to light, I had asked about the best way to reduce my risk of heart disease. His ironic response was, "Get new parents. So much of the risk of someone contracting heart disease is linked to heredity."

In the normal routine of every visit, we would cover areas of my life that affect my cardio health. Dr. Cunningham started with his standard checklist. "Okay, there are three major areas that contribute to your cardio health: heredity, diet, and lifestyle and/or stress."

We covered lifestyle and diet. I had made positive progress in both. He continued, "Family history . . . your mom had triple bypass at fifty-nine and your dad died at sixty-six from heart failure?"

"No, my dad died at fifty-seven from heart failure," I corrected him.

"How could we have gotten his age wrong in your records? Fifty-seven is not sixty-six, and it's not even close," he mused with irritation at the perceived error.

"You didn't get the age wrong. I had the wrong dad. I found out a few months ago, via a DNA test, that my dad isn't who I thought he was."

He pushed himself away from his keyboard and dropped his hands into his lap as he swiveled in his chair to face me. "What?" he said incredulously. "Are you kidding me?" His face registered total shock.

"No, unfortunately, I'm shooting you straight, Doc. Jack Osborne is not my dad. A Canadian guy named Peter Holmes is my biological father."

Dr. Cunningham wanted as much detail as he could get in the insurance-allotted time per patient, and then he blew past the allotted time to hear the rest of the story. Near the end of the appointment, he wheeled himself back to face the computer and said, "I have never had anyone ever come into the office and change all three heart health risk categories. This is a first for me." There was an element of humor, wrapped in empathy, in his voice.

One could say there was fortuitous serendipity in my DNA discovery. If not for Jack having a history of heart issues, I may not have paid much attention when I experienced the symptoms of a heart attack. Jack's death at the age of sixty-six had me on high alert for potential heart problems of my own. Given that Peter died of a heart attack even earlier, at age fifty-seven, it was fortuitous indeed that Jack had similar heart issues to Peter, and therefore I paid attention to my health.

CHAPTER 20

Life on the (One Way) Farm

People raised on love see things differently than those raised on survival. — Joy Marino

To fully understand how and why this situation gets as emotionally charged as it does, I believe you need to understand the decisions my mom and stepdad made during my teen years, the dynamics those decisions created in our home, and how horribly and negatively it affected their kids, especially Laura and me.

When I was nine years old, my mom and stepdad, Jerry, decided to open their home in Colerain Township north of Cincinnati to people in need. "People in need" were typically troubled adults and teens with a checkered past. Some of them had fallen on hard times and were trying to get their lives back together. Others were just questionable individuals.

I'm sure this decision to help others was influenced by Barb's own difficult upbringing. In her youth and teens, she was tossed between her parents, step-parents, and aunts. I've also heard her tell stories about how she was on the street. She was kicked out of her father's house by her stepmother because the stepmother discovered Barb's lipstick on her father's cheek and collar. (Yeah, I'm not quite sure what to make of that either, and I don't want to give it too much thought. I've already blown my therapy budget for the year.) Her experiences lead her to a place where she felt 'called by God' to help others. A noble sentiment for sure.

As is the way with so many high-minded concepts, there is a large gap between virtuous ideas and the reality of the daily and tactical implementation of said ideas. Simple things like where will all these down-on-their-luck people sleep? How will they be fed? And what might be the effects on my children, family, and marriage? Barb and Jerry's approach seemed to be: "Don't worry, God will provide." Who am I to question that approach? I do, however, question many of the decisions made by my parents.

Barb would regularly invite troubled adults to live in our home for extended periods of time. One of the first pictures I had ever seen of a topless woman was of the stripper who happened to be living in our house. She met a convicted murderer, who was also a frequent "guest" in our home, and they got married.

Our home was also a gathering place for teens. They would come into the house "carrying" (they had drugs on them). More than once, Gus, a friend of my oldest sister Kathy, overdosed in our living room. I was nine when I watched Barb and Jerry hold him down as he convulsed on our floor. Finally, an ambulance took him away. This was not a huge surprise to me as Gus was frequently tripping on speed or high on weed, while on our porch or in our living room.

Tom, another stray, was an extremely large, muscular, bald man who could star as a Nazi thug in any movie. He was a drug abuser and dealer. So too was his acquaintance, Ephesus. One afternoon, Tom beat Ephesus unconscious for god-knows-what in our front yard. Kevin, another frequent "guest" in our home, was taken away by the police for allegedly beating some other guy to death. Or it might have been for stabbing him, I'm not entirely certain. It didn't matter, as my mom felt these were all really nice people who just needed Jesus and a little love to get them back on their way.

I was eleven years old when we moved to Fairfield, Ohio. The house was set on a small, four-acre "farm." The property had a large old farmhouse which would become our family's home for the next five decades. It had a small field for planting, a large barn that we eventually tore down, and four smaller structures. Throughout my teen years we had a few horses, a couple of pigs, a few goats, and chickens. It was the kind of farm that any real farmer would make fun of.

Barb now had the space and resources to expand her outreach to troubled individuals. They named the place The One Way Farm, as they believed there was only one way to heaven and that was through Christ. At this point, Barb and Jerry felt called by God to extend their outreach by helping local troubled youth. This was another wonderfully virtuous and noble cause.

Two of the first individuals who lived in our newly-named home in Fairfield were serious drug users. To their credit, they had found God and were trying to get their lives on the right track. But drugs would continue to be a problem for them as well as others who came to live with us. David, a challenged young man, about 6'4" and 270 pounds, was a professional photographer, which I discovered was a euphemism for pornographer. David, *don't leave your camera and your portfolio lying around. Young kids will find that stuff and ask questions about what the lady in the picture is doing.*

By the time I left home at age seventeen, I had been, without my consent, forced to cohabitate with several more convicted felons. One had killed his wife and unborn child. But he too had found God, so I guess that would mitigate any risk of potential harm to me or any of the others in our house.

As I look back on the situation, I think the bigger issue I had was that some of these model citizens were sleeping in my bedroom. I understand my parents' desire to help people, but should they have risked exposing their pre-teen sons and daughters to drug users, drug dealers, pornographers, and convicted murderers? And it wasn't that we were just exposed to it; we were STEEPED in it like a teabag in a pot of hot water. I was living in it 24/7. There was no avoidance. There was no place to escape it. There was no possible way it could fail to affect us. A person can't walk through the junkyard in a white suit and not get some of that grime on them.

When I was thirteen, Barb connected with Butler County Children's Services to work out a mutually beneficial arrangement. Basically, if Barb and Jerry would take only minors, get some state certification, and fill out a bunch of forms, they could become a housing resource for the county and its troubled youth. This would mean a daily stipend for each child they housed in a temporary manner.

With that, Barb's ministry had found a dependable revenue stream. Her calling from God could be a sustainable, revenue-generating business. This would mean no more twenty-five- to thirty-five-year-old drug dealers or felons. Now we would house nine- to seventeen-year-old drug dealers and felons-in-training. Maybe this statement isn't fair to some of the kids who stayed in our home. Many kids who came to live with us were simply troubled youth who had gotten sideways with the law. Or who, by no fault of their own, found themselves in untenable living conditions caused by their guardians (i.e., parents who were drug abusers and/or violent felons).

The agreement with Butler County meant that my 12'x15' bedroom was converted into a dorm room containing six bunk beds—three sets of two beds each. These beds would sleep me and five guys to whom I had no relation. Complete strangers in each new face I met. Strangers at 8:00 a.m., roommates at 5:00 p.m. Options available to me: NONE. They would be there anywhere from a matter of days to years. The only thing they had in common was the emotional baggage and juvenile court records they brought with them and an endless demand for Barb and Jerry's limited time and resources. My parents, who already had seven children of their own, would now take into this old farmhouse up to seven additional troubled youth. How could anything possibly go wrong? How could anyone not see how this might be an issue?

Recently my sister, Laura, recalls seeing a photo of one of the temporary foster kids sitting on our mom's lap and wearing one of Laura's favorite dresses. That dress went missing when this girl left our house. The picture and Laura's comments about it are the quintessential elements that encapsulate the entire situation:

"I can't believe that Karen is sitting on Mom's lap, and she's wearing my dress. I never got to sit on Mom's lap. She was always too busy with those damned kids she took in. And then Karen stole my dress when she left." That about sums it up for both of us.

Living at "The Farm" was an education in the ways of the street. When I entered the seventh grade, my class was exposed to our first semi-adult topics in health class. Yeah, it was bit late, I know, but this was a private/Christian school. The curriculum was weak and outdated; the entire school was religiously uptight to the point of exploding if someone so much as said *damn*. We even had to spell the word S-E-X.

Our seventh grade teacher was Ms. Pond. I can't imagine she was more than twenty-four years old at the time. She came straight from the Christian college that many of my high school cohorts planned to attend upon graduating. It's a good idea to isolate yourself from the problems of the world. That way you'll never have to be exposed to or deal with them. Wait, that may not be right.

As the curriculum would have it, part of the semester was to be dedicated to learning about drugs, a topic in which I had a street-level master's degree due to my 24/7 exposure from the time I was nine. Innocent Ms. Pond barely knew anything more than what was written in the textbooks we were given. She would mention the proper name of an illicit substance; I would then offer up a half-dozen street names of said substance, its approximate cost, why it was popular or why it was fading in popularity, and the more common ways people used it.

My extensive exposure to drug users and dealers before the age of fifteen provided me with an unanticipated visit to the principal's office. I arrived there to find my mom already sitting in a chair. The principal began to express his concerns over the unusual depth and detail I had about street drugs and implied that I somehow might be engaging in the use or distribution of said substances. My mom waved him off and explained how I had gained most of that knowledge from my roommates. We were duly excused from the meeting. Barb found great humor in the situation. She enjoyed a good laugh about it. I, however, was furious. No teen wants to be in the principal's office under adult scrutiny and in the presence of his parent. What made it worse was this debacle was on them, not me. If they didn't want me to learn shit from drug dealers, they shouldn't have placed them in my goddamn bedroom.

Frequently, people who know or learn about the environment in which we were raised make statements such as, "It's amazing that you turned out the way that you did. Why are you not in jail?" I believe the reasons have to do with my dads' influence. I believe that Peter's DNA,

Jack's love, and Jerry's rigor and structure were my inoculation against the virus-laden environment we grew up in.

Jack hated The One Way Farm and the conditions Laura and I were living in on a daily basis. There was no way he couldn't feel that way. He loved us. He worried about us. He thought we were at risk of harm— emotional harm, if not physical, and he was absolutely right. He wanted us to come live with him and Mary Ann. Barb vehemently protested. The list of grievances she gave to us against living with our father was long. Barb argued that Jack and his friends did drugs and she couldn't allow us in that environment.

How unbelievably ironic and hypocritical that was, seeing as that was exactly the environment we were living in with her. She said that Jack ran with a group of ignorant low-lifes. If we lived with him we would be wasting our potential. All those reasons were complete fabrications on her part. I believe the real reason that Barb was against us living with our dad was she wanted to keep the child support money she would lose if we moved in with Jack, and she wanted control of our lives. Unfortunately, Laura and I never pushed the issue. We were living in Barb's sphere of reality-altering influence. She would speak and we would believe, often against all logic and visible evidence to the contrary. In many ways, we lived in fear of our mom and her propensity for emotional retribution.

At one point in our married life, Becky, who has a heart of gold, suggested that we consider taking in temporary foster kids. She knew that those kids could benefit from a bridge as they waited to find a new home. My response might have been a selfish one. I replied in an unequivocable tone, "No, I don't have any interest in that. I think I've done my time. I'm not willing to go back there." Alternatively, Becky led our family into multiple other community service projects, many focused on the youth in our area.

One of the positive outcomes of living at The One Way Farm was that I have never been tempted to do drugs. I've never smoked weed, never tried anything that might be considered mind altering. I can drink enough to get myself to that place. It's not a moral thing with me. I hold no judgment of other people's choices. It's just not for me. When someone has seen three different people overdose and get hauled out of their living room on a gurney before they are fifteen years old, drugs simply don't look like an attractive life choice. My early life experiences set me on a different path, a drug-free path. I guess I did get something of value from my time incarcerated in Fairfield, Ohio.

At the age of fifteen, I moved out of the communal bedroom and into what was a converted tool shed. The shed had a covered walkway to the main part of the farmhouse. The room/shed was roughly 7'x10'. I could fit my bed and a dresser in it. I had to climb on my bed to open or close the door. There was not enough room to open the bottom dresser drawer because the bed was in the way. I'm positive it did not meet the fire code as a bedroom, or any other code for that matter. It had only a space heater, a single window with a half-dead window A/C unit for cooling, and mice. But dammit, it was private and it was mine. I left the house about a month before my eighteenth birthday and moved into my first apartment. I planned on attending nearby Miami University and I was working at least two jobs to make it happen. It was the best living situation I had experienced since I was eight years old.

* * *

Fast forward to November of 2021, two months after the DNA test results brutally informed me that my past was based on a lie. The time had come to finally confront the only person left alive who knew the truth. A person who throughout my life had been less than honest, less than generous, less concerned about her children than she was about herself. Someone who could be manipulative, corrosive, and intentionally hurtful. Maybe the decades had changed her, but I held out little hope.

I set off alone on the thirty-five-minute drive that would bring me face-to-face with my mother.

CHAPTER 21

With Intent to Slay Medusa

Family quarrels are bitter things. They don't go according to any rules. They're not like aches or wounds, they're more like splits in the skin that won't heal because there's not enough material.
— F. Scott Fitzgerald

STEVE CONFRONTS HIS MOTHER

I knew there was a high likelihood that the impending interaction with Barb wasn't going to end well. I had driven the thirty-five minutes to my childhood home where my mother and my older sister, Carrie, still lived. I was nervous and angry. When I arrived, I started an audio recording on my phone to have an accurate record of what was about to happen, just in case I ever needed to play it for the police.

I entered the house to find my mother and my sister in the living room. Stilted salutations were exchanged. Neither one of them was happy to see me. I wasn't happy to be there. I hated the house and the memories it held. I had to practically throw Carrie out of the room so I could have some privacy with our mother.

I sat down on the edge of a couch opposite Barb, with a coffee table between us. "Why are you here?" she asked in a calm, detached manner.

"As I said on the phone, I have something I think belongs to you." I opened my portfolio and pulled out the pictures I had brought with me.

I slid a picture of Peter Holmes across the small coffee table. "You got anything you want to tell me?" I asked. I was trying to control the tone of my voice as I fought back the anger within me.

She picked up the picture and scanned it. Her eyes moved quickly between my face and the photo multiple times. She dropped the photo on the coffee table and said, "I don't know who that person is. Who is that supposed to be, your father?" Her response was disappointing. I thought we might have a gentle prelude of semi-truths and subtle evasiveness before the full-on lying started. But I was wrong.

"Is that my father?" I fired back in an incredulous tone. "Really? Of all the questions you could possibly ask about that picture, you ask, 'Is that my father?' Why would you ask that question? That's a stupid question. Of course, that's not my father. My father is Jack Osborne, right, Barb? I mean, isn't he?"

Barb sat quietly and shrugged her shoulders.

"I think you know that's my father. I think you've known it for quite some time, likely more than four decades. Yes, that is my biological father. His name is Peter Holmes. Does that ring a bell?"

"What can you tell me about him?" Barb inquired as if she had no role in this situation.

"What can I tell you about him? What can I . . . tell you . . . about him? I can't tell you anything about him. I wasn't the person schtuping him. That was you! What can you tell me about him?" I was in full seek-and-destroy mode. We were three minutes and forty-five seconds into the conversation and I'd gone full knives out. What a dumbass I was. *Have I no control?* I thought. There's a saying about catching more flies with honey. Clearly, I tossed that right out the window. Even fewer are caught with a flamethrower, but for some reason, that was the method I had devolved to ever so quickly.

Barb shrugged again.

"Please tell me you know something. Tell me you remember something! Tell me what the broom closet at the bar looked like. Or what the back seat of his car looked like. Because what I can tell you is I was conceived the week of your father's funeral WITH THIS MAN. So please, tell me something because the only image I have is of you and some Canadian guy wrestling around in the coat room at Stiff's funeral home."

Now, I know someone might be reading this and thinking, "Gee, that sounded mean." That's only because it was. In the moment, I had lost all composure, and I was selecting my words with intent to harm. I know it was a mistake. I know I should have been a better person than that, but that is how it went down. If I could go back in time, I'd do it differently, but I suspect I'd make the same mistake again.

"I can't remember much anymore. I've had a stroke," Barb replied.

My sympathy gauge didn't budge a single notch. I had heard that bullshit line so many times over the past twenty years. If I believed everything she said, this would be her nineteenth stroke. I can't count the number of times Barb was on her deathbed on a Monday and flying to Vegas to hit the casinos on a Thursday. The woman who cried wolf was crying it again, and I was having none of it. I was convinced she was thinking, "I'll hide behind the veil of weakness, feign illness, play the sympathy card, and hope he calls off the dogs." Well, I had absolutely no intention of accommodating her and her escape plan.

"You don't remember this guy?" I drilled her. "You don't remember him? Come on! Are you telling me you can't recall anything?"

"I'm not admitting to anything," she said defiantly, still trying to avoid the bullet.

"I'm not asking you to. I don't need you to admit to anything. I've got six independent DNA tests that tell me that this man's my biological father. If you say anything other than that, you're lying. I don't need your help to identify him. I know who he is and I'm sure you do too."

"Where did you get the picture?"

"It doesn't matter where I got it from. It's him and the resemblance is quite striking, don't you think?"

Barb mumbled something incoherently. I asked her to repeat herself but she didn't improve the quality of her voice or volume. Then she attempted a different defensive approach.

"You know, we did things in the fifties and sixties that we never thought we would have to explain today," she offered as some kind of reconciliatory excuse. I had no idea what to make of that statement other than a back-handed quasi-admission of the truth and a plea to dismiss the case. I'm guessing my blood pressure was 250 over 130 at that point.

She continued, "Who have you told about this?"

If there was one question that completely pissed me off, that was it. Her question was focused on who else might know and how much damage control she was going to have to do to protect her church lady reputation. The question had nothing to do with how I might be feeling or the damage I might have incurred. The damage she caused.

"Who else knows? You're worried who else knows? Who have I told? Is that your concern? You don't have to worry; I've already told everyone! Everyone in the family already knows. Everyone includes all your children, most all your grandchildren, and your ex-husband. I've told everyone but Carrie. I'll tell her in a minute if she can't hear me from where she is standing now. I've provided all of them with the DNA results and what we have found." I would not have gone at her that way if she hadn't provoked me.

And then my mother-in-absentia uttered the pièce de resistance of her arrogant self-absolution. "I don't know what you're so upset about. Look at your life. Everything turned out pretty well for you." Her fifth and final admission via non-admission. I'd had enough. I fast forwarded to the end of the exchange.

"So that's it? I've found some level of success in my life and that absolves you of any of your actions, your lying, your manipulation, the people you've willfully hurt?" I could barely keep my teeth behind my lips. If she was trying to short circuit our time together by stonewalling, lying, and deflecting, she had absolutely obtained her goal. I knew every second I spent there was a second with no value and time I couldn't get back. I shot across at her, "I can tell this is useless," and began to gather myself to leave.

By that point, Carrie had reentered the room. She looked at the photo and said, "Who is that?" As if she didn't know. She had been listening to the entire conversation standing right around the corner.

"That's my true biological father. His name is Peter Holmes."

"So, Jack Osborne is not your dad?" I wasn't sure if she was stating the obvious, confirming her supposition, or just slow on the uptake. Again, I'm betting on the latter.

"Correct. I found out via a DNA test a few months ago. You should consider getting a DNA test yourself."

"I know who my dad is," Carrie volleyed. She was referring to Ed Sayre, her father. Well, at least that's the currently accepted common story. But at this point, anything goes.

"Funny, sixty days ago I would have said the same thing, but I would have been wrong. You're likely wrong too." I turned to Barb and growled, "You've had five children with at least four different men. Should Kathy or Carrie return a divergent DNA test, you'll be five for five. That's batting a thousand. Those are hall of fame numbers. That's difficult to do in any endeavor. I hope you are proud of yourself."

She didn't respond. She just looked away.

I got up and left. There was nothing positive coming from this godforsaken charade.

So much for the loving, tearful mother/son reunion. The entire meeting lasted thirteen minutes and twenty seconds from entry to exit. Not much time to scorch the amount of earth we did, but we did a hell of a job of it. With gas prices the way they were, I wondered how much money I wasted with my thirty-five-minute drive. I put my car in reverse to head home. I had visions of the Hindenburg exploding into flames over and over in my mind's eye.

What the hell! She doesn't give a damn about anyone other than herself. What is the use in withholding information at this point? Her son is sitting in front of her, with insurmountable, undeniable scientific evidence. She knew why I was coming over. She had already figured it out. She knew forty years ago when she saw my senior pictures. She had to have prepared herself for this contingency. How f*****g hard is it to say, "I'm sorry"? And that is the crux of my issues with her.

NEW TRAUMA REVIVES OLD TRAUMA

As I looked back on the confrontation, I realized that the events of the day were not solely fixed upon the DNA results nor the lies I had been told. On the surface, I thought I was speaking rationally, logically, and passionately about my paternity. But my inner child had summoned the demons of my past along with the decades of hurt, anger, and betrayal. My emotions came forth in a Vesuvius-like display. Try as I did, I was unable to restrain a lifetime of negative energy and resentment. The years of my mother's parental neglect, the choice of securing her public glory over the safety and needs of her own biological children, pushed their way to the surface. The words I spoke were about my biological father Peter Holmes, but my aggressive emotions were avenging my dad, Jack Osborne, and my younger self.

I would not realize this dynamic was in play until months later in an early morning coffee/therapy session, one of the many Becky would help me through. When all the fat is boiled off, the only thing I really wanted from Barb were two words, which were "I'm sorry" (three words if you disregard the contraction). I'm sorry. Those are the words any DNA orphan wants to hear. A person can say anything before them and anything after them. Just fucking say them. She could have said, "I was in a bad place," or "I didn't know what I was doing," or "It was really bad judgment and I never considered . . ." or "I was just enjoying my life, and we lived in wild times. Hey, it was a party . . ." She could say ANYTHING SHE WANTED, and then say, "I'm sorry." I wanted acknowledgment that her actions hurt me.

And for any parent of a DNA Orphan, my advice is this: ask for forgiveness whether you feel you need to or not. This situation isn't about the parent— it is about the DNA orphan. It should sound something like this: "Blah, blah, blah, I'm sorry. Blah, Blah, Blah. I know my actions hurt you. I never meant to hurt you. I didn't know how to tell you. I'm sorry. I hope at some point you can forgive me."

I know now the only way the situation could have worked out is if she was focused on us, her and me. She didn't focus on us. She didn't focus on our healing or even my healing. She was focused on herself and how she would be perceived when word of her actions got out. Who cares who was sleeping with who? NOBODY cares! It was almost sixty years ago at that point. We have all screwed up in our lives at some point or another. Own it. Lean into it. Not for yourself, but for anyone and everyone other than yourself.

I look back now at the meeting and realize that I didn't get the information I wanted. I also realize the reason why it didn't happen. I set the tone and it was a dark one. I can see I put her on the defensive before she spoke the first words about Peter. I could have handled that better. As a sales professional, an adult learning facilitator, and a professional negotiator, I should have known better. I did know better. I let my pain, my fear, my resentment—and yes, my hate—control me. I went to the dark side and I dragged her along with me. As much as I want to blame my mother, I know it's my own damn fault. If given the chance, I'd do it differently. Who am I kidding; I'd probably just eff it up again.

CHAPTER 22

Family Secrets
Held Secret No More

Every secret has an expiration date.
— Josiyah Martin

Through some close examination of dates, documents, and events, we were able to determine that Barb displayed a very consistent pattern in her relationships with her significant others (mostly men). We were able to deduce that she was in a relationship with my dad, Jack Osborne, while she was still married to her first husband, Ed. This inference comes from the extremely short period of time between Barb's divorce from Ed and her subsequent marriage to Jack Osborne: three weeks. That close timing creates another whole area of speculation.

She was sexually involved with my biological father, Peter, while she was married to Jack Osborne. We are still trying to discern the start date and end date of their interactions, and those date markers are still moving as of this writing. We know that Jack and Barb were married for four years when I was conceived. We know that my younger sister Laura, confirmed as Jack's biological daughter, was born eighteen months after me. Barb and Jack would divorce almost two and a half years later.

She was then romantically involved with my stepdad, Jerry, while still married to Jack. Barb was providing daycare for Jerry's two daughters, who would eventually become my stepsisters. We know they were involved because Kathy, my oldest sister, has memories of it. Also because of a story that my stepmother, Mary Ann, conveyed to me multiple times over the years. It's one I remember happening as a child. The story goes like this. Barb and Jack were freshly separated, but not yet officially divorced. Dad came by to pick Laura and me up for a visit. I was unable to find my shoes.

"Son, you can't go without shoes. Where are your shoes?" my dad said.

"I know where they are. I left them at someone's house. I can take you there," I said confidently, or so I am told by my stepmom as she conveys this story. At four years old, I proceeded to instruct them to drive to where my shoes were. The drive took about thirteen minutes and consisted of eight different turns to deliver us to my soon-to-be stepdad's house. When we arrived, my dad asked whose house we were at. I told him mom's friend Jerry. We retrieved my shoes. Jack, realizing the intimate details the situation presented, was furious, as any man would be.

A decade and a half later, sometime during or after her marriage to Jerry (we are not sure), we believe that Barb was involved with various different women, four of whom I can easily identify, who were in her life for the next few decades. We (meaning most of her children) believe this to be true through Barb's own comments, comments vague and veiled at times, but clearly meant to convey that she no longer held any interest in men.

To me, a jaded observer, I believe Barb traded men like a thirteen-year-old trades video games at GameStop. She would play them for as long as they were entertaining and to see how many coins she could extract. She was constantly trying to level up in the social order, trying to increase her position and station. I guess we all do that through some means or method. Once she had extracted all the value she could, she would remove the current cartridge and head back to the market to get the next cartridge to insert into her PlayStation. I cynically imagine her thoughts as, "Let's see, I played this one for a while. Let's see if I can get more coins from this other one." This is just my opinion, but I think Barb used men like rungs on a ladder. She pulled herself up from one social station to the next, reaching, grabbing, leveraging, and eventually stepping on the men she married, and others in her life, as she attempted to pass them. As she grew older, Barb's obvious disdain for men became so clear to me and most of my siblings.

We all leverage the opportunities presented within our lives to advance our own wellbeing. There is no judgment in that. It is part of the human condition. With my mother, it seemed different. It seemed more calculated, maybe even a bit mercenary. The accumulation of data, dates, experiences, and her own dark comments on the subject create a complicated mosaic. As with all mosaics, people see different elements differently. I'm sure this is a similar situation. I have conveyed Barb's life as art and as I have interpreted said art. Others might disagree. I would surrender my position; there is room for interpretation. However, there is no contesting the dates, marriage and divorce records, birth records, addresses, and parties involved. Those items are concrete and the structure upon which all other observations are hung. They create the lens through which I view this picture, and it's not a pretty one.

WHAT DID BARB KNOW AND WHEN?

I've often wondered if Barb was confident in her knowledge of who my biological father was once she realized she was pregnant with me. I suspect she had sex with Jack shortly after doing the same with Peter to head off any questions that might arise should she become pregnant. Basically, to cover her tracks. At birth I looked like any other bald, white baby. By the time I was three years old, I looked NOTHING like Jack. By the time I was ten, I'm quite sure she knew. She saw what I was seeing, that I was different from my siblings. She was feeling the same things I was feeling. But the difference was she knew the truth and I didn't. By the time I hit my early twenties, and likely much earlier than that, she held no doubt whose son I was.

This is where I take issue with my mother. When I was fifteen years of age, she was ten years past the divorce with Jack. She had every opportunity to set the record straight. She didn't say anything, I believed it was because she wanted to continue to collect the child support Jack was paying for me, if not me and Laura. She also wanted to protect her "loving Pentecostal mother and follower of God" image. The truth would only be a huge black eye on her reputation and a hindrance to her as she tried to solicit funds from the local religious community for The One Way Farm. I doubt she ever considered what it might mean to me to know the truth, both good and bad.

INTO THE DARKNESS

Months went by after the encounter with Barb and I still had so many questions. Did she or did she not know Peter for more than a brief, and perhaps anonymous, sexual interlude? Did he know about me? Did I ever meet him? Did Jack know or suspect that I was not his son? Did she know I was Peter's son? Or more aptly, exactly when did she realize I was not Jack's son and likely Peter's son? Is this why our relationship has always been so difficult and strained? I suspect I was the daily reminder of a part of her life she'd rather forget. The saddest element of this Rubik's Cube was the fact that only one person remained alive who knew how to solve the puzzle, and she wasn't talking.

In researching Peter's life, Becky had followed many leads to people who had known Peter, but she couldn't find anyone who was still alive. Peter himself had died in 1982, the year after I graduated from high school. His ex-wife was dead. His second wife was dead. All his siblings and in-laws had passed. There was no one in his generation to shed any light on the situation between Peter and my mother. We learned that the son and daughter from his first marriage were adopted and extremely dysfunctional; in fact, we were warned by one of his grandchildren against attempting to contact the adopted children. I was grieving a father I had never met. Worst of all, there was no method of resolving this ambiguous loss. Time had eroded any hope of learning any more than the few facts we already knew.

My emotions regarding Jack were all over the place. In some bizarre way I was glad he was gone so that he didn't have to endure this shit show spectacular. But I desperately needed to talk to him. Such a large part of the Story of Me was a fabricated lie. But I believed a conversation with him would right our worlds. He would have the words that would settle me. They would calm me and give me perspective. He would hug me just like he did when I was young. He would hold me so tightly it would be difficult to breathe. He would tell me again that the only thing that mattered was that he and I were together with my sister Laura and our families. That would make everything right. But he's gone too.

There's no winning in this scenario. I am not too much of a man to admit that my tears are many and frequent. I am devoid of my dads, with Jerry being the lone exception. He is wonderful in his support and does all a stepdad can do and more. I hate the stepdad label in reference to him. He is simply Dad2. But Jack is gone. Peter is gone. Any hope for resolution passed with them. My mother, Barb, was uncooperative at best and intentionally deceptive at worst. Each day I slid a little deeper into the darkness. Healing for me had not begun. I didn't see it coming any time soon.

As time passed, the acute loss of Jack, the layers of information intentionally kept from me, mixed with the shame and guilt I was feeling concerning my conception, began to etch deeper into my psyche. I always had questions about how I fit into my family, but now I was questioning my self-worth. I wasn't worthy of Peter's involvement in my life. I wasn't enough to keep Barb and Jack's marriage together, in fact, I might have been the reason for their divorce. My wellbeing wasn't important enough to have my mother divulge anything she knew to help me process my grief. I was sliding into a dark place and the slope was steep. In the wee hours of the morning, or when I first awoke, I had thoughts that no one should ever think. Thoughts I would never act upon because of the harm that it would cause to my loved ones. I would banish those thoughts from my mind with a strong cup of coffee and a few tears.

When it comes to constructing your family tree, a birth certificate tells you who the government believes your parents and grandparents are. DNA test results tell you who your biological parents truly are. That can be a real shot in the genealogical acorns if those two data points do not match. It can destroy the mental image you have formed over your decades. You begin to wonder what other foundational beliefs in your life are also untrue.

I found out DNA often stands for "Did Not Anticipate." In my case,

DNA also meant "my Dad's Now Absent."

This type of loss is called a dissociative loss, one that is extremely difficult to reconcile in the mind. It is when we begin to feel disconnected from our own thoughts, memories, and identity. The loss from a death is different. I have experienced them both. Grieving a death has some honor to it. I lost Jack in March of 1999. But I was honored to carry on the Osborne name and his memory. The bond between us was strong, and my part going forward in life was to keep that bond, that memory, alive. Becoming a DNA Orphan is different and awful. There is a sense that the bond we shared, that honorable position as a father's son, is gone. It's not just gone; it was a lie. I felt a fool. Insult, meet injury— now sit over there with deception and loss.

CHAPTER 23

Can This Situation Possibly Get Any Worse?

On second thought, no, this is much worse.
— General George Custer

For anyone who has been through an event like the one detailed in this book, they can tell us how the associated emotions can, and will, well up out of nowhere. It can happen at the strangest times, and quite unexpectantly. Even after long periods of calm, the emotions can come upon us like a jump scare from a horror movie. About four months after my confrontation with Barb, I experienced exactly that.

One June morning as Becky and I enjoyed our coffee, the emotional swell overcame me and rolled me under its surf. My frustration regarding my meeting with Barb made me unbearably angry and resentful. She had stonewalled me. She lied to me. Correction, she CONTINUED to lie to me. Good god, I had her pinned into a corner. The jig was up. She knew that I knew everything. What was the purpose of lying at that point?

"This is so damn frustrating!" I said to Becky. "Why would she be that way? Why wouldn't she help me? I simply wanted to know what she was thinking back then." I was referring to 1963 when I was conceived and born.

"Maybe you should read her book?" Becky responded quite matter-of-factly.

In complete disbelief I responded, "I'm sorry, her what? She wrote a f*****g book?! She didn't write a book. I would remember that." My disbelief strapped on a rocket pack and hit the launch button. I have never known Becky to prank me, especially when I'm upset. There's no way this could be true.

Incredulously, I said just that. "That can't be true. I'm quite sure she doesn't know how to write." Yeah, I know, it's a bit hateful.

Becky wheeled around to her laptop, banged out a few keystrokes, tapped a few mouse clicks, spun her screen toward me, and triumphantly said, "Yeah, she did. It's right here on Amazon."

"She wrote a book?" In my head, disbelief was still leading the race against the presented evidence.

"Yes, as I said; right here on Amazon." Becky forced me to confirm, again, her excellent memory and ability to instantly conjure up the facts.

"When?" I know I stated that as a question, but it was really an alternative form of calling bulls**t.

"According to the publish date, back in 2010," Becky reported with what sounded like pride in her voice. I'm guessing the pride was because she once again was able to sleuth details within seconds, data that I would never find on my own.

Could this situation possibly get any more bizarre? Why on God's green Earth would that woman write a book, and who the hell would buy it? I had to imagine it sold tens of copies. But in fact, after a little research on Amazon.com, I saw that it just missed the top 100 books list. When I say just missed, I mean just missed it by 5,146,821.[1] That's the number of other books that have sold more copies than her book. I'm pretty sure that *The Complete and Unabridged Guide to Underwater Basket Weaving: A Continuing Education Course Catalog* (thank you to the author Lee Barrett for all your research) has outsold my self-obsessed mother's literary opus, her autobiographical tour de force, if you will. There are more than 4,000,000 books placed in front of Barb's book on the quantity sold list. Both of those facts are hard to get your head around.

"That's crazy. How did you know she wrote a book?" I asked Becky.

"I remember her coming to Renee's funeral and asking Jerry to sign a release for her so she could include him in her memoir." Renee was

---

1 Amazon book rankings as of February 12, 2024.

my stepsister via Jerry Condo; I adored her. She died of cancer in 2010 at the age of fifty. She was one of the sweetest people on the planet and God's gift to anyone who met her. Reene was a constant ray of sunshine, and we had shared a close bond. Of all my siblings, she and I were the closest in age and shared many interests despite the lack of any genetic relationship. As children, Renee and I would hang out together when she was on her visits to the Condo House.

My memory was yanked back to the day of her funeral. Becky was right. I remember the event Becky referenced, and it was horrible. My mother's actions in that moment told me a ton about Barb Condo. Her ex-husband had just lost his daughter to cancer. As he was standing, grieving at her casket, Barb approached him in the receiving line with a legal release document, expecting him to sign a paper to provide her with permission for a tell-all book she was writing. It was the most classless, selfish, and inappropriate act I had ever witnessed. I wanted to ask her to leave the service, but I had been taught to be civil and respectful, especially at life-end services. How could anyone be more insensitive, more self-serving? Jerry waved her off. It was not the time nor the place. But even at her stepdaughter's funeral, it was all about Barb. It was always all about Barb. Back to the issue at hand.

"Okay, we've got to get a copy of this thing," my voice painfully eked out the words.

"I'll order one," Becky chirped.

"Buy a used copy. I don't want her getting any money off this purchase." There I went again; clearly, I'm in need of therapy.

I hear the click, click, click of the mouse and then Becky says, "Done. It'll be here Tuesday."

I was sad but excited, mad but curious. What could she have written about? How real would any of the accounts I would read in this book be? Accuracy was not a hallmark of my mother's character traits. She often embellished stories to meet her objectives. When her objectives changed, so did her recollection of the story. Some people call this lying. Lying, however, requires intent. What I have found in dealing with narcissistic sociopaths like Barb (no, I'm not a medical professional, but I have played one on TV) is that the individual knows it's a lie as they speak the words, but by the time the sound reaches their ears, it has become the truth; at least the truth to them.

Forty-eight hours after she ordered it, Becky opened the Amazon package. She held up the book and said, "Shall we look through this?" There was unmistakably an element of excitement in her voice.

"Oh, good god. What fresh hell are we going to find in this drivel?" All this genealogical mystery and revelation is a great deal of fun as long as you are not one of the primary characters.

I abdicated the lead position, mine by birthright, with the words, "You start it. I'm not sure I can stomach it. If it is a waste of time, perhaps you'll just save me the trouble." I had near zero expectations that the 141 pages of musings from Barb could in any way change where I was standing in this familial bog.

"Okay, I can't wait to read it," Becky said as she picked up the book. She is an avid reader, from news stories in the morning to books at night, with recipes, magazines, and emails in between. She reads more than anyone else I know. She loves it. I'm sure there are others who read more, but I don't know them, and whoever they are, they need to get out more. Fortunately, she has passed this love for reading to our girls, and it has served them well. It has served me well, too, because she can give me the cliff notes so I don't have to read stuff. Everyone in our family has benefited.

Three minutes later, I was banging out some emails on my laptop when I caught a glance of her. She had a look of strong disbelief etched upon her face. Maybe that was confusion. I know, the two expressions are sometimes difficult to discern from one another. A minute later her head cocked to one side as if to question what she was reading. Then a furrowed brow. At this point, I didn't care what she was reading. Her facial expressions had become my morning entertainment.

Then the unexpected happened. She asked me for a yellow highlighter and began to highlight text within the book. This pained me for two reasons. The first is I paid a good $6.50 for a used copy. Her marking in it likely just cratered any chance of recovering my investment. The second, and likely more important, was Becky had found items she deemed important enough to highlight. Highlighting anything meant she intended me to read this drivel. Something was alerting her sensibilities.

Then she stopped. Her face was mildly contorted and noticeably pained. She had not been reading more than ten minutes at max. She closed the book and put it in her lap while keeping it slightly open to specific pages. The klaxon in the back of my head began to go off. I hear the "Warning! Warning! Danger, Will Robinson!" from *Lost in Space* in my head. Her look can hold no positive meaning for me. She transfixed my gaze and held my eyes locked into hers, something that is so easy for her to do. She intentionally changed her expression to something more empathetic.

"Sweetie, I think you need to read this. But I gotta tell you, you're not going to like it."

We'd been married for thirty years at that point. I recognized the tone in her voice. I knew the "Let me break this to you gently because this is a genuine train wreck" presentation style.

Damn! How bad can it be? I thought. I'd lived through almost everything in that book, I supposed. I know most of that stuff anyway; or so I thought. How bad can it be? Did she rob a bank? Did she rob a sperm bank? Did she sell drugs to preschool children dressed as a nun? Becky can't be five pages into that damned infernal thing.

"I'm at page seven, but I think you should start at the beginning." Okay, she was seven pages into it.

"At the beginning?" I said, disguised as a question, but it was really a complaint.

"Yes, start there."

"How bad can it get in seven pages?"

"You'll need to read it," was her only instruction to me.

At this point, I already know I'm not Native American. I already know Jack Osborne is not my biological father. I have already discovered that this Canadian dude, Peter Holmes, is my biological father, and this has been scientifically proven to be true. I know that Jerry Condo is my stepdad and that Barb was getting cozy with him while Jack was still in the house. What now? Do I have ten more siblings I don't know about? Why would I care? Fourteen siblings? Twenty-four siblings? What does it matter? I just don't get what could be the big deal.

"Okay, give me that damn thing," I made a waving motion towards the book. "Let's get this over with." The book was only 141 pages, self-published, larger print (hey, just like this book!), and grammatically correct—as long as English is not the reader's primary or secondary language. The entire book was written chronologically. It was almost completely devoid of proper names (I guess to protect the less-than-innocent). But since I was there for most of it, there was zero mystery in who or what Barb was referring to at any point on any page.

The first few pages were about Barb's life as a child and a teen. How she was bounced around between her mother, her aunts/uncles, and eventually her father and stepmother. I had heard all these stories before (in multiple versions). To be candid, I did read a few things I had never heard before. A couple of Becky's highlights were intended to point out some peculiar mentions and situations she wanted us to discuss, such as when Barb progressed through her teen years and early twenties into her first marriage. We were only now on page six. This page and the next one were bleeding highlighter yellow. Becky's highlights made the pages difficult to consume in the original intended order. My eyes jumped to the highlights, but I fought my way back to the top of the page to make sure I got everything in proper context. Remember, dear reader, we are only on page six . . .

Barb is discussing her life after her first divorce. Her marriage was covered in two sentences. The following text are direct quotes from her literary masterpiece:

"With two babies in tow, I was alone in a world of sin. It was always men, sex, and money."[2]

The two young children are my two older sisters, Kathy and Carrie. I am next in the birth order. As for the rest of that passage, let's just think about that for a minute. That sounds a little like prostitution. That can't be right. The Barb Condo I know is a very religious (Pentecostal) woman and sex was always a quasi-taboo subject. I know people change with time, but what the hell? I continued to read on.

---

2   Barbara Condo, "You Don't Know Where I Came From", self-published, 2010, page 6.

"I can still hear, 'Come on, Baby, we'll go to Miami this week. Get your mother to watch your kids. What is wrong with a little fun? Everybody is swinging!'" [3]

Ouch, that hurt. You never want to hear (or read) the word 'swinging' associated with your mother. Most people don't even care to have their moms utter the word 'sex'. There are some things that can't be unread. This is one of them. Imagine being the person who read that passage written by their own mother. Then imagine the amount of therapy they would need to pay for. The book continued . . .

"'Hey, you've got class. How about coming over to the motel? We've got some men coming in from out of town.'" [4]

That certainly didn't help the situation. The word selection of "men" is not a "man." Men is plural. It didn't say "come meet me," it said, "come meet men." I was reading this about my mother. This wasn't what I was expecting. The book continued on page seven:

"I started doing uppers to keep up the pace . . . I took one or two Black Mollies a day . . ." [5] (those are the amphetamines, not the fish).

Holy bat guano, Batman. I could not believe what I was reading. They were confessions written in my mother's own hand. It was mind-blowing and quite frankly, nauseating. As fantastic and outrageous as this sounds, you cannot make this shit up, and I am not doing so.

And then it hit me. My two older sisters were already born. Barb wrote that she was already divorced from her first husband. She was likely married to her second husband due to the ultra-short period between those marriages (measured in single digit weeks). But I was unsure because the book is irritatingly vague and poorly written. No matter, the critical point to be made is: I am the next child in the birth order. These events could very likely be occurring at the very time of my conception. As we were later able to deduce, not *likely* occurring, but *were* occurring. Combine that with the FACT that Peter Holmes is my biological father, and it became a very uncomfortable, genuine shitshow.

---

3 Same page as above.

4 Same as above, page 7.

5 Same page as above.

My thoughts were yanked back to Becky's instructions. I remembered the tone in Becky's voice. She had already read these pages, and she had already deduced the facts that I was just realizing. She knew before I touched the damned thing that it was going to scorch my psyche. She knew what conclusions this book would lead me to. She had already done the math, drew a line under the column of actions, and arrived at the sum. She knew there was no method that would bring me to a soft landing. I looked up from the book.

She was looking at me lovingly, sadly, compassionately. Her eyes said, "I'm sorry," before her lips formed the words.

"Sweetie, I know you can't be happy with what you just read. I know that must hurt you in ways I can't begin to imagine. Do you believe that any of that is real? Could she have made that up for some reason?" She shifted from accepting the facts as presented by the witness to the off-chance possibility that it might not be true. I think this was more a method to soften the blow of what I just read as opposed to any fiber of her actual belief.

"I can't imagine why anyone would make that up. Why would someone basically claim they were a swinger for cash or a prostitute unless it was in some way, shape, or form, true? Is there any benefit to making up a repulsive story like that?"

"I don't know. I know your mom is not one to stick too close to the facts. Does the rest of the book seem accurate?"

"I have no idea. I'm on page seven. I'm going to go pour bleach into my eyes. I'm not sure I'll be able to read much more after that. But to this point in the book, all the references to us kids, her marriages, all the other details seem to be what I know or remember. I don't have any evidence that these things you highlighted are wrong. I mean, this book has been out for over ten years. If it was wrong, wouldn't we have heard something about it by now? That is, if anyone other than you and I have read it."

"I really have no idea," Becky surrendered.

I think all of us would like to believe that we are alive because of some level of intent. A large number of us were born to a loving set of parents. Many of us were carefully planned, like down to the hour, and with a thermometer. Others of us are happy accidents of our parents' affection or their hormones, and that's wonderful too. Some of us were conceived with medical methods due to problems with natural conception. All those things are positive in their intent and outcomes. Conception and life are wonderful things.

And then there is me. According to what I had just read, I was likely the product of an out-of-state, multi-room, amphetamine-fueled, swingers' party. There is no better way to build one's self-esteem than to read those words in a book written by your mother. To be precise, those exact words do not appear in that order in the book. I parsed the sentences and stitched the concepts together. To arrive at those words, I had to know the facts and timelines that do not appear in the book. I could do that because I do know them. Anyone who does know the details cannot come to any other conclusion than I did. If there is any consolation to this tale, I'm guessing it would be that maybe she could pay the rent that week. So, perhaps the choices and actions which led to my conception served some other purpose.

There is no way of telling if these events happened before or during her marriage to Jack, or both. She states in the book that she "was alone in a world of sin . . . with two babies in tow." That points to the events occurring "before" she married Jack. She and Jack were married for four years when I was conceived, so that points to the "during" portion of their marriage. Combine the two and that places the preponderance of evidence into the "both" timeline. But the book is poorly written and intentionally vague. However, my birth certificate and their marriage/ divorce records are quite specific and all but dictate a significant overlap in her marriage to Jack and her relationship with Peter.

After reading a few pages of the book, I assumed the reason she couldn't tell me anything about Peter Holmes during our confrontation was quite possibly she had no idea who he was. There was no way to tell if she even knew him other than biblically.

To be fair to Barb, all these events occurred before she "found Jesus." The overall theme of her book is that she was once a horrible person with a horrible past, and her subsequent search for Jesus led her to turn her life around to help thousands of children.

PLANES, TRAINS, AND SEX-MOBILES

As a reader, I know it can be difficult to keep all the names, dates, and relationships Barb had in proper order. Hell, just keeping the names straight can be a challenge. It is difficult for me and I know all these people. My NPE discovery kicked off a paper chase and document search of biblical proportions. Becky began asking me about marriages, divorces, births, and ages or dates when these life milestones had occurred. Barb's life events ran extremely close together, many times overlapping with each other. It made maintaining a mental map impossible. We decided the only way to get a complete, and hopefully correct, picture was to lay the documents out on the table in some semblance of sequential order and aggregate the dates we found on the official documents. Here is what we found.

As Becky's genealogical research and document collection began to assemble the mosaic of Barb's life relationships, it painted an eyebrow-raising picture. Barb had five children with at least four different men: Ed, Peter, Jack, and Jerry. She married Ed, Jack, and Jerry. She was able to slip Peter in there somewhere. If at some point my two older sisters produce DNA results divergent from each other, it would mean Barb had five children with five different men. I must admit it would not be a shock given what we have learned to this date.

One peculiar pattern which arose from the information we gathered was the occupations of the men Barb shared children with. When looking at the occupations of these men, what I see is this: we believe Ed drove a cab, Jack drove a bus, Jerry drove a truck, and Peter worked for British Airways. This is either some bizarre coincidence or Barb seemed to have some sexual fascination with the transportation industry. She slept her way through the whole "Planes, Trains, and Automobiles" thing. I guess if it moved fast, she would have been interested in it.

* * *

Kathy's Birth	Carrie's Birth	Steve's Birth	Laura's Birth	Adam's Birth

| 1956 | '58 | '60 | '62 | '64 | '66 | '68 | '70 | '72 | '74 |

Barb Married to Ed	Barb Married to Jack	Barb Married to Jerry*

Involved w/Jack	Involved w/Peter	Involved w/Jerry

*Barb and Jerry divorced in 1995

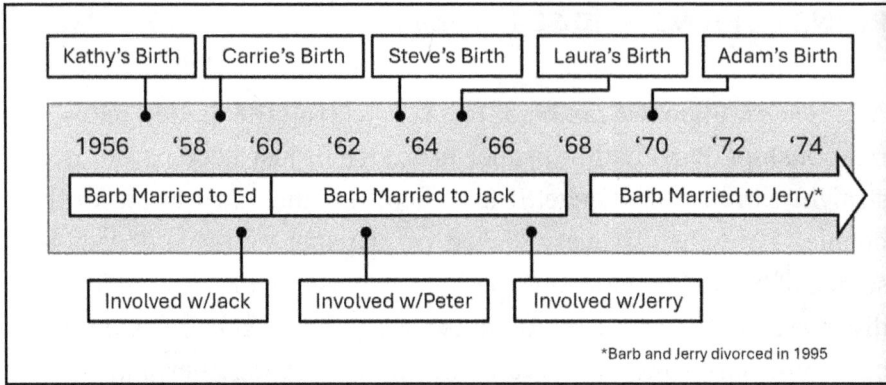

I GET BY WITH A LITTLE HELP FROM MY FRIENDS

After reading as much as I could from my mother's book, there was something that stood out to me. The word "Miami" stuck in my mind for some reason. In all the generic, nameless, white-washed writing Barb did in her "tell-it-all" tome, Miami was strangely specific. In fact, it was the only specific reference made in what I read. The idea that someone would jet off to Florida back in those days, or anywhere for that matter, was equally odd.

In the early 1960s, working class America was not jet-setting to Miami for the weekend. Air travel was an expensive luxury. People dressed up to get on a plane. Men were in suits. Women wore dresses. This didn't fit my image of my parents, who were living paycheck to paycheck. Miami might as well have been Europe, Fiji, or the moon. Why is the name of that city so out of place? Why is it so peculiar? Its specificity nagged at me. Like a specter, I could see it in my peripheral vision, but when I turned to look directly at it, it wasn't there. It was as if the answer was playing in my head, but the volume was too low to discern the words. But I could hear the beat. The beat . . . the beat was familiar.

About a week later, my four friends, John, Paul, Ringo, and George, delivered the answer. It was a beautiful, sunny day and I was driving with the top down on my convertible. I heard the Fab Four on the radio singing one of my all-time favorite Beatles tunes, "Back in the USSR." It started with an unmistakable guitar riff and the sound of a passenger jet's engines whining in descent, and then their lyrics describe a flight back from Miami Beach, Florida, via BOAC. How they could not sleep and how happy they were to be back in the USSR.

Oh, my frickin' God! BOAC! What most people don't know is that BOAC stands for British Overseas Airways Corporation. Most people know BOAC as British Airways, the company my biological father, Peter Holmes, worked for. Flying to Miami for the weekend was far too extravagant and too expensive for the working class in 1963. That is, unless a person was traveling for free, accompanying an airline employee. All my life I have loved the song "Back in the USSR" and played it repeatedly. I always stopped channel surfing when I heard it on the radio. I would instantly crank the volume up to an uncomfortable level for anyone other than myself who happened to have the misfortune of being in the car with me. I had no idea it would be the key to me understanding what the hell had happened back then. And in a way, understanding how I came to be.

The reason Barb's reference to Miami Beach was strangely specific, and not accidental, is because it was very likely a real event. This connection is way too strong, too specific to be random chance or an arbitrary selection of words. Peter, my biological father, must have asked my mother to travel to Miami with him for some extracurricular activities. Both he and Barb were married at the time, but my mother would often take my two older half-sisters to Big Bone Lick, Kentucky (yes, that's really a place and no, it's not what you think), and leave them there with her mom for three to five days. My oldest sister, Kathy, would later confirm this actually happened.

The Greater Cincinnati Airport (CVG) is in Northern Kentucky. It gets its CVG designation from Covington, Kentucky, which was its nearest post office at the time. For Barb, jetting off to Miami with Peter for a few days really wasn't too difficult. All she had to do was drive about an hour south to my grandmother's shack in Big Bone Lick and drop off her kids, then go another twenty minutes to CVG. There she would meet up with Peter, who took care of all her travel arrangements. There was no one checking up on her because Grandma Brock didn't have a phone (or for that matter, a toilet or running water). Thank you,

Fab Four, your piece of musical history was the Rosetta Stone that allowed me to decode the mystery of my genealogical hieroglyphics. I know you didn't write it for me, but I thank you all the same.

PART FOUR
The Road to Redemption

CHAPTER 24

First Holiday as a DNA Orphan

New beginnings are often disguised
as painful endings. — Lao Tzu

Three short months after we had decoded the DNA mystery (a wedding, a funeral, and a ninetieth birthday party later), the Christmas holiday was upon us. Holidays can be tough, but Becky helped me get my mind into a manageable spot. I'd been talking about the situation with our friends (too much) as a form of inexpensive therapy. Yes, family, holidays, and therapy, it just seems like a natural collection. Some might say cluster.

YOU ARE STILL MY LUKE

About the holidays: Becky and I and our family always make the effort to get together with my sister Laura and her husband Greg. It can be difficult because Greg and Laura have moved around the US quite a bit while Becky and I have been rooted for thirty years in the Cincinnati area. As the rotation would have it, Greg, Laura, and their grown boys and families were all coming back to Cincinnati for the holidays and renting a house less than ten minutes away from our home.

Laura, my once-full-now-half-sibling, never let on in the three months after the news broke, but I think she struggled with the news much more than she was willing to show. The memories of the typical sibling rivalry and the irritations of being the little "sister," I suspect, were dredged up and exacerbated by my DNA surprise and the events of the past few months. If this was true, she never mentioned it. Either way, I wanted to apologize to her. I suspected she never said anything because she is too kind, too loving, and too focused on others to make a fuss in any way. Laura was well aware of how this news hit me like a broadside salvo from the big guns. I was devastated. But I think she was hurt too. Perhaps in a different way. However, the only concern she was showing was how I, her big brother, was getting through this mess. Selfless. She's a great human being and a gift of a sister. I love her dearly.

When we were young, we had our tiffs and fights. I was a demon of an older brother. I was unkind, uncaring, and an irritant whenever the opportunity presented itself. Being raised within our home, or should I say within the business of The One Way Farm group home, we were forced to compete for resources. For money, for time, and for our parents' attention. Attention which was spent mostly on the foster children whom our parents took in on a temporary basis.

Laura and I were at odds with each other in our youth. We were at odds right up to the point where someone else was mistreating her. Then we were unified, and I would bare my teeth. I could torment my sister to no end, but don't *you* ever pester her. I can make her cry, but don't *you* look at her cross-eyed. Not to say she couldn't take care of herself— quite the contrary, she was very capable. She was (and is) strong and smart and ironclad. But like all of us, occasionally she needed extra firepower. That was me.

There was an obscure sci-fi movie released back in 1977, kind of a cult classic, popular with a certain audience. It was about a brother and sister who teamed up with their cohorts, mostly aliens, to fight the forces of evil. If I remember correctly, the movie was called *Star Wars*. I was Luke, the young, blonde rebel, and a fighter. She was Leia, the cultured damsel, not-so-much-in-distress, very independent, needing very little help. But when she did, she looked toward Luke. Laura often referred to us as Luke and Leia. It was a reference I cherished and still do to this day.

Now we found ourselves forty-five years later, still fighting the forces of evil, but the person in need of rescuing was me. I was lost, damaged, taking on water, and listing to port. I'd taken more hits than I cared to count. My closest and most valued family connections were severed or at risk of evaporating. I felt alone and isolated. Honestly, I was frightened and vulnerable. But we were getting ready for Christmas dinner and I was set to my assigned task—the task of setting up the bar. I am assigned that task because I believe everyone sees me as the most qualified. Alcohol and I have a familiar and intimate relationship.

Chaos reigned in this small house that Laura's family rented for the week. There were a dozen and a half people, including some small children scurrying around, prepping for the evening. Food was being prepared. The tables were being set. I was still working, assembling the bar, when I realized Laura was standing close behind me. Not just close, but so close as to embrace me from behind, her arms around my waist and chest. She pulled me close and whispered in my ear, "You are still my Luke and I still love you." Each word seemed like a paragraph. She held me tightly for a few seconds longer. I could feel Dad's embrace channeled through her arms. I began to tear up. Tears of relief. Tears of solace. For the first time since I learned of my origin, I felt safe. I was safe because I had been rescued by my sister Leia (Laura). Yes, the force is strong with this one.

A CHRISTMAS PACKAGE FULL OF LOVE

Just a few days after the evening with Laura and her family, Becky and I were at home with not much going on when we received a delivery at our door. Curiously, my oldest half-sister Kathy had sent me a present, a Christmas box. This was unusual as we had stopped gift giving between us decades ago.

I opened the box. To my delight, there was a wonderful collection of items she had chosen for me. The first was a crocheted blanket that she had made for me (I have slept with it every night since I received it). What followed was a litany of items that could only be assembled by someone who knew me as a sister would. Butterscotch hard candies, blueberry jam, and bacon wrapped something (it wouldn't matter if it was a rock . . . wrap it in bacon and I'll eat it). All kinds of eats and treats and tiny treasures. And there was a note. A loving, hand-written confirmation of her love and support. I called her immediately.

"Sissy . . ." I began

"Yeah, Stiv . . ."

"I got the box you sent. It was so wonderful of you to do that for me." I said the words, trying not to allow my voice to quiver.

"Yeah, well, I just thought that this year you could use a little extra love. You need to know that nothing has changed between us. We are not going anywhere, and we are not going to let you go anywhere. You're still my little brother. I know this thing with Jack is hard on you. I know it hurt you. But I'm here for you. I love you more than ever. You'll be okay. I promise." Kathy had always been there for me my entire life. This situation was no different.

Love and time heal all wounds. The Christmas box had accelerated that process. Merry Christmas to me.

* * *

VACATION TO AMI

As Life and Fate would have it, in October of 2021 we booked a vacation for the following May to a wonderful cottage on Anna Maria Island, Florida. We had heard about the charms of this place, and it was on our bucket list to visit but no plans had been made.

It came about when Becky was texting with a friend who mentioned their friends had recently backed out of sharing a duplex with them. Would we want to take it? It was on Anna Maria Island. Normally it takes us weeks to put together a vacation plan, but something propelled us to throw caution to the wind and book it the next day, sight unseen. It just felt right.

This occurred only weeks after we received my DNA results and learned of the existence and identity of my biological father, Peter Holmes. After the fall came winter and with it my descent into the pit of DNA orphaning. I struggled emotionally almost daily through the dark and cold of the season. As spring arrived, we looked forward with great anticipation to the sunshine and warmth of Anna Maria Island, known by most who have been there simply as AMI. The upcoming vacation would be a great break from the day-to-day drudgery of our normal routine. The chaos of our hectic days of business and commercial real estate ownership keeps me in my computational and tactical frontal lobe. Vacation allows that part to fall into an idle background state and allows my more spiritual self to come forward to see the sun. Introspection and reflection (combined with some quantity of alcohol), more times than not, have ushered in my best ideas, highest creativity, and sharpest clarity for our many life plans.

May came and we eagerly packed for our week in AMI, but first there was a little detour north to Chicago for the wedding of our son-in-law's sister. Whoo! More Wedding Stuff in Chicago! It was a lovely weekend celebrating the nuptials of the happy couple with our daughter's in-laws, whom we love. The morning after the wedding dawned wet, chilly, and gloomy. We lifted off from O'Hare anxious to reach the sunny skies of Florida.

A beautiful day awaited us upon landing in Sarasota, and we quickly reached AMI. Just a few blocks from our duplex we passed a sign that said, "Welcome to Holmes Beach." What? Unbeknownst to us, our accommodations were actually in the area known as Holmes Beach. It suddenly made sense why this vacation came together in just a few hours—Peter was directing it for us.

AMI is of a size which invites walking almost anywhere in town. It is very doable even for those who are not avid walkers. But that didn't stop Becky and me from renting a golf cart for the week. Golf carts are legal on all streets and are a part of AMI life. Becky and I began driving the cart throughout the town, truly meandering aimlessly street by street, breezing past shops, restaurants, and beaches as we came upon them. AMI was completely drenched in sunshine and awesomeness. After four or five hours, multiple beaches, multiple beers, and a giant cinnamon roll, we found ourselves in a residential area with only a general idea of the direction we needed to head to get back to our lovely little cottage.

"Where are we going?" Becky asked. We knew where. The real

question was how were we going to get there?

"Heading south," I replied. "We will find 59th street at some point."

"Do you have any idea where we are?"

"Generally, yes. Specifically, no."

"Stop and let's look at the street signs," she suggested so we could get our bearings.

It is so very easy to do it in a golf cart. I slowed and pulled the cart within three feet of the street signs. I read the signs. They read: Holmes Boulevard and 63rd Street. We'd already received a huge surprise when learning we were in Holmes Beach, but now it got even weirder: Holmes, the surname I could have had; 1963, the year I was born.

"You have got to be kidding me," I said in disbelief. "Is this Holmes dude following us somehow?"

"Isn't that cool?" Becky said in her lovable, giddy tone. It was the only time we had stopped to read a street sign. Becky said it was time to snap a picture. Some would say Holmes and 63rd are simply a strange coincidence.

Fate smiles.

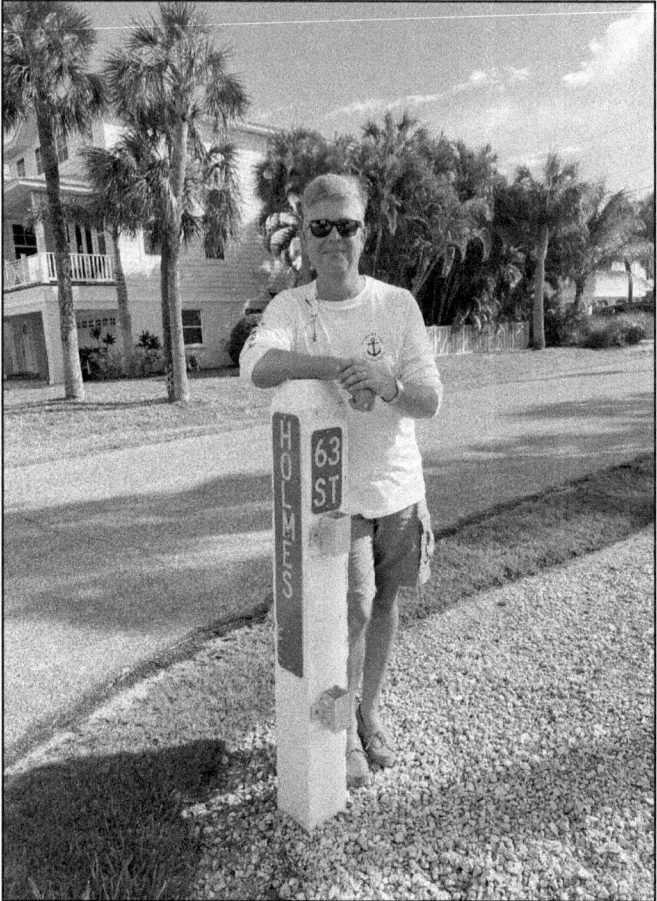

Anna Maria Island: A sign from Peter.

CHAPTER 25

The Gift of My Four Fathers

My father gave me the greatest gift anyone could give another person: He believed in me.
— Jim Valvano

I believe at some point in our lives we are all compelled to ask, "Who am I? How did I become the person I am? Where do my traits, strengths, and weaknesses originate from? Did I create these attributes or was I imbued with them?"

The cataclysmic events surrounding my DNA orphaning caused the introspective self-examination to push its way to the top of my to-do list. *Who am I?* The most detached answer I can muster is that I am, like all living creatures, a sum of my collective experiences combined with my base genetic material. There is new research pointing to a much heavier reliance on the nature (DNA and genetics) side of the equation as the primary determinant to much more than simply eye color, height, and weight.

My characteristics, attributes, and aptitudes come from the building blocks gifted to me at conception. My knowledge, skills, and abilities come from my environment, experiences, and personal investments. I am, as we all are, the combination of our genetic foundations and the accumulation of our choices and actions. We are finished by the investments made in us, some by ourselves, but also by others. Investments made in us because of their love for us. Some are due to the serendipity of collision between our life's paths. Some by obligation, meaning they got compensated for it. No matter how or why or their intent—they invested. It is what we do with those investments, those experiences, those base talents and genetic blueprints given to us at conception, that determine the paths, destinations, and successes of our lives. No matter the cause, it seems that Fate, like Gravity, pulls life's matter together.

I attempt to take a pragmatic inventory of myself. I work to deconstruct myself to see my individual elements. I attempt to divine their origin in terms of parental influence, both biological and adoptive. I have come to realize that I am an amalgamation of these men (in chronological order): Peter Holmes, Jack Osborne, Jerry Condo, and Fred Brower. Capt. F. F. Brower, United States Marine Corps, is my father-in-law. I haven't spoken of him to this point because the focus of this book has been on the men who served as father figures in my youth, but Fred's influence upon me and my adult life mandates his mention. These four men have each imbued me with the majority of whatever positive qualities I may possess. As I evaluate the inventory, I can see with ease the origin of a great many of my characteristics.

My ability to love those close to me, and to openly communicate those feelings, comes from the headwaters of Jack Osborne. My generosity, compassion, and occasional display of empathy (some would argue it's rare) also come from Jack Osborne. From my stepdad, Jerry Condo, I learned my work ethic, organization, tenacity, mechanical inclination, and strength of character. My focus on family, personal strength, business acumen, and recently obtained steadiness are from Fred Brower.

Subtract the above and that leaves some qualities unassigned. My intellect, my drive, my rogue devil-may-care attitude, my irreverence and casual disregard for authority and structure, my stage presence, desire to teach, and my all-out love for aviation, specifically military aviation, which was present within me before I could spell my own name, must come from someone else. Their origin could only be from my biological father, Peter Holmes. These items were assigned to me at conception via the medium I refer to as DNA memory.

In the world of MPEs (Misattributed Parentage Experiences), these seemly odd coincidences are not coincidences at all but are known as synchronicities. They come from deep, underlying patterns or connections. In the context of MPEs, the similar characteristics, likes/dislikes (i.e., favorite color/food/music, career paths, political views) are common between genetic family members and a genetic family member raised outside the family. This is what Peter Holmes and I share. He gave me the pieces of myself not found in my other parental contributors.

Peter gave me these items along with a family history of cardiovascular disease and colorblindness. Not everything we inherit is positive. I found out through Becky's genealogical research that most of my male predecessors died relatively young, at fifty-seven or younger. I was fifty-seven when Becky conveyed this disturbing fact. Fortunately for me, we already discovered that I, too, suffered from this medical threat. I had cardio-bypass surgery at the age of fifty-four. Again, not great, but hey, I was able to get in front of it and hopefully, I'm good to go for another thirty-plus years.

* * *

WHAT IS YOUR NAME?

In the days of my rambunctious youth, I can recall multiple occasions where I did something stupid and/or destructive. Nothing criminal, but things I knew I should not have been doing. Most of those times, my actions went unnoticed. If they were noticed, they were not associated with me. But it was not always the case.

I was in my mid-teens when late one Saturday afternoon, our neighbor approached Jack in the driveway of the Osborne House. Seeing the two of them talking in the driveway was not uncommon. However, the tone and body language of their interaction was. I noticed the occasional glance in my direction as I stood in our yard. I would soon learn our neighbor had seen me pushing fifty-five-gallon drums and throwing glass bottles into a local river and then sinking them with a .22-caliber rifle. Neither the drums nor the bottles belonged to us.

Once they had finished their conversation, my dad, Jack, came to me and explained the inappropriateness of my actions. I didn't need the explanation. I was aware of it as I was doing it. He also explained to me the nature and depth of the apology I was going to make to our neighbor, the owner of the drums. He also introduced me to the word "restitution" and the actions I would undertake to compensate for my adolescent poor judgment. Unlike other dads of our day, he didn't take off his belt and give me a few good lashes. With Dad, a tone and a look could hurt as bad as a belt—just not in the same place.

When we arrived at what I thought was the end of the conversation, Dad transitioned to another one. He looked at me with steely eyes and asked, "What is your name?"

"What do you mean?" I shot back. Why was he asking this question? He knew my name as well as anyone.

"I'm asking you: What is your *name, boy*?" The clear emphasis was on the word "name." The word "boy" was added to ensure I understood the hierarchy between us. It was clear I was not at the top of the pyramid.

"Steve," I answered as I slightly shrugged my shoulders to indicate my answer was my best guess. I wasn't sure what he was getting at. I knew he was displeased with my actions but what did that have to do with my name?

Dad cocked his head to the side and furrowed his brow. His wordless expression was clear: *Think harder about your answer.*

After a few seconds I responded, "I mean—Osborne." I believed I had divined the meaning of the question.

Dad nodded his head in the affirmative. The vertical motion was minimal, slow, and deliberate. It communicated a deep, meaningful focus on the topic: my name.

"You know, that's my name too. When you are out in the world, remember, you carry my name. You carry *our* name with you. *Don't mess up our name, boy.*" He spoke as if he was delivering a great revelation, which in many ways he was. Dad was proud of who he was, the values he held, and of our family name. He made me realize my actions not only displayed the type of person I was, but they also reflected upon him. Our conversation was meant to convey a key point:

if I didn't respect my own reputation, I damn well better respect his.

That day our name, Osborne, gained a new importance to me. It was not simply an identifier. It held value. There was an element of pride in it. I needed to make it mean something. I needed to do something with it and with myself. Unfortunately, throughout my life, I have not always made decisions that would make my dad proud of me. There are times I hurt the family brand. Recovering from those mistakes has not always been as easy as a simple apology. But no matter how difficult the journey, I have been committed to repairing the damage, not only to my name, but to those I have hurt in the process.

Growing up, my mom made me hate the name "Jack." The vitriolic poison she harbored for my father was associated with his name, and by association part of my name. As proud as Jack was of our name, Barb despised it. She demonized my father at every opportunity. She twisted my view of him into some disfigured monster no sane person would want to be associated with. She had some success with this during my mid-teen years. But truth often prevails, as it did with my image of my dad Jack. His loving kindness overcame her endless attempts to disparage him. I learned to embrace my name and attach the same importance to it.

My name is J(ack) Steven Osborne. I am proud to proclaim it as fact.

POWERFUL MAGIC

I remember when I was nine years of age, there was a confrontation between Jack and Barb. It was a heated phone call where Jack made the statement, "I'm not sure he is my son." It was the only time in my life I would ever hear him question my paternity. I'm not certain that he really questioned it or if it was just a tactic that came out in a moment of conflict.

Either way, at nine years old, I didn't understand the ramifications of the statement. All I knew was that when the call ended, Barb looked at me and said, "Your father wants to send you to the hospital to have your blood drawn with a needle because he doesn't want to pay for your child support. Do you want to go to the hospital and get stuck with a needle?"

What nine-year-old is going to answer that question in the affirmative? Of course, I didn't. I was nine and petrified of needles and she knew it. With me crying in the background and begging not to be taken to the hospital, she called Jack back to tell him what a horrible father he was. And while she was at it, she berated him with the old, "How could you possibly do that to your son" attack. Point Barb. Jack zero. It was aways point Barb.

The way Barb would treat my father for the remainder of his life is one of the primary reasons I held such negative feelings towards her. Jack Osborne may not have been my DNA dad, but he is my dad in every other way. He was not a perfect man, but he was as damn close to a perfect dad as a boy (at least this boy) can want. He showed me as much unconditional love, faith, and pride as anyone can. Yet Barb did everything she could to drive a wedge between us. On occasion she would intimate that he was a drug dealer, a criminal, and/or even a child molester. Of course, nothing could have been further from the truth. Jack Osborne was a good, lovable, hardworking blue-collar man.

I can forgive any transgressions against me. I'm armored and battle-hardened. Very little gets through to my core. But she took relentless and mean-spirited aim at my dad. And his return volley? Nothing. He never once attacked her when speaking to me. He never spoke harshly of her to me. He knew his best defense, his only defense, was to stay on a very specific path. That path was to show his true and unconditional love for me. "I love you, son," was his defense against the arrows she fired at him. Whenever I would tell him of some vile accusation that his ex-wife had levied against his character, his response would be, "Boy, I think you know your dad's not like that. I'm not sure why your mom would say those things. Just remember that I love you." "I love you, Boy," is the talisman that kept me safe from the poisonous lies spewed by a bitter ex-spouse. The talisman that kept his hope of a good relationship with his boy alive. Powerful magic, Jack Osborne, and very well played. Very well played, indeed.

Dad gave me the greatest gift a man can give to his children. He gave me true, complete, and unconditional love. It was my dad's love for me that gave me a foundation for the successes I have enjoyed in life, both in personal relationships and in business. His love made me feel safe. His love made me confident. All my positive traits are laid upon the cornerstone of Dad's love.

Jack went even further with his altruistic approach. While he was alive, Barb and I had become estranged. He knew I had no active relationship with her. Despite all that she had done to him, our estrangement didn't sit well with Dad. From time to time, he would ask if I had talked to my mom. He would suggest that I needed to reconcile with her no matter how difficult I thought that might be.

"Dad, how can you possibly suggest I reconcile with her after all she did to you; after all she did to hurt us? She worked endlessly to drive a wedge between us." Barb had some success in separating us. There were a few years in my mid-to-late teen years where I bought into her lies of, "Your dad's a godless, drunken, drug-dealing, wife-beating, child molester, with a temper like Godzilla." During that period, I would refuse to go see him. I was reluctant to talk to him. She used me as the weapon to hurt him. I was complicit. I didn't have the strength of intellect, nor the strength as a person, to stand against her. Dad's concern for the woman who was attempting to assassinate his reputation was beyond my comprehension.

"Dad, I can't understand where you are coming from," I protested. "I hate her! I hate what she did to us," I said, my voice spewing a mixture of resentment, trauma, and tears.

Dad's rebuke came without hesitation. "Boy, don't you ever talk about your mother that way. She's your mom, no matter what you think she did—and I taught you better than that. What she did doesn't matter. We are here, together, you and me, and we're good. That is the only thing that matters. She's still your mom. You need to get past the anger you have for her. There will come a day when you'll regret it if you don't. If you keep hold of that hate, it will eat you up." Dad didn't go to church, but it's hard not to see those words as Christ-like.

Throughout our lives, Jack taught me through his actions that love is patient and love is kind. It's not selfish or easily angered. It keeps no record of wrongs. Love does not delight in evil but rejoices in the truth. But most importantly to me: Love bears all things, it believes all things, it hopes all things, and it endures all things. Love. Never. Fails. That is, by definition, my dad. That is Jack Osborne. He never failed me. (Yes, that may sound familiar—1 Corinthians 13:4–8.)

This dynamic between the three of us is the origin of the acidic cauldron I held for my mom. It can still be heard bubbling within me from time to time. There are some things I'm still working through. I'm far from a perfect person. Hell, I'm not even sure I'm a good one. I'm certainly not my Dad1 or Dad2, but I aspire to that pinnacle.

LOVE DECLARED

"I love you, Son." Words that are great to know, but when I was fifteen and with my teenaged cohorts close by, those words could be just a bit embarrassing.

My friends would raise an eyebrow when they heard it. "You'll never hear that from my dad," any one of them would chirp. It seemed a little soft and not very manly. It was certainly unusual. None of my friends' parents said it to their kids while in public, especially their fathers. It was different. I know I always wanted to hear it, but at times it was awkward in front of my friends. I finally pressed him for his reasoning.

"Dad, why are you so insistent in saying, 'I love you'? You do it every time you leave me or before we hang up the phone. You say it a lot."

His response was sage wisdom that would go on to affect hundreds, if not thousands, of lives. "Boy, words have meaning. Unspoken words are meaningless. So, if you've got something to say, you need to say it. Wait too long and you might not get the chance. It never hurts to remind someone how much you care for them—and, yes, real men say, 'I love you.'"

Think about that statement. Words have meaning and unspoken words are meaningless. He has a point, and it is a strong one. He would later tell me that in his mind, those words were the only way he knew to combat Barb's attacks on him. He thought if he said it enough times, their meaning would sink in and permeate me. He was right. It became such an important part of our relationship that it would last until Dad's final days and beyond. I once told him how lucky his granddaughters were to have him as a grandpa. I heard his words coming out of me as I told them daily, constantly, how much they meant to me. How much I love them. I still tell them to this day.

And it is not just my wife and kids. I say it to my sisters. Those are easy ones. I say it to my friends, male and female alike. There are at least thirty-five men that I say, "I love you, brother" to on a regular basis. And the wonderful thing is they have become comfortable saying it back. My daughters say it to their friends, and their friends have taken the practice back into their own families. Jack Osborne's "love declared" has touched more lives than any of us will know.

WINNERS NEVER QUIT AND QUITTERS NEVER WIN

Drive and tenacity are two attributes I inherited from, and had developed within me, by my fathers. These character traits have been critical success factors in my life. When faced with adversity, it can be easy to give up or give in. There is not much quit inside of me. I abhor losing or failing in anything I do.

It was often said that the easiest way for me to get something accomplished was to tell me that I couldn't possibly do it. That statement would strike two chords within me: my ego and my tenacity. I always wanted to prove myself worthy of my fathers' adoration, and accomplishing the things others thought could not be accomplished was a way to prove myself to anyone watching. I think some of this came from a lack of attention and/or need for attention. The Condo House was a foster home with a dozen-plus kids, so to get a modicum of attention from my parents, I needed to be either standing in front of a judge pleading a misdemeanor, or I had to be exceptional in the areas where I focused my efforts. I was rarely in front of a judge.

I believe my tenacious approach to life and business was forged when I was ten years old. It was the year I first played pee-wee football. Candidly, I was far too slender of build to be playing football. There were kids twice my size and weight playing in our league. The laws of physics worked to my severe disadvantage. 'Thin' would be an understatement. I was downright skin-and-bones type of skinny. No matter how much I ate, and I ate a ton for my age and size, I could not gain a pound. Fifty years later, I no longer have that problem.

Football is a violent sport which requires strength and speed and mandates intentional collisions and tackling. I had speed but lacked the other aforementioned requisites. However, even with my physical deficiencies, I was a starting player at the tight end/wide receiver position. Maybe the team was short on players. Those positions required the ability to catch and run with the football. Those things I did well.

I was not a rough and tough kid. I preferred to watch cartoons, or catch frogs, or page through one of our family's three encyclopedia sets. There were sports much better suited for my build like bowling, darts, or chess. Yes, chess would have been perfect for me: more cerebral, less physical. Football's daily push-ups, wind sprints, blocking, tackling, and the frequent act of getting the wind knocked out of me, were getting to be too much for me physically and mentally. I was tired of getting knocked on my butt. I decided I was going to tell my stepdad, Jerry, that I wanted to quit the football team. We were about one third of the way into the season when I decided to broach the subject. I was nervous about approaching him.

Jerry was eating dinner. He had just pulled his Swanson's Salisbury Steak frozen TV dinner out of the oven and sat down to enjoy this culinary delight in its partitioned aluminum tray. I approached him with great trepidation.

"Dad, I want to quit the football team. It's too hard for me. I hate getting hit," I said, trying unsuccessfully not to cry. I'm not sure I was crying because I hated the physicality of the game, or if I was afraid of his response, or that I feared he would refuse my request.

Jerry paused. He looked up from his dinner, pointed his fork at me, and with genuine disgust he said, "Boy, winners never quit, and quitters never win. Now I'm not sure which you are going to be in your life, but you figure it out and figure it out right now. You choose now. Be a winner or be a quitter. I don't care which but make up your mind now. My dinner's getting cold."

The complexities and nuance of his declaration were lost on me. The manner in which the words turn back upon themselves to create meaning was too complex for me to comprehend. Years later, I would analyze it and discover the multiple facets. Winners don't quit because they enjoy winning, so they keep going. If they were to quit, they could never become winners in the first place. Quitters never win because they stop before the contest is over, therefore, they lose by default. They face adversity and they give up. Being a quitter is, by default, being a loser. What I did realize was that winners are strong. Quitters are weak. Quitters are losers. I thought to myself, *To hell with that! I'm no loser.*

Jerry's response wasn't the compassionate permission to surrender my shoulder pads and helmet I was hoping for. In fact, it was the opposite. I felt it was mean-spirited. It made me angry. I walked away angry at him and at the fact I had to continue to play this physically painful sport. I carried that same anger to practice every day and to every game. I began to hit my opposition the way I wanted to hit my stepdad that day. I became a better, more physical football player. But I also became a better young person. I realized I couldn't give up because something is difficult. Life is hard. Get a helmet and get after it. If I get knocked down, get my ass back up. And maybe think about taking the fight to the opponent. In life there are many things that are worth fighting for. That fight may not be easy, but neither is life—so man up! Tenacity, determination, and aggression sprouted their seeds within me from that experience. Those traits have served me well when I have tempered them with compassion, empathy, understanding, and wisdom. Thanks, Jerry.

Yes, I finished the season. The Mount Healthy Dairy Bar Rebels won the city championship that year. We were undefeated and even unscored upon. It was a pretty good team of little ten-year-olds. Football and Jerry's response to my dilemma taught me a valuable lesson. The next year I signed up for . . . the chess team. A more cerebral sport. It was a little more my style. In the greatest of ironies, having survived football with no major injuries, I would break my ankle walking down the stairs at a chess tournament. Life is strange. We just never know how it will unfold.

NATURE VS. NURTURE

My dad, Jack, was a bus driver for Queen City Metro, Cincinnati's city bus company and my stepdad, Jerry, was a truck driver for Holland Motor Express. Two blue-color, hard-working guys, working honorable professions. Salt of the earth kind of guys. Both very likable, honest, all-around good men. Great examples for a boy to look up to and model himself after. Both with high school diplomas but no collegiate experience.

Yet here I am, a serial entrepreneur with two degrees, someone who has started multiple companies, some successful and some not. In fact, I think I've had more failures than successes. But business ideas are a lot like high-odds bets. A person only needs to hit on one or two to make the trip to the table a profitable one. And I was able to hit on a couple which enabled me to provide a more than reasonable standard of living and put food on the table for our family. Becky and I were able to send both of our girls to excellent Ohio universities. I've been fortunate enough to be elected as a city councilperson in our small city of Mason, Ohio. I learned from mentors how to acquire and invest in commercial real estate. We've been blessed.

But I have often wondered where my entrepreneurial streak came from. My two dads, Jack and Jerry, didn't have the entrepreneurial drive within them. Not to say that they weren't hard workers, because they were. And while they were both smarter than the average bear, neither had extensive financial or corporate business savvy. They were both outgoing people who loved a good time, but neither was considered the sales executive type. Neither of them would choose to be on stage presenting to an audience of hundreds; if there was any way possible, they would avoid it, even if it meant scheduling a conflicting proctologist appointment. They certainly wouldn't have chosen the roles of sales trainer or industry speaker, yet this was the path of my life. I find the dichotomy of my dads' careers and mine to be strange. My love for aviation is also well out of line compared to my paternal examples. Neither Jack nor Jerry held any interest in flight, military or commercial, whereas I became an aviation wonk.

I'm saying all of this to say I didn't have someone at home as a role model for many of my personal characteristics. I didn't have someone who would set me on the course I took in my life. Yet, to be successful in business, I needed problem solving skills, tenacity, sometimes a complete disregard for rules and authority, and most of all, creativity. Those qualities came from somewhere and those qualities, along with the ones that I did gain from Jack and Jerry, have been key to whatever success I have enjoyed.

To bring this together into tight focus, my daily role models were good, hard-working, blue-collar guys. The man who sired me, who I never met, was a sales professional, sales trainer, and industry speaker who worked for British Airways. I don't drive a bus. I don't drive a truck. I've become an entrepreneur who started a sales training/sales technology company called Top Gun Sales Performance, a company that utilizes an aviation motif/storyline/educational model to deliver selling concepts and build selling skills within its students. I spent much of my career speaking on the topics of sales and sales technology. I have spoken frequently at industry conferences. I have had the pleasure of coaching, training and working with thousands of selling professionals. I do not believe that is a simple coincidence. I find the commonality of Peter's career and my own to be flat-out bizarre. For me, this is all the evidence I need to be convinced DNA has a memory and I am a product of that specific scientific theory.

OFF TO A WORLD OF HIGHER LEARNING

There are a couple of stories that convey how I demonstrated the aforementioned qualities, which I attribute to my biological father, Peter Holmes. One of the most dubious was how I gained entrance into college. I was the first in my family to graduate from college, seeing a degree as the ticket to a good paying, white-collar job that could propel me out of the lower-middle class caste I was in. My choice of a learning institution was Miami University, about thirty minutes up the road in Oxford, Ohio.

I filled out the application and sent it in along with the necessary recommendations.   However, gaining admission was going to be a challenge. According to the Miami University admissions office, I was not what they called "Miami material." Those were not the words I read in the rejection letter, but that is what "We regret to inform you . . ." meant.

My high school GPA of 3.2 was not the problem, it was the fact I graduated in the lower 50-percentile of my senior class that flagged me for rejection. I had attended an extremely small, private school and finished sixteenth out of thirty students, therefore ranking in the lower half, or the "doesn't make the first cut" group.

What made it worse was my status as a white trash, hillbilly kid from Fairfield, Ohio. I had no connections: I didn't have a parent who knew the president of the university, we were not major financial donors, nor was I a fraternity's alpha chapter legacy. I was much more akin to a character from *Animal House* who would have been led to the back room and sat down with Pinto and Flounder. It was, however, a familiar position for me and one that had never been a personal deterrent before. It wouldn't be a deterrent this time either.

Saddled with these challenges, but sporting a *screw these guys attitude*, I decided I would have to hack my way into Miami University. "Hack" is a nebulous, somewhat ambiguous term. My friends preferred the term "scammed," as in "he scammed his way in." My wife simply explains it like this: they wouldn't let me in the front door, so I just walked through the back door instead.

Truth be told, I'm not one for rules and procedure. I like to learn the rules for the sole purpose of gaining advantage when playing the game. I do not learn them for the sake of adherence to them per se. I look for holes. I look for conflicts. I look for unintended consequences of the rules when applied with a little creativity. Becky says other people hate me for the way I approach rules. I disagree. They hate me for different and certainly more valid reasons. This is just one way that is easy to point to. I fully subscribed to the stance taken by Marilyn Monroe: "If I'd observed all the rules, I'd never have got anywhere."

So, there I was, just seventeen years old due to my early graduation (cough, cough) from high school. I had a void in parental guidance, a lack of common social graces, and a level of street smarts that would make me the de facto gang leader at any juvenile detention center.

But back to the admissions process . . . in order to gain entrance into Miami and get that degree, I only needed to overcome four small obstacles:

1. I was not an accepted or registered student with the university. Miami didn't want me. They had formally rejected my application, and by extension, me.

2. I had to sign up for classes that were already full of students named Biff or Buffy or the like. They wore Izod Lacoste sweaters and penny loafers. These would be the 'preppies' of the 1980s and they were already enrolled in an established, university-approved major.

3. The enrollment process included waiting in long lines with literally hundreds of people. This was before online registration, back when everything was done with pencil and paper and then manually keyed into a computer. I know, I'm old. This was not acceptable, as I was not willing to wait in line.

4. I had no money and no scholarship to offset the cost.

Other than these four small barriers, I was ready to attend my first class! Difficulty level in overcoming these obstacles: Should Be a Piece of Cake.

Established in 1809, Miami was a university before Florida was a state. Often referred to as "the Harvard of the Midwest," MU boasts an incredibly beautiful campus. In the late 1960s, Miami established two branch campuses in the nearby cities of Middletown and Hamilton. I lived in Fairfield, a short ten-to-twelve-minute drive to the Hamilton campus of Miami University. Being so close, I would be able to commute to classes and avoid the cost of university housing (remember Obstacle #4, no money).

Back in 1981, the Hamilton campus had five buildings. The main building was Mosler Hall, which had five stories of classrooms and labs. The first floor housed the university administration, a large student lounge, and the university bookstore. This is where student registration occurred and was the real focus of my reconnaissance.

One of the rules (God, I love rules) was that anyone who was accepted at one of the branch campuses and completed a certain minimum number of credit hours was automatically considered a student at the university. Their diploma would be issued from the mothership, Miami University, Oxford, Ohio (righteous!). Therefore, as a registered student of a branch campus, Obstacle #1 could be overcome. Armed with this knowledge, it was time for some reconnaissance.

After borrowing gas money from my sister, Kathy, I parked my Mercury Capri (that's a car) in the student lot and walked into Mosler Hall. The place was huge. It was registration week—I could tell by the throngs of students in a line that extended out of the administration offices and down the hallway. The insanely long line of people, four and five abreast, told me that I was in the right place. The people in the line were older (by a few years), smarter (they got accepted to MU), better dressed, and had more money than me. Anyone with any amount of money had more money than me. There is no way I would stand in that line with those sheep. I would have to figure out another way.

I walked up to someone about twenty feet behind the front of the line. "Registration?" I asked. He nodded with that slow, lifeless nod of a prisoner in for life. He then pointed behind himself and down the hall which was about seventy feet long. I looked down the hall and saw that the line took a turn around the corner and then stretched another thirty feet and out the door. That damn line was over 120 feet long. I could die of starvation before I could get through that line. Who thought that was a good idea? Not me, that's for damn sure.

"Thanks, dude," I said to the Izod wearer.

"Yeah, no problem," he replied and turned back to his conversation with his peers about Men at Work and their new cassette release.

I decided to loiter off to the side of the registration area but still in sight of the front of the line. I scanned the registration tables. About a half-dozen staff members were processing the zombie-students. I noticed that, after a brief conversation with the administrative staff, some students would pick up a small 5"x8" form and walk away. There was a stack containing hundreds of these forms sitting on the front table. I stopped one of the persons who had taken a form and asked,

"What is that form you picked up?"

"It's the Add/Drop slip," he replied, showing me the form. *An Add/ Drop slip . . . that has possibilities*, I thought. I walked toward the registration table. There was a very kind looking, grandmotherly lady working the registration line. She had a nameplate in front of her that read: Mary Rose Williamson (not really her name, but why indict her as an unwitting accomplice?).

I addressed the person who was next in line, "Excuse me, do you mind if I ask Mary Rose a quick question?"

He made a hand motion communicating his approval of my imposition.

I asked, "Mary Rose, can you help me? This Add/Drop form, how do I complete it?" It was the dumbest of questions because the instructions were clearly printed on the form.

"Love," *(ah, she called me 'Love')*, "just print your name, the name of the class, use the catalog code for the class, check the box whether you are adding or dropping the class, and get the professor to sign it.' She said this as stoic as a statue. Her hair was as white as Christmas snow, and her voice sounded like she consumed two packs of cigarettes and a bottle of cheap scotch as a daily regimen.

"How do I know if the class is already full?" I knew this answer already. All the classes I wanted were already full of mindless zombies who were moaning and swaying from side to side in the line behind me.

"It doesn't really matter. The professor can decide if they are willing to add you to the class. People often drop after the first week or so. If you can get the professor to agree and sign, you're in," she explained.

This was exactly what I was looking for, which was a way to bypass that damn line and get into the classes that were full. This was gold. But I wasn't finished. I'm still not a registered student at the distinguished Miami University. I scanned the table in front of my newfound friend Mary Rose, and noticed her bottle of Diet Pepsi.

As not to be too obvious, I continued, "Thank you so very much Mary Rose. I'm headed to the cafeteria. Can I get you a cup of coffee?"

She pointed at her bottle of caffeinated diet cola and right on cue she responded, "I don't drink coffee. But thank you."

"No, thank you for your help." I turned to the student zombie who had granted me access and said, "Thank you, too. I appreciate it." I then left Mosler Hall and took the very short forty paces to the Rentschler building where I found the cafeteria and purchased a diet Pepsi.

I walked back to the registration table in Mosler Hall and approached the table where Mary Rose was assisting the current undead line trudger. I quietly set the bottle down near Mary Rose without words or eye contact. I turned and walked away. At about fifteen feet, I stopped and turned back toward her table. Mary Rose was smiling at me. I returned her smile, turned around, and out the door I went. I grabbed a semester schedule with all the available class offerings AND six Add/Drop slips, the same number as the number of classes I wanted to take. Obstacle #3: Eliminated.

In the ensuing weeks I would attend the classes I wanted to take but which I had not yet registered for. Without fail, after the first few sessions, 10 to 20% of the original students would drop out of the course. At that point I would retrieve one of the Add/Drop slips and ask the professors for their approval and signature. Clockwork. Trains should all run on a schedule as tight and dependable.

Obstacle #2: Removed.

With six authorized and approved Add/Drop forms in hand, I made my way to the first floor of Mosler Hall and Campus Administration.

"Hello, Mary Rose," I greeted my new friend with a smile.

"Hey there! Good morning. You know, I never got your name." We had seen each other a few times as I had passed through Mosler Hall; I never stopped to chat but always smiled and waved.

"I'm Steve Osborne."

"Very nice to meet you, Steve Osborne, and thank you for the Diet Pepsi."

"It was my pleasure. You were so kind to help me."

"I saw you pick up the Add/Drop slips. So, you figured it out, didn't you?" she said with a sly smile. Now I'm on my heels. It hit me. Holy hell, I didn't figure that process out on my own. She telegraphed it to me right in front of God and a hundred plus people, and I totally missed her intentional messaging. I thought I was smarter than the average bear, but Mary Rose had Jedi Mind Tricked me. This lady and I are going to be quick friends and for quite some time.

"Almost nobody figures out that little work around. You picked it up quickly. Good for you."

"Only with your help, ma'am." I said genuinely.

"Well, how can I help you today?" Mary Rose asked.

"So kind of you to ask. Those slips I picked up . . ."

"You have them signed and you want to add those classes," she interrupted.

"Yes, ma'am."

"You don't have to call me ma'am"

"I'm afraid I do, ma'am. My father raised me a certain way. He requires it. His words: 'Always respect a lady, your elders, and your betters.' I believe I am in the presence of all of three of those."

"You could leave out the elder part next time."

"Yes, ma'am, per your direction."

"Let's get your classes added," she turned to the computer terminal.

That morning, Mary Rose entered me into the system as a 'non-registered student,' an oxymoron if ever I heard one. A status that would eventually be converted to official student and would entitle me the right to earn a sheepskin, the ultimate goal. Obstacle #1: Removed by the lovely Mary Rose of the Hamilton Campus Administration.

I went home to tell my mom and stepdad that the third sign of the apocalypse had occurred: I had made it into a real university. "Guys, I've gotten into Miami University, and I am registered and taking classes at the Hamilton Campus. But I've got to find a way to pay for it." We resolved that Barb and Jerry would pay for my first semester and books, a total of $625 dollars. I would be responsible for the rest. That would mean applying for student loans, which I did. I funded the next year and a half of my tuition with student loans. I paid them off over the following ten years per my commitment to the US Government, the lending institution, and my fellow taxpayers. Obstacle #4, the final obstacle to my college education, was laid to rest.

I worked multiple positions at two retail jobs to eke my way through college. With this minimum income, I could eat while I learned. I graduated in 1983 with an associate degree in System Analysis and Design. I opted for the associate degree because I was out of money, and I had been offered a job that could pay my rent and provide more than Frosted Flakes for my meals. I just couldn't afford a four-year degree at that time.

In the late 1980s and early '90s, I continued my education and earned a bachelor's in business administration from Embry Riddle Aeronautical University (there's that flight theme again). At the time, I was working for GE Aircraft Engines (aviation, again) and I took full advantage of their generous tuition reimbursement program.

In the end, I became a student at Miami University without breaking any of the rules, and only causing the guidelines to spend six weeks in the ICU. Article 12, Section 137, Item 6, Subparagraph C states: "The system has accommodations for, and allows the admittance of, a non-standard student under conditions and exceptions evaluated on a case-by-case basis by administration."

Perhaps the rules maker had seen me coming. And yes, I just made up all that Article/Section stuff. It's not real. No one really cares about how they handle a few misfits like me.

MY FAIT ACCOMPLI

Should anyone at Miami University with any influence or administrative power stumble upon this book and read the accounting of my early interactions with our beloved institution, I would ask they not be too quick to retroactively cancel my diploma. I was young, just seventeen years old, when I arrived. I had grown up in a group home. I had no guidance, no direction, and no mentor. To that date, I had been raised by wolves, and survival was the order of the day, every day. I meant no harm and was never found guilty of such (I was acquitted). I hope that Becky's and my recent financial contributions and commitments to the Speech and Hearing Center and the University Fund can atone for any transgressions, real or imagined, that may have been committed by the younger version of myself.

Deus, ignosce stultitiae meae (Latin translated: God forgive my foolishness).

I owe all the actions detailed above to the DNA that I inherited from Peter Holmes. Credit or blame—reader's choice.

CHAPTER 26

A DNA Gift Most Unusual

*Once you have tasted flight, you will forever walk the
earth with your eyes turned skyward, for there you
have been, and there you will always long to return.*
—Leonardo Di Vinci

Note to Reader: The following story details one of the many ways I
feel connected to my biological father, Peter Holmes. It is a story
about aviation, WWII fighter planes, and an extremely serendipitous
experience I had during a business trip. It is a detour from the core
DNA story. If you love this stuff, please enjoy. If not, feel free to skip
ahead to chapter 27.

I am about to convey a story as factually and accurately as I can
possibly remember. Some will read it and say, "What's the big deal?"
Others will say, "That's not possible. It can't be right." I promise it
is. As you, our cherished reader, knows by now, I am a big aviation
fan, especially military, specifically WWII. I attended Embry-Riddle
Aeronautical University as a business major, specializing in airline and
airport management. I am not a pilot, nor have I ever taken any flight
instruction. I have never flown a plane before.

And with that prelude, here's the story . . .

On a gorgeous, late summer morning in 2013, I took an early
morning flight from a small, regional airport in Cincinnati to an equally
small, regional airport in Morristown, New Jersey. I was headed to
Newark to see a client that afternoon. Morristown airport is so small
that there are no rental car agencies on site, therefore I had to arrange

for a taxi or town car to take me to my destination. Uber and Lyft were not yet part of my travel lexicon back in 2013.

When we landed, I headed to the terminal exit, stopping briefly to grab a quick cup of coffee. As I left the terminal, I saw the town car I had requested sitting at the curb; the name OSBORNE was clearly visible in the passenger window. I also saw two jackasses not named Osborne climb into the back seat of the car. Before I could intervene, the town car drove off without me, its intended fare. Jumping another person's town car was not completely uncommon at Morristown, though it is a total dick move. I called the transportation company to report the theft of my ride. They acknowledged the wrong people were in the car. The dispatcher apologized appropriately. He then apologized again for the ensuing thirty- to forty-minute wait that I was going to endure due to lack of available cars and rush hour traffic. No worries on my end as my appointment wasn't until 1:00 p.m. I decided to just enjoy my coffee and the beautiful morning by taking a stroll to kill the time.

I walked around to the end of the building where there was a bench that faced a row of high hedges in front of a chain link fence. Nothing glamorous, nothing unusual . . . except for the view of a vertical stabilizer (the tail of the aircraft). I could only see the very top of it, maybe only the top two feet, but that was more than enough for me to identify the entire aircraft as a WWII B-24 Liberator. Yes, I only needed to view two feet of the plane's tail because: a) I'm an aviation geek and b) the tail of a Liberator is unique. It's shaped like a Ritz Town House cracker—the oblong ones, not the round ones. Only the B-25 had something similar but not exactly the same.

I began walking to get a better view when I spied a gate that was open to the tarmac. *This just can't be*, I thought. As I continued toward the gate, I caught sight of the tail of a WWII B-17 Bomber. It was just like the model aircraft my dad, Jack, had given me for Christmas when I was fifteen years old. I walked through the gate without seeing so much as a hint of security.

Once inside, I could see a small squadron of vintage military aircraft. To my left was a folding table with literature and other marketing items. It appeared some kind of air show was being set up. There was a middle-aged lady sitting at the table.

"Excuse me, ma'am, what is all of this?" I asked with a broad sweeping arm motion to encompass the air force before me.

"This is our vintage air fleet. We are the Collings Foundation, and these are our babies," the nice lady explained to me in a very pleasant voice. I felt as if I had died and gone to a candy store in Heaven with someone else's credit card.

"Those are absolutely awesome!" I was stunned. "That's a Liberator, yes?"

"Yes, sir."

"And that is a gorgeous B-17."

"Yes, it is. For $15, you can get in and walk through it," she said with mild enticement.

"Really?" I said. In my mind, I had already taken the money from my wallet and paid.

"For $450, you can go up in a ride for thirty minutes," she continued.

I was already in my pocket locating my wallet. This was a once in a lifetime opportunity. Just then, I caught the sun glinting off something silver and shiny in my peripheral vision. I turned to identify it and could not believe what I saw.

"Is that what I think it is?" I asked with baited curiosity.

"That's a P-51 Mustang" she said. My heart skipped three beats.

"Is that for display or . . ." Hoping the next words out of her mouth completed my aeronautical fantasy.

"Oh, no, not just display. We fly it. We've put a second seat in the back and for [a ridiculous amount of money] you can ride in it for an hour. It's also dual controlled so you can fly it from that second seat and for [a pornographic amount of money] you can fly it for an hour."

I was in for $15. Then I was in for $450. Then I was considering an amount I simply couldn't justify, but it was in the low four-digit range. When she said fly, I knew that meant a qualified pilot would be in the plane with me who would take off and land the aircraft. I would get to touch the controls at some point. That was more than enough for me.

"Do you have a slot available before 11:00?"

"Let me look," she quickly turned and read a schedule. "Yes, sir we do. We have a flight time now."

"I have just one more question. Do you take American Express?"

"We certainly do, sir." I pulled my wallet from my pocket, extracted my AmEx in a split second, and tossed it on the folding table with only one word.

"Next!" I filled out the seventeen forms and waivers in triplicate. I believed I understood the risk I was taking.

Once the forms were completed, the nice lady directed me to the P-51 Mustang and said, "Your pilot, Jim, will meet you by the plane in a few minutes. Enjoy your ride!"

As I stood by this mid-century technological marvel, I remembered that this was the fighter that helped turn the tide of the WWII air war in Europe. If someone says "World War II fighter", the image most likely to come to mind is a P-51 Mustang.

"Good morning, Steve, I'm Jim, your pilot."

I turned to see exactly what I expected: a very fit, middle-aged man with dark aviator sunglasses.

"Hey, Jim. I'm Steve. Very nice to meet you." I continued, "Jim, she is gorgeous. Is this a 'B' model?"

"Funny you would say that. It's a 'C' model, but we painted it with 'B' markings," Jim responded.

Jim and Steve (me) in front of the glorious P-51, Betty Jane.

There's not really much difference between the B and the C; mostly just where it was manufactured.

"So, it has the Merlin engine in it, not the Allison?" I asked. The Merlin was the major engine upgrade that made this fighter a bona fide killer in the air war over Europe.

"Why, yes it does. Good for you," Jim said.

Jim and a member of the ground crew gave me a flight briefing. The only things I remember are that I wouldn't have a parachute, Jim would take off and land, and I was given a plastic bag in case I threw up. Other than that, I was told to get in the plane, which was lovingly referred to by the name painted on her nose cowling: Betty Jane.

The ground tech strapped me into the rear seat of the Mustang and helped me put on my headset. I was strapped in the cockpit wearing suit trousers and a white, button-down Oxford shirt. Not the typical flight suit. I left my jacket with the ground crew. Because of the angle of the craft when it is on the ground, the view was nothing but a few clouds and a ton of instrumentation in front of me.

From my time at Embry Riddle, I knew about compass points, altitude, rate of climb, temperatures, and pressures. What helped even more was the week I spent at the Air War College in Montgomery, Alabama, a few years prior. The Air War College is an annual event where the Air Force invites a limited number of civilians and international allied military guests to the base for presentations and demonstrations. While I was there, I had the opportunity to sit in and operate an F-35 simulator.

The F-35 is nothing like a P-51. The two planes are four generations of aircraft apart. Yet, the cockpit somehow felt familiar to me. The difference is akin to grilling over a campfire or using a microwave oven. They both cook food. But knowing how to do one provides almost no reference as to how to do the other. Flying a simulator versus flying a real plane is like thinking you can ride a horse because you sat in a saddle once, whilst on a fence at your uncle's farm. I scanned the array of forty-plus instruments, gauges, and controls, which I had never before encountered. Why did I feel like I knew what they all were?

Jim brought the P-51 and its Merlin engine to life. The sound alone made me want to lose control of a certain bodily function, and they didn't give me a bag for that one. The Merlin engine roared like an angry beast desperately wanting to break the bonds of gravity. I could hear nothing but the roaring drone of the Merlin and Jim in my headset.

"Steve, how are you doing back there?"

"Great!" I responded.

"Do you see your gauges?"

"Yessir!"

"See your oil temp and pressure? Upper right."

I quickly scanned the upper right of the instrument panel. "Got it." I was learning in real time.

"When we get to the proper levels, we'll taxi out," Jim informed me.

"Roger that."

Before we began to taxi, Jim continued to review and quiz me on the instrumentation. Then I heard the Merlin increase in RPMs and decibels. We moved forward, slowly at first, and then at a crisp pace as we taxied to the end of the runway and called for clearance.

"Tower, 251 Mike X-ray, clearance," Jim squawked into the radio.

"251 Mike X-ray, you are cleared for takeoff, runway 05," returned the static-free voice from the Morristown tower.

Jim wasted no time advancing the throttle forward and Betty Jane along with it. I quickly found my mobile phone and began snapping pictures as fast as I could knowing that Jim had full control of the Mustang. We sprinted down the runway and lifted off with power and force that shocked me. I thought I had an idea of what that would be like. I grossly underestimated the marvel that was Betty Jane.

We were barely 600 feet off of the ground when Jim came over the internal radio. "She's all yours," he said.

I did not have my hands on the controls nor my feet on the rudder pedals. I was snapping pictures out the side of the canopy with my phone. I was hoping he really didn't take his hands off the controls. I gingerly put my feet on the rudder pedals and my hand on the stick. Jim felt the pressure I applied via his tandem controls.

"Take her out due west. Keep the same rate of climb. Once you get above 10,000 feet, you can do whatever you'd like," Jim said casually.

He couldn't see my eyes because he was sitting in front of me, but if he could, they were the size of silver dollars. I thought, *Okay, Mav, time to do some of that pilot shit.* Jim said due west. I knew the compass points for North, South, East, and West are 0 (or 360), 90, 180, and 270 respectively. I found an instrument on my left that was displaying similar numbers but missing the trailing zero. So, to head west, I needed to turn the plane to 270 degrees on the compass or 27 on that numbered thingy on the dashboard—I mean, instrument panel.

I remembered Jim said, "same rate of climb." I found the altimeter, and below it was the rate of climb indicator. *Just keep the plane going up at that same rate and don't do anything stupid that might make that gauge change.* The altimeter would also show me when we reached the 10,000 foot mark. *Hey, this is easy, right?* We continued to climb west. I remembered thinking, *I paid all this money, so I might as well get my money's worth.*

"Jim, what can I do in this plane?"

"Practically anything you want. This plane is the Porsche of World War II fighters. She's incredibly responsive," Jim said boastfully about his girl, Betty Jane.

"So, if I want to roll it . . . ?" I asked.

"Just push the stick over to the left or right. She'll roll right over. You don't have to move any control too much. She moves."

Okay, Jim, if you say so. I pushed the stick maybe five inches to the left. Jim wasn't exaggerating. The Mustang responded instantly by making the Earth rotate on our nose and made it exchange places with the sky, and then continued to roll until they returned to their rightful place in the universe, at which point I centered the stick.

"Holy cow, dude!" I exclaimed. It was effortless, scary, and exciting.

"I know, right?" She's a ton of fun." Jim had the best job in the world. I continued to do ever increasingly complex maneuvers, as many of them as I could think of from my limited experience. Rolls, corkscrews, jinking, banking, split-S, all things that I suspect Jim thought were routine or maybe even tame.

"Can I loop her?" I asked, suspecting that I might be bumping up against a limitation.

"You sure can. Let's start at 10,000 feet. Just push the nose down. Once we hit 550 knots of airspeed, pull the stick straight back into your lap and she'll go right over. We should come out of it above 6,000 feet."

Jim said those words with so much confidence and encouragement I just had to try it. But I was about to point this sixty-year-old aircraft toward the ground, violently reverse the course by pulling straight up into a climb, and continue onto our backs until we were completely upside down. Then continue to pull the loop until her nose was pointed directly at *terra firma* and hope I could pull her out of the inverted dive before we hit the green stuff below us. Oh, and I knew this was going to be so totally badass, I knew I was going to do it with one hand on the stick because my other hand would be holding my phone recording video of all this badassery. (This move would later cause my daughter to scold me: "You told me to never text and drive, but you pulled that stunt in a plane? You were using your phone to record video while flying a plane, upside down? Really, Dad!? What the hell is wrong with you?" She had a point.)

I was right. The loop was totally badass. I captured the whole thing on my phone. We pulled just a little over 4Gs (four times the force of gravity). My phone recorded all of it, even when it started to pixelate and scramble the image a bit due to the g-forces.

After successfully completing the loop, my confidence and curiosity surged. What else could I do? I wanted to do a barrel roll. After all we had done to that point, it seemed kinda lame, but it was the maneuver I was having trouble figuring out.

"Jim, how do you do a barrel roll?" I asked a bit sheepishly.

"A what? A barrel roll? Why would you ask?" There was confusion in his voice. "Why would you ask that? What kind of plane do you fly? How long have you been flying?" He asked. His voice was showing the first signs of stress.

"I've been flying this Mustang for the last forty minutes. That's it," I confessed, not wanting to mislead him.

"What? You told me you were a pilot!" he protested.

"No Jim, I never said that. You never asked if I was a pilot," I corrected him.

"Are you @%$!@ kidding me? You HAVE to be a pilot!"

I assumed he was saying that given all he had seen me do to that point, combined with my knowledge of general aviation and that of the plane and cockpit, he had quickly come to the conclusion that I was a pilot. I could see how the misunderstanding could take place. I knew too much aviation terminology and history not to be a pilot. At the very beginning of the flight when he ordered direction, altitude, and rate of climb, I had complied without asking questions. Despite his dismay, Jim let me keep the controls as we continued the last twenty minutes of our flight, returning to Morristown and marveling at the beauty of the morning at 10,000 feet.

At one point Jim said, "Steve, look up and at your 2 o'clock. That's a Gulfstream G5. How cool is that?"

"Jim, I can guarantee you that everyone in that Gulfstream is looking at us saying, 'A P-51 Mustang! How cool is that?' We definitely have the better ride, bro."

As we made our approach to Morristown, Jim took control of the Mustang. After clearing up any confusion regarding my flight expertise and experience, there was no chance I was going to get the opportunity to land the plane.

As we climbed out of the plane, Jim pressed me again, "You're just messing with me. Surely, you're a pilot."

"No, sir, I am not. I'm sorry." I know Jim was going over in his mind the fifteen to twenty times I had the aircraft upside down or pointed at the ground, barreling toward Earth. He was probably thinking *I will never make that dumbass assumption again.*

I convey this story to make this point—I believe that DNA has a memory. I believe that Peter and his exposure to aircraft at British Airways had found its way into my being. My love for aviation, my ability to quickly analyze, decipher, and adapt to complex problems, and the trait of being comfortable in uncomfortable situations does not exist in my other paternal figures. I know Peter's sales and presentation skills are in me. I'm convinced that DNA has a memory, and I have the genetic memory of Peter Holmes.

I often think about the events that led me to this place, a place with four fathers: Jack, Jerry, Peter, and my father-in-law, Fred Brower. I think about how it has affected me, how it assembled me. I know the events are not optimal. I know the situation left me with many flaws. I am fractured in many places. I still have holes in my personal development. But in other ways, I have been blessed. I would like to think that I was able to take some of the best qualities from these quality men and integrate them into my person. I have been fortunate for the many inputs into my design, and I am grateful for them. In a strange way, I feel bad for others who have only one dad. But upon further thought, it's easy to imagine that having the one right dad is as good as having four really good dads. So, I think we are all where we should be, which is blessed.

CHAPTER 27

All Cards Face Up

The truth hurts, but silence kills. — Mark Twain

There is an acceptable amount of time that spans the discovery of a DNA surprise and the point at which you feel compelled to let family members know what has been found. I think there is a grace period from the time a person learns of such a significant discovery until they are required to communicate it to their affected family members. That grace period is necessary as it provides the person with the time to confirm that the details of the discovery are accurate. Everyone would want to eliminate the possibilities of misunderstandings or misinterpretations. Then there is time needed for subsequent research to fill in the gaps. In my case, after I found out that my dad is not my dad, but before I told too many people, I wanted to be able to anticipate questions like, "Do you know who your real dad is?" or "What do you know about this guy?" or . . . this list can be long.

The initial grace period also covers the shock and processing required to digest the life-changing news. How long this takes varies as much as the stories that are discovered. For some people, it's weeks. For others it's months, or even over a year. But at some point, personal privacy and reluctance to reveal the uncomfortable details becomes deception by omission. I'm not saying everyone must write a book and tell the world. (I mean, what kind of a crazy person would want to do that?) However, we can all agree the DNA orphan's closest relations probably should know, notwithstanding any extenuating circumstances. These decisions are personal and for each person to make. But each one of us who had an NPE or is a DNA Orphan, we will know when we are near the end of our discovery and at a sufficient point in our emotional processing. There will come a point of quasi-comfort when we can discuss the topic with those whom it affects, no matter how uncomfortable that conversation might be. I believe the acid test is this: if someone close to me finds out about the news from a source other than me, would that person say to me, "Why didn't you tell me?" If the answer is, "I wasn't ready. I was still working through it," then it's still the grace period. If the answer is, "I don't know, I just didn't want to," that person may be delinquent in their actions. This is just my personal opinion and not one of a trained professional.

But there is another school of thought on the topic which is: there never seems to be a good time to tell someone this type of news, especially if they are our children. I honestly can't say that I have a perfect answer to this dilemma.

For me, that time of disclosure had come. It was hastened by the realization that my DNA test results and the uncomfortable truths they conveyed were already public information. Becky was the defacto family genealogist and had frequent conversations with the Osborne clan trying to extract details of marriages, deaths, locations, and the like. Becky heard through the grapevine that some of the family didn't like her poking around or rooting through the closets. She was asking a lot of questions and with good intentions. But she became sensitive to the quiet criticism of my family. I couldn't care less what they thought. Becky had mentioned to multiple members of my family that I had taken a DNA test but stopped there when the results had returned with bold neon question marks.

I said to Becky, "You know at some point, someone in the Osborne clan is going to take a DNA test, or they already have. Many of them were aware that I have taken one. Because I don't share a common Osborne ancestor, I'm not going to show up on their DNA matches report like everyone else. I will be conspicuous in my absence. Eventually, the light is going to go off in somebody's head. We need to be ready to answer that question, not if, but when, it's asked." This was unquestionably one of life's situations where it is better to play the tune rather than be forced to dance to the music.

CONVEYING THE TEST RESULTS TO MY STEPMOM* AND STEPBROTHER*

It had been almost a year since my DNA test discovery. I knew the time had come for me to face the music with my stepmom*, Mary Ann. Other than telling my own daughters, and the confrontation with my mother, this would be the most difficult conversation I would be forced to have. I genuinely had no idea how the conversation would turn out. The potential range of responses was across the spectrum. I feared more for how it would affect her personally than any negative energy directed at me.

Mary Ann was Jack's second wife. They married when I was twelve, so she had been my stepmom most of my life; nearly fifty years. I always called her Mom, which I know only adds to the confusion for those reading this book. She is a wonderfully kind, gnome-like little woman who had an upbringing as rough as 60-grit sandpaper. But she was never anything but kind to Laura and me, Jack's children with Barb Condo. She had to endure the collateral damage of Barb's spiteful ways. Barb's attacks were always targeted at Jack, but Mary Ann was always within the blast radius. Any pain caused to Jack was at least a frustration to her if not worse. But, again, she was always able to separate Barb's actions from our relationship with Jack and herself. No evil stepmother to be found here. Mary Ann was the best stepmom we could wish for. She loved my dad and took great care of him. Almost too good. There were times I told him to stop asking her to do things and get up and do them himself.

But she was about to become a stepmom with an asterisk; the asterisk indicating the fact that my DNA test had removed the biological connection with Dad1, her husband, Jack. Therefore, we no longer had any formal family relationship. Our fifty-plus years together was based upon a lie told by my mother.

On the day I decided to come clean, I called my stepbrother*, Jerry, because I was reasonably certain he could tell me Mary Ann's whereabouts and anything she had scheduled for that day. He was geographically the closest child and the one who took care of most of his ninety-one-year-old mother's needs. I called Jerry's mobile.

"Hey, Steve, what's going on?" he answered.

"Hey, brother!" Our normal chit-chat ensued, but I quickly got to the point. "Do you know if Mom is home today? I'm going to be down your way for a meeting, and I thought I would stop by." That wasn't entirely the truth. I didn't have a need to drive the forty miles and forty-five minutes for anything other than to meet with them. I was hoping to catch the two of them together.

"Mom is at a doctor's appointment right now. I'm going to pick her up in about thirty minutes and then take her home. Then I'm going to take her out for lunch later," Jerry informed me. This was the perfect scenario. The timing would work out just right, and I would have them both together. "Frannie's at the house, too," Jerry continued. Frannie was another of my stepsiblings*. Even more perfect! All three of them.

"Great, do you mind if I stop by about 10 o'clock? I want to say hey to everyone and catch-up." Again, not 100% accurate, but the information I needed to deliver wasn't going to be delivered over the phone, and I couldn't afford to tip my hand.

"I'm sure that's fine. I'll let Mom know when I pick her up, and we will see you around ten. I'll let you know if anything changes."

I got a knot in my stomach and a lump in my throat. I was committed now. Difficult discussions are always, well—difficult—hence the name.

I arrived a few minutes early. I didn't want any chaos to enter the picture, and time is the enemy in these situations. I grabbed my portfolio with my DNA test results and exited my car. I thought about the document in my hand. I knew what it meant to me. I didn't have a clue what it would mean to them.

Here goes nothing, I thought as I entered the house. Jack and Mary Ann had purchased this house in 1972, and Jack lived there until his death in 1999. Mary Ann continued to call it home. It was filled with decades of knick-knacks and pictures, mostly pictures. A good number of the pictures were of Laura and me through the years. I was happy to see that even though my dad had died over twenty years prior, Laura and I still held our positions on the walls and bookshelves along with the rest of our stepsiblings/second cousins*.

The salutations and small talk were brief. I made them so. The faster we got to the heart of the matter, the faster I could see the result, whatever it might be. My tone and posture changed from casual to serious. I had no other plan than to address this head on. We sat at the kitchen table that had been there as long as the residents. Jerry was to my left, Mary Ann to my right. Francene was upstairs getting ready for an appointment. I decided to push forward with Mary Ann and Jerry. I drew a deep breath.

"Guys, I have something to tell you and I don't know any other way to say it, other than to just say it."

Their eyes grew wide as they looked at each other and then back at me. Their expressions conveyed they were mentally bracing themselves.

I continued, "I recently took a DNA test." I patted the portfolio to signal I had the results with me. "The test showed that Dad, Jack, is not my biological father." I paused to let that settle for just a few seconds. "My biological father is some Canadian guy named Peter Holmes." There was a long pause. My eyes were fixed on my stepmom.

She shot Jerry a glance and then leaned back in her chair.

"Is that it? Is that what you drove all the way here to tell us?" she asked.

"Yes, ma'am, it is." My tone was conciliatory and apologetic. This is where the road will fork.

"Oh, hell, Steve! I thought you were gonna tell us you and Becky was gettin divorced!" There was relief in her voice, almost disappointment in the anticlimactic nature of what I had just revealed. There was a distinct relaxing of her body language. Her sweet Kentucky drawl was soothing to me.

"Uh, no, ma'am. Becky and I are fine. We're still married. No changes there." I was a bit shocked by her lack of shock. She quickly shifted from the non-divorce discussion to the topic at hand, my bastard status.

"Steve, your dad wouldn't care none about that. He loved you and Laura more than anything. Hell, if he was sitting right here, he'd tell you the same thing. It don't make no difference to him. You're his boy. That's all he cared about. He was so proud of you. He was your dad. You're his son. That's that and nothing can change that." She was emphatic and certain, practically dismissive of all other elements of the conversation.

I was so relieved by her response I wanted to cry. Of all the scenarios I could conjure in my mind, there wasn't one that was this positive. I turned to look at Jerry. He had his head cocked to the side the way people do when they have a question in their mind. He reached out and placed his hand on my shoulder and gave it a compassionate squeeze.

"Brother, are you okay?" Jerry asked the $64,000 dollar question. The first question that should be asked of any DNA Orphan, "Are you okay?" There is such incredible healing power in that question. It delivers so much healing goodness to the injured.

"Yeah, Jerry, I'm working through it. I'm much better with it now."

"You've known this for a while, haven't you?" Jerry asked the question in a knowing tone. It really wasn't a question.

"Yeah, Jerry, I have. I'm sorry. I just didn't know what to say or how to say it. I'm sorry I didn't tell you sooner. I just didn't know what to say. Why do you ask?"

"You knew at Mom's surprise birthday party last year, didn't you?" His question hit me square in the face.

"I did, Jerry. I had found out just a few weeks before. How did you know that?"

"I was watching you, and I said to Johnny, 'Something is wrong with Steve.' I could tell," Jerry explained.

"How could you tell?" I was embarrassed that I was so transparent.

"You were drinking a lot at the party."

"Hell, Jerry, I always drink a lot."

"You were drinking a lot even for you. I could tell something was bothering you," he confided. "I was worried about you."

"I'm sorry, Jerry, I just didn't know what to do. I was wrestling with it, and we had so many unanswered questions at that point. And I didn't want to ruin Mom's birthday." If only my head was truly that clear on that day. Jerry looked at the papers I had pulled from my portfolio.

"Are those your test results?" Jerry asked.

"Yeah," I said sheepishly. Jerry picked them up and waved them as if they were Exhibit A in a courtroom.

"This . . . I don't care what this says. There is no piece of paper you can show me that will tell me that you and me are not brothers. You have been my brother from way back since we were kids. This paper don't make no difference, none."

I had just received the official Kentucky triple negative. This meant that I was certified and in the clear. My eyes welled-up, and I quickly dabbed at my tears.

My stepsister, Frannie, came into the kitchen, and we had a quick recap of the DNA discussion. She was stunned. We continued for the next hour to go through the sordid details of my conception. There was no time lost before the venom for my biological mom came out. The things she had done to Jack, and by extension, Mary Ann, were enumerated, ranked, and graded. Not to mention, but it was mentioned, the almost fifteen years of child support that Jack paid to Barb for me, someone not really his child.

The time we spent together was a blessing but also an emotional drain on me. And there was something bothering me. Deep in my psyche, I was wrestling with something; but what? I could not put my finger on it. Did this seem too easy? Was this situation dismissed without the expected emotional and psychological wrangling? Why was my stepmom so quick to dismiss this situation? Where was the shock? Did Jack and/or Mary Ann already know? That would explain a lot.

Jerry and I were determined not to let these events drive us apart; we vowed to stay closer than ever. We started to play golf together monthly as the weather would permit. Those days were a gift. It allowed me to stay in touch and to show him I was not going anywhere.

At the next birthday party for Mary Ann, one year and a few weeks after my discovery, I caught up with my stepbrother*, Johnny, and said to him that I expected Jerry had brought him up to date on all things DNA-related.

Johnny, never one to miss an opportunity for a good jab, said, "Yep, Jerry told me. He said Jack's not really your dad and we aren't really related. That's gotta be a tough one. Anyway, we all got together and talked about kicking you out of the family, but we figured it was just too much damn trouble at this point. So, I guess we're just stuck with you."

It's always nice to know I'm wanted, even if somewhat reluctantly. Sometimes the path of least resistance can work in our favor. Thanks, Johnny.

CHAPTER 28

John Watson Comes to Cincinnati

Our first meeting was like Fate bringing two people together against all odds. — Unknown

Throughout the first year following my DNA surprise, our relationship with my new Canadian cousin, John Watson, continued to grow. John would end up being the only substantial new addition to my family resulting from the discovery. John is two years older and notably shorter than me. He is a wonderful man, very spiritual, kind, and loving. We stay in frequent contact via text with him and his wife, Kathy. They now live in Prince Edward Island, Canada. That's about 1,300 miles from us as the crow flies.

Becky and I decided we wanted to meet John, so we asked if he would consider coming to the States. He could stay with us and we, of course, would bear the expense of the flight, since this was a large request on our part. John agreed. Almost one year to the day of our discovery, John made the international trip to Cincinnati.

But John's trip would have a dubious start. His incoming flight on Air Canada was fraught with successive delays. We were getting text updates on the flight arrival status, which was originally scheduled for 9:30 p.m. EST, which became 9:50, which became 10:45. Becky and I decided to leave for the airport so that we could be there when the flight landed. We arrived only to find out that the flight was now scheduled for an 11:20 arrival. We waited for John just outside the secured area near the arrivals exit. Then 11:20 became 12:15 a.m. This situation had become irritating, but perhaps there might have been some divine providence at work.

Fifteen minutes past midnight came and went with no sign of Mr. Watson. But at 12:50 a.m., we were delighted to see our longtime friend, Kelly Bennett, coming through the secured exit from the concourse gates. A Delta Airlines "Redcoat," Kelly's family had lived across the street from Jack and Mary Ann in Burlington, Kentucky. We occasionally spent weekend summer days with Kelly and his family at Dad1's pool. Kelly is a wonderful salt-of-the-earth kind of guy who looks like a retired linebacker. He is exceptionally nice. He and Dad1 truly cared for each other.

Surprised to see us, Kelly asked, "Steve! Becky! What are you guys doing here so late?"

"We're here to pick someone up," I replied.

"Who's that?" Kelly asked.

He's not shy and we are practically family. No question is off limits. Becky and I shot a look at each other to silently probe each other's thoughts on whether to disclose the revelation about me and Jack, Kelly's beloved former neighbor. Becky's face and body language said, *What the hell, go ahead.*

"We're here to pick up my cousin from Canada."

Kelly knew the Osborne family well enough to find that answer very odd. His brow furrowed and his head tilted. His next questions were not unexpected.

"You have a cousin from Canada? Who is that? Who moved to Canada?"

"No one moved. Kelly, I found out via a DNA test that I have a cousin in Canada." I paused to let him digest that tidbit and then continued with, "That same DNA test told me that Jack is not my biological father." It seemed to me that the entire airport fell silent as Kelly processed those words.

"What? Did you just say that Jack's not your dad?" The shock rippled through his face and then his entire body. He involuntarily took two steps back and covered his mouth with his hand. "Oh my God, Steve, are you kidding me?"

"No, my friend. I'm sad to say, I'm not."

Kelly continued to process for a few seconds, but very quickly. "Are you okay? That had to be devastating to you." Kelly knew firsthand how close I was to Jack.

He was spot on with his assessment. Devastating—the one-word definition for the entire mess. The conversation continued for about ten minutes as we conveyed the story's details.

Then Kelly resolved to the point that anyone who knew Jack Osborne does. "Steve, here's all I can tell you. Your dad loved you more than anything. He was so proud of you. I can tell you that if he were alive today, it wouldn't make one ounce of difference to that man. Knowing him for almost thirty years, that man is your dad. Jack Osborne IS your dad and there is no two ways about that."

I know Kelly well enough to know that he was not blowing sunshine up my skirt. He's a straightshooter, and he believed every word he said. I did too.

At about that time, which was 1:30 in the freaking morning, John Watson came through the concourse exit. It was the first time we had seen each other in person. We could see him coming from about fifty yards away. He was tired from his extended day of travel, as anyone would be, but when our eyes met, both his face and his pace stepped up. Becky and Kelly were there to record on their phones the first meeting of my cousin and me at this late stage in our lives.

"Hey, Cousin," I said as I walked toward him with my arms open to embrace him.

"Hey, Cuz," John said as we came together in a tight and extended hug.

The trip for him was a nine-hour ridiculous travel ordeal. It was a milestone for both of us. Until that moment the connection between us had only existed on the Internet, with a few Zoom calls and scanned pictures thrown in. We finally had the opportunity to move beyond the virtual world and into the physical one. It held a deeply significant meaning for me. The circle was complete. We both began to cry.

Becky and Kelly joined us in a group hug. It was surreal to have complete strangers embrace in an airport. It is a moment that I will take to my grave. Thank you, John Watson, for everything you did for me and for all the effort you put forth to help me find my family. If it wasn't for you, I would still be wandering around blindly, without hope of ever unraveling this mystery. God bless you, cousin.

John would spend three days with us enjoying the local flavors of Cincinnati: Skyline Chili, Graeter's Ice Cream, and other caloric/cardiovascular nightmares we associate with our hometown. We took great pride in introducing John to our daughters, son-in-law, and other family and friends. As Fate would have it, my stepdad, Jerry Condo, had traveled from Florida and was staying with us while John was here. We spent a couple of late nights on our back deck detailing and dissecting the family tree and comparing the information Becky had found with the oral history John knew. We even recorded John telling the story from his point of view, perhaps for a future documentary on the topic. It was a very special time.

The highlight of John's visit was the short trip we made to Anderson Township, the Cincinnati suburb where Peter and his wife Helen raised their family. It was a community we were familiar with for various reasons, never knowing the hidden connection nestled on one of its residential streets.

We easily found Peter's house and set out to walk the street. We hoped to get a feel for what he might have seen and experienced during his years here. Not one to be shy, I knocked on the door of the former Holmes house and spoke to the current owner to explain why we were there. She, unfortunately, knew nothing of the prior occupants. But through a stroke of luck, a neighbor sitting outside watching us directed us to a home whose occupants had lived there during Peter's time. We knocked, they answered. Yes, they remembered Peter vaguely but hadn't known him well. They did recall attending the raucous party that took place at the house after he divorced Helen and she remarried a nice man. It was all we learned.

From there we drove to the address that had first clued Becky into Peter's residence in Cincinnati. It was the initial discovery that would eventually solve the mystery of my biological father but hadn't begun to shed light on the man himself. The address had once held an apartment building but now was simply a parking lot. Across the street sat a new, upscale condo community for seniors. In another crazy coincidence, Becky's aunt lived in one of those condos and had hosted us there several times. It was frustrating to think we were so close to another of Peter's former homes and yet no nearer to knowing him.

John would spend three wonderful, conversation-filled days with us. Then it would take an additional three days to get him home to Prince Edward Island due to the never-ending delays and cancellations from Air Canada. I've flown over two million miles in my career, and I have had plenty of flight cancellations, but nothing anywhere near the three-day cluster that John's trip home became thanks to Air Canada. I can only hope he felt it was worth the trip.

CHAPTER 29

Memory Shards
That Make the Mosaic

The greatest discoveries are those that shed light unto ourselves. — Ralph Waldo Emerson

No matter how many times I tell my DNA orphan story, everyone asks the same question: Have I ever met my biological father, Peter Holmes? I have no concrete evidence that a meeting ever took place, but I guess it's possible. The first question is, did he even know of my existence? Did Barb know him for anything other than a one-night stand? Did she know his name? Was there any contact after the torrid night that produced yours truly? Was she able to discern I was Peter's son? An affirmative answer to the above questions would be prerequisite to us having met. I have no solid answers to any of them, and the person who knew the answers wasn't telling (or telling the truth).

I still try to piece together anything in my past that might be a fragment of a clue. What I am about to disclose is a thin hypothesis to say the least. Its evidentiary value is practically nil and would never be admissible in court. It, like the word "Miami," is a tightrope of reasoning that I am walking in the absence of any other concrete facts.

WHAT DO YOU WANT TO BE WHEN YOU GROW UP?

With those caveats in place, here is what I do have. I have a memory, a vague memory, that might support the possibility that Peter and I met at least once. It is one of my earliest memories. It only holds its place in my cerebral archives due to the commonality of its trigger. The trigger being one of the most common questions every small child gets asked: "What do you want to be when you grow up?" A fireman, an astronaut, or a baseball player were all popular answers of the day. They were role models represented in the media, people kids saw and admired.

My answer was less than common for my age and that era. I would say, "I want to be an aeronautical engineer." Those are not words that a three-and-a-half-year-old would acquire from his Saturday morning cartoons. "Aeronautical engineer" were not words that were bantered around the Condo House, nor did I pick them up at the bar on Friday night (I was a severely underaged drinker). But at almost four years old, when people would ask me what I wanted to be when I grew up, I suddenly began to answer, "aeronautical engineer." Of course, I had no idea what those words meant. I must have picked them up somewhere or perhaps had been coached to say them. Not by my dad, the city bus driver. Not by my older sisters. They wouldn't have known any better than me. I can only imagine that I might have heard those words from my biological father, Peter Holmes, a former employee of British Airways.

The aforementioned vague memory is of me sitting in the front seat of our family car, a blue Ford station wagon, with my mother at the wheel. We are parked and the windows are down. It's a hot summer day. My mom is talking to a man I don't recognize. He's standing outside the car, bending over, leaning on the door, looking and speaking through the driver's side window.

This is where the evidentiary value of the story goes out the window and supposition takes center stage. In an attempt to pull him away from his family, my mother introduces Peter to his son. Peter would be the next rung on my mother's social ladder, her next step in an improved life. She extolled the resemblance. She noted the absence of Jack's physical traits within me. She told him how smart his little boy was. (It was something I heard from her most of my life. I always felt it meant, "See what great babies I produce?")

"If he's really that smart, he could be an aeronautical engineer," the Canadian employee of British Airways possibly comments.

"Aeronautical engineer," his son parrots back to Peter. He and Barb both laugh. Kids pick up things so quickly and then repeat the words they hear. No matter how that happens, real or imagined, Peter and Barb likely do not see each other ever again. Within a matter of months, Barb would leave Jack Osborne for Jerry Condo. The interaction within the car that day is perhaps wishful thinking combined with a manufactured memory. I can't be completely sure. But over the years, I would watch an 8MM video of me saying those words: aeronautical engineer. The evidence is undeniable. My older sister Kathy, seven years my senior, and with a much better memory of that era than I, remembers those words, too—AND the blue Ford Country Squire station wagon.

* * *

LIFE AND FATE PULLS SIBLINGS TOGETHER

Kathy and I used to be so close, but as with many siblings, geography, spouses, and kids had put time and distance between us. We had forgotten that Kathy and her husband moved to Kentucky until a massive EF-4 tornado went roaring through her new hometown of Mayfield in December, 2021. That's when Kathy and I began our efforts to revive our relationship.

The renewal of our brotherly/sisterly bond would prove providential. On a road trip to Chattanooga, Becky and I decided to go a little out of our way to visit Kathy and Bob and to check out their tornado-ravaged town. We hadn't visited them since they left Cincinnati years prior. They decided that while Becky and I were with them, they would renew their wedding vows. After all, we were the ones who fixed them up thirty years earlier, so it made sense for us to be there. It was a wonderful opportunity to strengthen our ties and see the extremely happy home they had set up for themselves in Mayfield. Bob was blessed with a wonderful job working for fantastic people. They seemed set to ride out Bob's few remaining work years in glory.

Six weeks later, my cell phone rang very early one morning in May. It was Kathy. "Stevie, didn't you see my text?!"

"No, I didn't. I wasn't near my phone," I replied.

"Steve, my husband died this morning! Bob died!" Kathy wept violently on the other end of the phone. My heart immediately broke for her. She and Bob had discovered so much love together after each suffered a bad first marriage. What a joy it had been to see them so happy and know we had played a small part in it.

Within days of that phone call, Becky and I set out on the five-plus-hour journey from Cincinnati to Mayfield. The Masonic Lodge where we'd so recently celebrated their happy union and vow renewal was now the scene of Bob's funeral. Photos from the vow renewal sat on the front table.

The following Christmas, the owners of Bob's employer, Marine Solutions Inc., invited Kathy, Becky, and me to their holiday party in Lexington, Kentucky. They wanted to honor Bob for his significant contributions to the company and make sure that Kathy still felt part of the Marine Solutions family.

Kathy, Becky, and I met for drinks in the hotel lobby on the afternoon prior to the evening event. We were discussing our plans for the holidays and Kathy's plans to move back to Cincinnati to be closer to us and our half-brother, Adam. I was delighted at the thought of having her back home where I could more easily reciprocate the care Kathy had given me in my teen years.

After an hour of catch-up with Kathy over drinks, Becky looked at us and said, "I'd like to go up to the room and start to get ready. It takes me a while to get beautified."

That wasn't true. She is beautiful when she wakes up. Becky sensed the need for Kathy and me to talk about our past family matters. Becky's EQ is almost otherworldly. I attribute this to her hearing impairment. Growing up, she could not always hear the words of others, so she would read the non-spoken, visual clues.

"Thanks for the drink, Sweetie," she said with a smile and a wink as she turned and left us.

Kathy and I continued the conversation covering an array of topics. Central to those topics was how we both cherished our renewed closeness in the last few years. Those confessions came with tears. Tears of happiness for our closeness, cojoined with tears of sadness for the time that we had spent apart. I know I own the transgressions of separation. We are brother and sister, no matter who our respective fathers may be. Kathy took the opportunity and directed the conversation to some of her own memories.

A FRIENDLY STRANGER IN A BLUE SEDAN

"Stevie, I've been thinking more about this thing with Mom and your father, Peter. You know when you are young, things happen, and you don't really know what's going on. Well, this happened with me and Mom. I remember her on the phone with someone. I had no idea who, but I know she used the name Peter multiple times. It meant nothing to me, and I was so young. I never thought a thing about it. It never made any sense to me. But now it does."

"Sis, that doesn't shock me one bit at this point."

"I also have another memory that I want to tell you about. I remember Mom taking Carrie and me to a pool, like a public pool. I remember her talking to a man, a tall man with a dark complexion and really dark hair. I'm almost positive his name was Peter. Why would she do that?"

"Why would she meet him in public?" I asked. "She was rather bold; I'll give her that. Hide in plain sight, I guess." I turned the conversation slightly. I needed to fill in more of the mosaic. I needed to augment my memories by melding them with hers. I wanted to triangulate the things I thought I remembered with things I knew she would remember.

"When we were living on Aspenhill Court, in Forest Park, Mom and Jack had a car—" I began.

"Yep, a blue Ford sedan, a really long sedan," she interrupted, which I didn't mind a bit. For the most part she had just confirmed my memory of the vehicle.

"I thought it was a station wagon," I added. I was willing to concede this difference. I would have been three or four years old. She would have been about ten. Certainly, she would have a more accurate recollection.

"It was a really long sedan," she corrected me. I don't know exactly what a really long sedan is but nonetheless.

"But we had a blue Ford, yes?" I asked.

"Yes, sir, we did. In fact, that is the car you were almost killed in." Kathy was referring to an accident that happened the winter I was five years old. Barb, my younger sister Laura, and I were in the blue Ford and were coming home after skating on a pond or lake. I have no idea where we were when Barb hit a patch of ice and slid left of center into oncoming traffic. We hit another car head-on. Neither Laura nor I were wearing seatbelts—no one did back then. Barb was able to protect Laura by reactively extending her arm out to stop Laura from being thrown forward. But I was on the far side of my sister and out of reach. Into the dashboard I flew, face first. I spent the next two weeks in Good Samaritan Hospital. My face was bruised, battered, swollen and I had a severe concussion.

We continued the conversation about Barb and Peter with questions

Jack Osborne and the blue Ford station wagon.

about the incident still floating in our heads. Our memories were too distant, and we had no touch points to help bring them forward.

After the Christmas party in Lexington, Becky and I returned home, and the next day I was in my office at work. I spent most of the day facilitating two separate office suite renovations and general maintenance (toilets always leak) in the two multi-storied office buildings that we owned.

Becky had come into my office and asked me for a few spare folders I might not be using. I turned to a box near my desk where I had recently stashed some odd items and found about a dozen or so old pictures that my sister Laura had sent me months prior. I never really looked at them very closely because they were old and small and seemingly inconsequential. This time, one caught my eye. It was my dad, Jack, shirtless and barrel-chested with a beer in his hand. Standard issue Jack. He was sitting on the open tailgate of a . . . holy bat guano, Batman! It was a blue Ford Country Squire station wagon. I quickly snapped a picture of the picture and sent it to Kathy.

"What do you see in this picture?" I texted Kathy.

"Your dad having a beer. Looks like he is pulling a trailer?" she responded in a text message.

"WHAT is pulling the trailer?" I am making a point without making the point for her.

"Blue station wagon."

"The blue Ford station wagon we talked about in Lexington."

"It is . . . OMG!"

I didn't want to drive home to her that the Ford wasn't a long sedan. I texted back, "The picture is dated March of 1967. It's the exact car that I remember. The one that Barb and I were sitting in when she was talking to Peter. This picture was probably taken within a few months or weeks of the situation I described to you: me and Barb in that car talking to a man I believe was Peter Holmes."

"I remember the car now," Kathy continued. "That is the same car that we were in when Mom dropped me off at the pool and was talking to that tall man with black hair. I keep thinking about it."

"I'm pretty sure that car was totaled when Laura and I were in the accident with Barb that winter. Do you remember that?" I texted.

"Yes, I remember it like it was yesterday. You were in such bad shape, Stevie. We were so worried we were going to lose you." Kathy continued the text but not the topic, "Can't wait to get back to Cincinnati, we have a lot to talk about. Love you."

"I can't wait either. Love you too."

The picture referenced was fifty-six years old. It had drifted through our family shoe boxes and other archives for decades, never discarded. My sister Laura held it for who knows how long. When I requested that she send me some pictures to help put this whole 'you-can't-make-this-shit-up' story together, this picture was one in my discard pile. At first glance, it held no relevance. It would hold none until Kathy and I renewed our relationship, until we had multiple conversations about Peter, until my faint memories of a blue station wagon crept out of my semi-pickled, gray matter, and then, only then, would it reappear.

Gravity, matter, Life, and Fate. My person, my story, my chaos, once a supernova, are coalescing to form a new world.

CHAPTER 30

It Was All Part of the Plan

I love it when a plan comes together.
— John "Hannibal" Smith

About a year after my DNA surprise, I had lunch with one of my oldest and dearest friends, Matt. I wanted to share my discovery with him, primarily because he knows so many of the people involved in the story. He knows me like a brother. He is my non-DNA-sharing brother. My brother from another mother. I knew that Matt would have an attentive ear and a kind heart. I knew he would understand how badly this DNA surprise had hurt me. He was very aware of the closeness between Jack and me, as well as the struggles in my relationship with Barb. We met for pizza at one of our favorite local restaurants. Pizza makes everything better, even DNA nightmare stories.

I led Matt through a review of my extended and convoluted family vine (Arlene, Darlene, Charlene, and the eleven other siblings, etc.). He laughed and told me that the story never gets old because it's so hard to believe, but he knows it's real. He's heard it dozens of times.

"Well, hold on to your seat, my friend. It's about to get wilder than a drunken roller coaster ride." I tell him about Becky researching my family tree looking for some Native American link, then her ultimate frustration and suggestion that I take a DNA test. I tell him how the test results show no Native American DNA, but a cousin in Canada. I tell him about the "Harold's Me Uncle Theorem" and how that disappointingly failed and how "Jack's not my dad" reality took center stage.

All the time, Matt was making appropriate comments and expressing concern for my emotional state. I take him through my confrontation with Barb and the subsequent discovery of my rather distasteful origin story. I introduce him, virtually, to Peter Holmes. I show him the picture of Peter that makes any DNA test results superfluous. As I do all these things, my angst and frustration with Barb and her inability to come clean boils over into our meal. Matt attempts to draw away and divert the negative energy.

"Dude, you can't be mad at your mom," Matt pressed. I wasn't sure why he believed that, but I was certain I would convince him otherwise.

"Oh yes, I can. In fact, I've become rather good at it. I'm like an expert, almost Yoda-like at being mad at her. Did you know I teach a 300-level class on being mad at my mom, at Miami University on Thursday nights?"

Matt ignored my exaggerated response. "Ozzie, first of all, no sane person would ever give you the opportunity to influence America's youth. That's just crazy talk. Let's stop with that nonsense. But that's not the point."

"What's your point?" I was sure he couldn't have a convincing one.

"Ozzie, you are a different kinda dude, bro. You always have been. You've always stood apart from everyone else. Since the day I met you, what, thirty, thirty-five years ago? You do things I've never seen anyone else do. You have the ability to make stuff happen like no one else I know. Look at the stuff you've accomplished. I'm not blowing smoke, Bro, you're a different dude and you know you are." Matt was in his best sales mode. I wasn't buying it. Not to mention I think he grossly overstated my abilities and my successes quite a bit.

"And so, I just roll over? I just accept this bullshit and brush it off? Matt, you sound just like her. I can hear her in my head, 'I'm not sure what you're so upset about. Look at your life. Everything turned out pretty well for you.' What does that have to do with anything?! It certainly doesn't absolve her of her actions. It doesn't change the fact she has hurt the people she hurt," I protested strongly.

"Bro, I think you need to step back. I think there is a bigger picture here. A much bigger picture. The reason you can't be mad at her is because this was the plan, all along, from the beginning."

"I'm not tracking." My confusion was genuine.

"Like, before you came here, before Barb and Peter came here, they planned this. They planned you. They planned to get together in this life and they planned to have you. The things that happened were the only way that they could create you, as the person that you are. You are here because this was the plan. Their getting together, or whatever you want to call it—it was the plan."

"You mean like in the spiritual world . . . before my birth? Before their births? Like a we-are-going-to-Earth-so-let's-get-our-stuff-together type of plan?" I was incredulous.

"Exactly, my friend, exactly! A plan where each of us set out how we are going to experience life. The things that will help you grow as an entity, as a being. Also, who you're going to do it with."

"Okay . . . ?" I still wasn't 100 percent on board with this concept.

"And here's the kicker. It's my belief that you were there, too. You were in on the planning. This was part of your life plan before you came to this physical plane." Matt paused to let the percussion from that mind bomb subside. "That's why you can't be mad at her because you were in on it. It was your plan, too. You chose this. That's what I believe with all my heart."

I knew that Matt did believe it. He is a deeply spiritual person and his beliefs are genuine, even if they don't run parallel with mine.

Well, that perspective certainly was a new one. It had the element of having never been considered before. I am not a very religious person. More harm, more deaths, and more evil has been committed in the name of 'religion' than anyone can imagine. That is because religion is man-made. It's man's perversion of spirituality. Spirituality is a person's relationship with their Maker; whatever or whomever a person believes that to be. And while I am not 'religious,' I'm spiritual. Spiritual enough to be open to Matt's interpretation of the events. If Matt is the least bit accurate, and I somehow had a say in these events, then perhaps I should consider cutting my mother some slack. Very little slack.

I looked up and the pizza was gone except for a single slice. How did that happen? Who ate that entire extra-large pizza? There is never enough pizza when Matt and I get together. Matt is a true and dear friend. I surrendered the last slice to my friend (I would normally say 'my brother,' but there are too many of them in this book already).

CHAPTER 31

The Day Arrives

Everybody is going to be dead one day, just
give them time. — Neil Gaiman

Becky and I had just finished a year-end financial planning meeting with
our investment advisors and our attorney, Kevin. We don't consider
Kevin our "attorney" as much as we think of him as an extremely close
family friend who practices law. Kevin and I met in 2011 when the
senior partner at his firm introduced us. The senior partner was going
to retire, and Kevin would take over as legal counsel for our multiple
companies and eventually become a senior partner himself. Kevin and
I, despite minor differences in political views, favorite bourbon, and
the like, became fast friends. We both grew up in the same part of town
that carried with it certain attitudes and ways we viewed the world. He
became, and to this day still is, one of my closest confidants and knows
more about the entirety of my life than anyone other than Becky. Our
daughters refer to him as "Uncle Kevin—Attorney at Law."

The three of us were sitting in a specialty brunch restaurant
recounting and commenting on the previous hour's meeting when my
phone buzzed. It was a text from my sister, Laura. I quickly scanned the
message alert summary.

I knew that Becky and Kevin wouldn't mind if I quickly responded,
as it would give them a chance to talk to each other without my
interference. They were fond of discussing family issues and the most
recent events in our collective children's lives; softer stuff that I tend
to have less to comment about. Before I could read the message, Laura
was calling in.

I motioned that I needed to step away for a few minutes to take the call. "Hey, Sis, what's up?"

"Stevie, Carrie just called and said that she thinks Mom just died."

"Don't tease me," I said lightheartedly. Throughout the years I had found Carrie's assessment of Mom's health condition to be inaccurate and prone to extreme exaggeration.

"No, I think this is for real." Laura's response was missing the trademark breathy chuckle she has when talking about our typical family craziness.

"Okay, I'm in a meeting at the moment. Give me a few minutes and I'll call you back." I was not quite sure of the appropriate protocol for the situation. I didn't want to interrupt or end our lunch, but there was the death of a close relative involved. I quickly typed out a text on my phone, not to send, but to show Becky discreetly under the table. It said: "That was Laura. Barb has died." Becky reached over, took my hand, and gave it a squeeze. Both of us were debating in our own minds the best way to handle this situation.

I realized we were with one of our closest friends. If I can't be completely transparent in this situation; where could I be? I looked up at Kevin from my phone. He was looking over his reading glasses with an inquisitive smile and his head tilted forward as if to say, "What's up?" I shot Becky a glance, and she gave me an approving nod.

"Well, that was my sister, Laura. She was calling to inform me that our mother died this morning." The tone of my voice was sterile as if one attorney was speaking to another attorney.

"Oh, no," Kevin responded. He was fully aware of the strained and dysfunctional relationship between Barb and me, as we had spent hours discussing it over the course of our years together. "How are you doing with that? How are you feeling?" Kevin asked, as he always would in potentially emotional situations.

"Honestly, I don't know exactly what I'm feeling. I guess I'm shocked at how strongly I do feel about it. I had convinced myself that when this day arrived, I would feel nothing or even a bit relieved, or even, perhaps, a bit of elation." That last thought was as cruel as it was stupid. I was just presented the hard truth that she was gone, and I was feeling the finality which goes along with death. The sadness was registering within me in a much greater quantity than I had expected.

"I think you told yourself you might be happy, but that was just you fooling yourself in the moment. No one is truly happy with this loss, no matter the condition of the relationship. No matter what, she is your mother. She gave you life," Kevin correctly assessed.

I spent the rest of the day in and out of a state of mild melancholy in the shadow of the loss. I would say I genuinely "grieved" for less than fifteen minutes. The relationship didn't warrant more than that. If it did, our recent interactions eroded any compassion I had for her. My anger and angst easily defeated any fond memories that still survived within me.

CHAPTER 32

A Celebration of Life

Always go to other people's funerals, otherwise
they won't come to yours.
— Yogi Berra

In the days following our mother's death, the text messages continued between Laura, Kathy, and me. As Laura and Carrie continued to discuss the topic, they concluded a memorial service for our mother would be the proper course of action.

Carrie had posted on social media that Barb had died. Her acquaintances in the area were appropriately kind in their responses. Three people liked the post; I don't think they truly "liked" the announcement of her death as much as acknowledged it—but who really knows.

I was surprised by how quickly the gallows humor entered our text exchange, including the text from one of my sisters suggesting I should be the person who paid for Barb's funeral in its entirety. Everyone was aware I was going to receive absolutely nothing from the estate. Barb and I had been estranged for far too long for any inheritance to be even a remote possibility. My other sister asked if the sister who suggested the idea had been drinking. I suggested our third sister, the one most likely to receive Mom's entire estate, should be responsible for paying the funeral expenses. Doing so would ensure that there wouldn't be a funeral.

The issue of whether there should be a service and why were points of a philosophical divide. Laura, being the kind and loving peacekeeper she is, always wanted to do the right thing, the appropriate and respectable thing. I honestly didn't care. With each passing moment and each additional text on the topic, my resolve to NOT attend whatever service they planned grew. I was resentful her death was a topic of conversation that appeared on my phone. I was resentful of doing anything out of obligation to her or her memory.

Laura again asked about my well-being. I told her I was doing okay. I was sadder than I imagined I would be. I was reviewing my memories of our life. The good things she had done for us and the questionable things she had done to us. I told Laura my gratitude was in a knife fight with my resentment. I think my resentment had brought a gun.

SHOULD I STAY OR SHOULD I GO?

A Celebration of Life for Barb was set for February 18, 2023, at the Eagles Lodge. We found out about the service via the local newspaper, not from a phone call or email, a fact I found not overly shocking considering my estrangement from Barb.

Laura was lamenting that she was having trouble finding any reasonably priced flights back from Salt Lake City to Cincinnati. I encouraged her not to come. She, too, had eventually left the Barb Condo cult, and I feared she would be considered persona non grata.

There was nothing that would make me feel better about going. My reluctance was based in the feeling of what I felt she was owed. My relationship with Barb was not due my attendance.

I finally made up my mind. I was not going. PERIOD! In the days leading up to the gathering intended to celebrate my mother's life, Becky asked me if we were planning on attending. My answer was a consistent, "Hard pass." I had no intention of going. My heart had not softened one bit, and I felt no obligation to go and play nice with people whose opinion of me had been formed by speaking with my estranged mother. I didn't need the side-eye stares and whispering I anticipated would happen. Not to mention any interaction with my older sister, Carrie, who was with Barb when we had our final showdown regarding my misattributed parentage.

"Are you going to your mom's service?" Becky asked the question again just a few days before the event.

"No, I have no intention of going. In my mind, it's a waste of time." I was still firmly set in my position.

Finally, the day before the funeral, Becky suggested, "I think you should consider going. You might see some people you haven't seen in decades. It might be nice."

"That's why I'm not going. I don't want to see those people."

The morning of the service, Becky asked, "Are you going to your mother's service?"

"No. Why are you asking that?"

"Because you should. Get dressed. We're going."

I knew she was right all along. I was being resistant. I can't stand to be obligated to do something I don't want to do. I guess it was time to be an adult. That, too, can be unfamiliar territory for me.

* * *

Becky...

We had often talked about what we would do if/when my mother-in-law passed. I say "if" because for the past twenty-five years, she seemed to survive one medical crisis after another. Each one was supposed to be her final demise, but she'd inevitably pull through. I honestly thought she would outlive us all.

For me, Barbara's death was a relief from the negativity of her remote but constant presence. Over the thirty-plus years Steve and I have been together, I've been privy to countless stories of her neglect, lies, and egomania. I'd personally seen several examples of how she always considered herself the most important person in the room: at my bridal shower, at our wedding, and even during the birth of our first child. In her mind, she was the star of all those events.

At the end of her life, her refusal to tell Steve anything about his biological father or the details of her relationship with Peter was totally in character for her, but still deeply disappointing. She could have given her son some answers about his origin—something everyone has a right to know. It could have done so much to repair their deeply damaged relationship. But she chose to preserve her reputation over helping her son.

In those frequent conversations about how we would respond to Barbara's death, there was usually a debate around whether we would attend the funeral or not. That sounds callous, but if I thought Steve would experience more emotional trauma than healing closure by attending her funeral, I would certainly support his not going to it.

However, I've seen enough of life to craft my own motto: weddings are often temporary but funerals are permanent. I try to never miss a funeral. Therefore, I explained to Steve that we had to attend. Naturally he was resistant. Understandably he did not want to provide her with any respect. But in the end, he knew he had to be there.

Despite Barbara's long insistence on her Christian beliefs and lifestyle, the Celebration of Life was not held in a church. It was at the Fraternal Order of Eagles Lodge in the county seat. She had apparently not been connected with any one church for many years. When the day of the service arrived, Steve and I approached the FOE location with much trepidation. Who would be there? Would Steve receive any kind of backlash from Barb's few remaining allies? We weren't even certain what type of reception we'd get from within the family. We'd had no relationship with Carrie and her son for years. We didn't even know who the man was who would soon become her fourth husband. And Laura, who had for so long been Leia to Steve's Luke, had seemed somewhat distant since the DNA reveal. Supportive, but distant.

As we approached the front door of the venue, we passed a large young man in funeral clothing standing by the curb talking to what appeared to be a homeless person who was smoking. They seemed like an odd pair to have something to chat about on this occasion. As we continued up the few concrete steps to the door, Steve reached out to open it only to find it locked. What?? Suddenly the nicely dressed young man was at our side and reaching for his cell phone as he, too, tried to open the door. We heard him say into the phone, "Hey, I'm outside, come open the door." We quickly recognized him as Carrie's son, Allen, whom we hadn't seen in over a decade. Thanks to Laura's updates, we knew about Allen's dependence on welfare, his fathering of several children by different women, and a general lifestyle of living off the largess of others.

A rather heavy-set young lady opened the door for us. No introductions were offered, no acknowledgment was made between uncle and nephew. Allen simply pointed to the stairs and said, "It's down there."

Sometimes when arriving late to a party, everyone stops and looks up. It's a terribly awkward feeling and exactly what we experienced when we entered the crowded, noisy room at the bottom of the stairs. Thank goodness someone actually made the effort to welcome us. Laura's mother-in-law jumped up and gave us each a big hug. She had recently lost her husband, and I inquired as to how she was doing. It was a relief to engage in warm conversation with her.

Similarly, Laura's sister-in-law popped up from her chair nearby and made a beeline for Steve. She had also recently discovered that her father was not her father, and she could hardly wait to compare notes with Steve. I immediately knew we had made the right decision to attend.

Over the next few moments, I surreptitiously scanned the room to see who was present. Steve's sister, Kathy? No. His brother, Adam? Nada. Barb's live-in companion, Bonnie? Nowhere to be seen. Who were these thirty-five or so people?

Over the course of the next ninety minutes, I met several former employees and one-time foster children of The One Way Farm. Steve enjoyed reconnecting with people despite the unhappy and distant past they shared. Some attendees made it clear they loved and/ or respected Barb; others were simply cordial and murmured their condolences. A collection of photos and some food were laid out on a small table on one side of the room, but no one seemed to be taking any interest in looking at mementos or eating.

Eventually we joined up with Laura and her husband. Our conversation was mostly about their family and the recent death of Greg's father. Missing entirely was any mention of Barb.

I had virtually no happy memories of my mother-in-law and certainly did not want to look at her photos. One of them had been enlarged and was also on the cover of the small event program. With short blond hair replacing the long dark tresses of her youth and middle age, she appeared exactly as the cold and aloof person I remembered from my early married days. I had so wanted to forge a close and loving relationship with her but instead had been met with a brick wall. I came to learn it was all she was capable of.

SHOCKING BUT NOT SHOCKING

We arrived at the Fraternal Order of Eagles Lodge in Hamilton. I must be honest; it was not my cup of tea. It embodied so many things I had tried to distance myself from. It screamed Late-Last-Century Appalachia, but so did most of my family, so I guess it was a fitting location.

As we moved toward the entrance, we converged with two young men. Neither one I recognized even though one of them was my sister's son. We gained entrance to the building, which was locked, when my nephew called someone who was inside. I assume it was one of the multiple women who had borne his offspring. Nothing says "Welcome to our loving service" quite like a locked door.

Once inside, we were directed to the basement. As we entered the room, my sister Carrie approached and put her arms around me and began to cry.

"I'm so sad she is gone," Carrie said.

I have no idea what she thought she was doing. We are not that close, and she knew I didn't want the public display. Within seconds of Carrie separating herself from me, I was able to turn away and get a few more feet into the room.

I saw one of Laura's sisters-in-law approaching. I quickly remembered that Laura had told me her sister-in-law had experienced the same "your-dad-is-not-your-dad" NPE trauma. We spent at least fifteen minutes telling each other the details of our stories. I was sad for her, yet we were both comforted by the company of our misery.

Becky was right. Going to the service was the right and appropriate thing to do. It was quite an unusual event. I did see people I had not seen in over forty years, and it was good to see them again. At end-of-life events, people tend to focus on good memories and pleasant conversations.

As could be imagined, I was a little shocked by the candor some people openly displayed. I heard, "There were two sides to Barb. The Christian side and the side you got to see when she didn't like what was happening." I also heard, "Your mom had a causal relationship with the truth." While I agree with that statement, I was surprised that someone would actually say those words in a group of ten to twelve people about the recently deceased. Hell, even I wasn't going to say anything like that.

The coup de gras was when someone who had worked for her, whom I had known for decades, sat down next to me and her first words were not, "I'm sorry for your loss," but instead, "You know, I hated your mom." I had never heard anyone talk like that at an end-of-life event before. This person knew I was estranged from Barb. They were also aware of the recent DNA revelation and subsequent conflict, but damn, that's going straight at it. No beating around the bush. I don't think I want to be at my funeral. I can only imagine what mean things people will say about me. If it happens, I guess I deserve it.

The event and the day ended predictably. It was unsettling and emotionally wrought. A life milestone had been reached. The event had been completed. The tables and chairs were folded and stored. The leftovers were packed for later consumption. Someone turned off the lights. We each returned to our respective homes. I was left with my thoughts. Sixty years of memories and dreams of what could or should have been, wrapped in the chaos and pain of the prior sixteen months. I can't truly remember the weather that day, but my mind's eye tells me it was overcast.

RIP Barbara Jane Melton-Sayre-Osborne-Condo
(1937–2023)

On January 31, 2023, Barbara J. Condo died in Fairfield, Ohio, at the age of eighty-five. Any efforts made by her or me were insufficient to bring about any meaningful reconciliation . . . in this life.

PART FIVE
Moving Forward

CHAPTER 33

All That I Feared
I Would Lose

Eventually, everything connects.
— Charle Eames

Many years ago during the holiday season, our oldest daughter, Samantha, and I were in a big box store, something like a Walmart. Sammie was five years old. Old enough to wander in the store and be excited by the holiday lights and displays. It was a joy to watch the wonder in her eyes as the shiny objects caught her attention.

She continued to move from display to display as she scampered around the store. She became so engrossed with whatever was in front of her and whatever was next to her that she lost track of me. I never for a moment lost track of her. She moved to a place where a four-foot display had come between us. Her line of sight to me was blocked, though I was no more than six feet from her and watching her like a hawk.

In that moment, she looked up from whatever item of interest she had been looking at and she could not see me. She looked left, right, and then her face crumpled. She seemed to think I had left her. She panicked, as any five-year-old would do, and began to cry. I stepped around the display to come into her view. She extended her arms up toward me. Tears were already coming down her cheeks, though my perceived absence could be measured in single-digit seconds.

I picked her up and asked, "Baby, what's wrong?"

"Daddy, I was lost," she sobbed. I held her tight and wiped her tears.

"No, Sweetie, you were never lost. I knew right where you were the whole time." I wanted her to know that even when we can't see each other, I will always be there for her. I will be there for her, her mother, and her sister no matter what, even in death.

Being lost (or suffering loss) was a matter of perspective. She thought that I had left her, and she was alone. It was an illusion caused by a distraction placed between us. In this case, it was something shiny and a display taller than her. In my DNA journey, it was my temporary belief that a set of DNA test results meant Jack Osborne was not my dad. I had lost him to a spit-filled vial and an auto-generated email. Our disconnection and my loss were my reality in the moment.

In the end, I realized I had not lost Jack Osborne. I had simply misplaced my connection with him amid the stack of negative emotions and turmoil my DNA discovery had placed between us. Not only did I not lose him, but over time, I gained a greater appreciation for him, a greater desire to be Jack Osborne's son. It is a closer and stronger bond. All that I thought I had lost, I had gained.

My dad was my biggest fan. Throughout my life, he was the audience I was playing for. Making him proud was the nexus of my drive for success. Making Jack proud meant more to me than I ever understood until the day I lost him. And now I hold making him proud as a badge of honor I strive for daily.

The day I became a DNA Orphan, I feared I would lose my siblings, my family, my connections. Instead, the opposite happened. Each of the valued relationships, which were at risk, grew stronger. For many of my family connections, whose consanguinity was severed, we jointly decided to replace our connection of genetic obligation with a connection of choice based not on DNA, but on our love for each other. When I feared I would be expelled from my clan, my clan told me not to get any ideas about leaving. They would sit on my chest and hold me down if that was required to keep me close. I am truly blessed to have my family.

I am aware not every DNA Orphan experiences what I have. I know there are some people whose DNA test results set off a string of reactions, events, or decisions that bring great pain and/or significant loss. For those people, I extend my heartfelt sympathies. I pray they will find the family they were always meant to have. Perhaps we will meet someday, and they can add me to their extended family. I certainly will welcome them with grace, acceptance, and fully open arms.

DNA NUCLEAR DÉTENTE

As stated before, I am very different from my siblings in many ways. The most significant way was one that was never spoken of, the one that Barb held within her our entire lives. I am now aware that she likely knew I was Peter's son from the time I was very young. The circumstances around my origin, the dynamics it created between her, Jack, and Peter, were acidic and painful for her. It is my belief that early in my life, Jack suspected my true paternity. That suspicion likely contributed to Jack and Barb's divorce. It killed their relationship, but not the relationship between Jack and me.

At the time of my parents' divorce when I was four years old, his love overrode any issue of paternity. If he knew I was not his biological son, it didn't matter to him. That relationship was not going to change, and he made the decision to keep that information from me in the hopes of protecting me from the chaos the information would eventually deliver.

I have come to understand that Jack, Barb, and Peter each had a vested reason for protecting the secret of my paternity. Jack did not want to lose his only son of whom he was so proud; Barb couldn't afford to ruin her reputation as a religious benefactress to wayward children; Peter was not interested in upsetting the upper middle-class family life he had carefully constructed over the years. And together, the three of them most likely believed that keeping the status quo intact was the best course of action for me as well. They truly felt justified in their disassociation with the truth, and I can understand that. But in the end, it was me who paid the price for their deception.

Jack's desire to maintain a relationship with me, coupled with Barb's need for financial support, combined with the added complexity of my sister, Laura, Jack's true genetic daughter, whom he also loved dearly, made the complete decoupling of the parties unpalatable for everyone.

We believe that Barb was unable to convince Peter to leave his wife and adopted children to be with her and their biological son, so she kept him out of my life with the threat of revealing his infidelity to his family. Jack chose to ignore the facts of my true paternity in favor of keeping our relationship intact, a relationship that has paid endless dividends to both him and me. A relationship that is my bedrock. This dynamic held risks and costs for all three of them. It also held advantages for each. It was a three-way nuclear détente that became more and more difficult to alter or unwind with each passing year. Sadly, they would all carry this burden and their secret to their graves.

To Barb, I was the daily reminder of her choices and the interpersonal dynamics those choices created. I was the salt in the wound that would never heal. I don't doubt that Barb would look at me with pride. She would see a little boy with great potential, and at the same time be reminded of the manifest dumpster-fire of a part of her life she'd rather forget. I was an object of love and pride, as well as endless conflict, all rolled into one. Barb admitted in the end that it was this dynamic, those conditions, that created the negative energy within her. That energy caused a lack of closeness and a bitterness which led to the eventual rift between us, which lasted decades. Some things in life are a radioactive mess, and there is no cleaning them up. I guess I am one of those things.

Sometimes the greatest acts of love are to protect others at all costs. Sometimes the most selfish acts are to protect oneself at the expense of all others. Sometimes the two are indistinguishable from one another.

CHAPTER 34

Moving Forward

*You will find that it is necessary to let things go; simply
for the reason that they are heavy.*
— C. JoyBell

WALKING THE PATH

It took over two years for me to process the tectonic shifts brought on
by my DNA test results and to arrive at a place where I could say I am
okay with all the associated changes. After those two years of healing,
my personal saga has become a serious yet funny story I tell somewhat
frequently because it's so bizarre. But as I was living it, it was anything
but funny. Becoming a DNA Orphan (or NPE, if we're trying to be
official) in so many ways is like living through an earthquake.

In an instant, the walls began to shake and the earth shifted below
my feet. The violent shifts in reality knocked me on my ass and jolted
everything from the walls and shelves. I wondered if I was going to
survive. I immediately sought cover. When the shaking stopped, I felt
rattled, confused, and afraid. I looked around and saw the mess that
was previously my tidy world. I saw the chaos. I saw the life I knew the
day before, lying on the floor with little hope of putting it back together.
Then, when the aftershocks finally subsided, I did what I knew I must.
I picked myself up, collected the valuables, and swept up the broken
glass. I started putting my life back in order—a new order.

Some things left my life. Some new things entered. Eventually, I
went on with my day-to-day living, and most people couldn't see that

anything had changed. Oh, but it had changed dramatically for me. It was both earth-shattering and a non-event all at the same time.

In the end, I am settled with my new reality. I've accepted it. I've embraced it. Not that it doesn't still hit me emotionally from time to time, but generally, I'm good.

There were multiple good things that came with that DNA gut punch. The validation that I wasn't crazy is one of them. Well, I might be crazy but thinking that I was different from my siblings has been eliminated from the list of potential reasons. Now that I know why I'm different, I'm perfectly okay with the difference. I'm at peace with it. We all are.

I have had people inquire, "This had to be a devastating event for you, but you seem okay with it now. How did you get there?" The truth is, I didn't get there by myself. I was taken there. I was taken there by the love and compassion of my family and friends.

My wife Becky did much of the heavy lifting with significant contributions from my sisters and my daughters. Our closest friends were forced to hear this story dozens of times as it evolved. It was a form of self-therapy. They, too, helped move me forward in my healing. Thanks, guys, you saved me thousands of dollars.

The lunch I had with my friend, Matt, who framed these events as "all part of the great plan," helped me release much of the resentment I had previously held. Resentment is corrosive, and it will eat you alive if you continue to harbor it.

I owe so much of my healing to my wife Becky. She pressed the genealogical research. She suggested the DNA test. She found Peter Holmes (no small feat). She stood by me, and for me, when I could not stand upright by myself. She helped rebuild me. The process of losing Dad1, losing my family relationships, losing myself, and then finding us all again, was not unlike emotional chemotherapy. It was painful and difficult, but in the end, I am better for it. She held my hand and my head through the unsought and unplanned treatments I underwent to rid myself of the decades of emotional cancer. It was a familial cancer that had grown within me. She righted my ship. She was and is my keel. She saved my life. She saved my soul. She has done all these things with patience, loving kindness, and grace. There is a reason my loving name for her is Grace. It is because I have, undeservingly so, been blessed by God to have shared my life with her.

Should I ever make it to the Pearly Gates (the odds are heavily against it—I suggest you take the under on that one), I fear the tab I have accumulated. My debt to her and to my Maker for placing her in my life is beyond my ability to repay. Hence the name: Grace. I love her more than I have words. I'll love her even more tomorrow.

FORGIVENESS

People often ask me if I resent my mother's actions. They ask when they correctly identify something in my tone that sounds harsh. But the harshness is only tangentially related to my Non-Paternal Event. What people hear in my voice and misidentify as resentment for her actions is actually my frustration with her inaction. She had hundreds of opportunities to tell me what had happened. She knew I was seeking the truth. She knew I was struggling with not knowing. There are dozens of reasons I needed to know, not the least of which is medical history. She chose not to be honest with me, even when confronted with the insurmountable scientific evidence and data which displayed the facts.

But here's what I know: Life is screwed up. It's far from perfect. Each of us is far from perfect. People do some really stupid shit. They make bad choices. They can hurt others unintentionally or intentionally. The only redeeming path is to seek forgiveness for yourself and provide forgiveness to others. It is vital to our emotional well-being, our connections, and a healthy life.

It has taken me a great deal of time and introspection, but I am at peace with all the events that I have described in this book—EVERY ONE of them. Over time, I have even been able to get to a place where I am at peace with my mom. At one point, Becky asked if I had forgiven her. I said I had forgiven her. But my forgiveness is not what anyone might expect.

SHE DID THE BEST SHE COULD

Barb had a hard life and faced hard choices without the benefit of loving parents and wisdom to guide her. I do know this: she gave me my life. I must acknowledge that when she realized she was pregnant with me, she had a choice. She chose life for me. I'm here and I'm grateful. She loved me as best as she could as the person she was. How can I resent that? What is there to forgive in that?

As for her actions and choices, I will never truly know her motivations nor her thoughts. She may have done what she did because she needed money and thought that was the only way to pay the rent. Maybe she was just having a great time and didn't think twice about the ramifications of any of it.

As a friend of mine said when he heard this story, "Hey, it was the sixties. All that 'free love stuff' was common back then. Who knows, maybe your dad knew about it." His statement took me back to the original confrontation with Barb where her de facto defense of herself included this gem: "We did things back in the fifties and sixties and never gave a thought that we might have to explain them today." I guess that's as valid as any other position.

I do not judge or condemn my mother for her actions. I realize that there is no way I can. I am not her. I did not live through the events and challenges of her life. I was not there when she had to make her most difficult choices. It's clear that her youth and early adult years were extremely difficult. Those experiences forged and shaped her, as our own experiences shape each one of us. She made choices, and whatever those choices were, they were what she thought were the best ones given the tools and resources she had available to her at the time. She made choices that she wanted to, or was forced to, in order to survive. I know she had a difficult life. She did her best. Therefore, in many ways, there is nothing to forgive her for. I know she worked to give us kids a better life than she had. That is what every loving parent strives for. She exceeded that goal, and not by a small margin. I am thankful for that. Was it perfect? No. Was it the environment I would create for my children? Hell, no! Did she love us? Yes, I think as best as she knew how.

I do not need to forgive my mom. She did her best. I only need to love her. That would be the best I could do and what she deserves. So, I'm gonna go with that. Yeah, I'm just going to love her and I'm good with it. I'm good with all of it.

* * *

I started this path unaware. In the beginning I harbored anger and resentment. I felt disconnected, distant, and alien. I was confused and bewildered. I was ill at ease with most of what I knew myself to be. Like gravity, Life and Fate pulled at the elements of my past and pressed upon the wounded and troubled parts of me. They drew together the shards of my memories, my injuries, and the incompleteness of my person. They led me, or forced me, on a painful journey to revisit the source of my voids. They helped me discover the answers to the questions I didn't know how to ask. The journey disassembled me. It deconstructed me. Like a supernova, it scattered me to the cosmos. In many ways, it destroyed me. Only love and family resurrected me. They reconstructed me. But this time, the pieces I was previously missing were replaced with pieces graciously given to me by the people who love me. I am not saying I am perfect now. I am anything but that. But I am better. I have answers. I am at peace. I've lost the negative energy and the poison I previously harbored within me. Life is good and I am grateful.

Life and Fate and mass and gravity—I owe so much to
the forces that have guided my journey.
I am forever grateful.

CHAPTER 35

The True Definition of Family

It's the family you choose that counts.
— Andrew Vachss

DNA—IT'S FUNKY

Why do we put so much emphasis and weight on our DNA test results? Do we really need to? While our DNA does make us unique, DNA itself is massively more common amongst all living things than most people realize. For instance, most people don't know that humans and chimpanzees share about 98.8% of their DNA. Or that humans share about 50% of their DNA with a banana. Yes, a fricking banana! Those facts certainly help put this DNA crap into perspective, eh?

DNA is ridiculously common, and the DNA between us is ridiculously common. We each have so many individual elements of DNA (known as nucleotides, approximately three billion in the human genome). It requires science to "pick the fly shit out of the pepper," if you will, to simply match us to our lineage. Each DNA test is splitting hairs. In reality, it's splitting the same hair about 100,000 times. We are all much more alike than we are different.

I learned that family is not what we have been told it is. A birth certificate tells us who the government says is our legal family. A DNA test result tells us who science says is our family. Neither of those are correct. Our family is who our heart tells us our family is. They say, "you can't choose your family." That's just bullshit. We do choose our family. Family is not an obligation, not an edict, nor a mandate. Family is a choice. We choose our family, and they choose us. Only love and commitment defines family. My NPE experience has taught me this, and I believe it with all that I am.

Family are the people who love us because of who we are, but also in spite of it. They are the people who selflessly give of themselves to help us survive and thrive and never expect a goddamn thing in return, other than the hope that we might love them. They hold us in their hearts, and they hold our heart in their hands. They are the people that when the shit hits the fan—and we are on our knees—they are the ones who we know will run through a brick wall and place themselves squarely between us and our troubles. They pick us up. They brush us off. They kiss our head. They set us back on our way. That's our family. Genealogical lines are nice, but not required. A DNA connection is great, but not necessary. The people who care for us, who laugh and cry with us, whom we can stand completely emotionally naked in front of and know we are safe, that is our family.

Do not give up hope but instead let Life and Fate use their gravitational forces to pull us together with the family we deserve. Let us never forsake the people we love. Never let them go. Love the hell out of them. We must all find our family. We must find our peace. It is what makes us human. It's what gives us a voice. It is what makes us whole.

I Love You.
Blessings!

AND THEN THE STORY ENDS THERE BECAUSE . . .

The purpose for this book is two-fold. The first is I heard that writing is a great outlet for people who go through traumatic events such as I have (and it saves thousands of dollars in therapy). From that standpoint, it has helped me to see, understand, and process what I have gone through.

The second reason is that perhaps these words will help other DNA Orphans such as myself. The formal term may be NPE, which stands for Non-Parental Event, but I like DNA Orphan better. It's simpler, not as sterile as NPE, and I made it up.

However, when I think about how many times this journey could have ended, simply derailed, it is mind boggling. There were dozens of places where this story could have sputtered out, and we never would have found out the truth. If my mother had never told us her BS Native American story, this search never begins. If I never take a DNA test, this story ends before it begins. If my DNA test comes back with any significant amount of Native American genetic material, this story ends. If John Watson never takes a DNA test and there is no DNA match, no reason to question my heritage, this story ends. If John Watson never responds to the online message, we never make headway and this story ends. If Barb doesn't approach Jerry Condo at the funeral and ask him to sign a release for the book she's written, and Becky hadn't heard and remembered it, this story ends somewhat incomplete. Fate and gravity made sure that all the pieces and particles of this story drifted towards each other to complete my mosaic.

I am one who believes situations like this happen for a purpose. It is my belief that Fate or The Universe or God (for those who are spiritual) had a plan, and in these events, I saw said plan unfold. I don't know what that purpose may be for us. I hope it will, in some way, make a positive impact on the lives of others.

Maria the Medium

We have decided to include this additional content because it is something that happened to me along my DNA discovery journey. It is the transcript of a forty-five minute session with a spiritual medium. We are well aware that some people do not believe in the spiritual realm. If paranormal stuff is outside of a person's belief system, as it is with me, they shouldn't feel obligated to read this epilogue. My hope is that the readers have enjoyed what they have read to date. God bless. Or continue reading if curious about what the spiritual medium revealed.

I would consider myself an extremely healthy skeptic at a minimum. I am not one for psychics, mediums, or anything of that nature. I am too much of an engineer and logician to fully embrace the unseen, untestable, and untouchable. Having said that, I will not dismiss something simply because I don't understand it. Just because I can't get fully invested in the concept doesn't mean it can't be true.

* * *

When the defecation hit the rotating airflow device with regard to my DNA story, Becky decided to seek information from another source—outside of typical documents and records. Becky visited a local medium named Maria but didn't tell her why she was there. I listened to the recording of her session and candidly, I was shocked at the accuracy of the information Maria was able to communicate to Becky. With no prompting or leading from Becky, Maria was seemingly communicating with my parents, all three of whom had passed. Becky booked her appointment in hopes of hearing from my biological father, Peter, but my mother, Barb, pushed her way through. Barb communicated through Maria things that even Becky did not know or understand. But when I heard the recording, the messages resonated with me, the skeptic. I was able to explain the references Maria had made and they were unbelievably specific. Things a person would never say, or risk saying, if they were cold-reading a person because the odds of being correct are way too small.

After Becky experienced such a productive call with Maria, she asked if I would be willing to have a session with her. I gave a less than lukewarm answer (I meant "no"). It's just not my bag. Nonetheless, Becky decided to purchase a session for me as a Christmas present. She knew I would never schedule a time with her on my own volition. She gently forced my hand. I'm sure she thought it might help my journey or provide some form of relief or closure. I did not hold the same opinion. But when someone we love believes in something, and goes to the time and expense she did, a person must respect it, therefore, respect it I did.

I scheduled the meeting with Maria via her portal. I provided minimum information via the webform (and much of it intentionally false). I didn't want to give this person any foothold from which she might launch any investigative effort prior to the call. I am cynical and suspicious of potential charlatans. I am by no means leveling accusations toward Miss Maria, but I do believe there are individuals who are hurting and seeking a connection or comfort, and there are hucksters trying to separate those individuals from their money.

As the session began, I refrained from providing any information about who I was or how I had found Maria. I limited every answer possible to a very monotone "Yes, ma'am" or "No, ma'am." Our session was conducted via a Zoom call, using a guest account not associated with my ID, and a ginned-up email address. I turned my camera off so that Maria would have no visual clues about me or how I was responding to her reading. The only thing I presented was a monotone voice response. I also recorded the session for later analysis. I was confident she would say or do something that would give her away. No one can make blind guesses about your family and family situation for forty-five minutes and not get something materially wrong. The recording would help me identify any errors.

* * *

The session began with Maria quickly saying hello and adding a few pleasantries. Within the first minute, she asked if I was ready to proceed. "Yes, ma'am," I responded.

Maria explained how the session worked and that she wanted me to provide her with only limited feedback. She didn't want to hear details from me that might influence her. That was good to hear. That was already my plan. *Ok, let's get after it*, I thought.

Steve: Good morning. How are you?

Maria: I'm doing very well, thank you. How can I help you this morning?

Steve: That's a great question. I'm not sure. I don't know what else to say other than that.

Maria: Okay, so have you ever had a mediumship reading before?

Steve: I have not.

Maria: Okay. Are you interested in talking to your spirit guides? Do you want to talk to a trusted loved one? Do you want to find out about a past life? We can do all these things.

Steve: I guess, for me, I would be most interested in talking to anyone who has passed before me. [*Let's see where she goes with that*, I thought.]

Maria: Okay, is there anybody specific you're looking for? The only reason why I asked that is if you have a specific intention, and if I bring through someone else, it can cause you to feel some disappointment, and I just want to make sure that we are coming in with an open mind.

Steve: Probably not. I'm going to be somewhat vague. My ancestors, whoever that may be.

Maria then explained how the session would work, how she senses thoughts and images, how she would convey them, and how I could respond or ask questions, but only if I wanted to. I acknowledged the information with the same monotone "Yes ma'am."

Maria: Okay, do you have any questions before we get started?

Steve: No, ma'am.

Maria: Awesome. Can you say your name for me please?

Steve: Steve.

Maria said a prayer to begin the session.

Maria: Steve, as I step into your energy, the very first thing I see is a lot of question marks over the top of your head. I asked spirit what are all these question marks for? It's interesting . . . I don't know how old you are, but I'm in my fifties, and so they're doing this almost like the Riddler from Batman. It's like, riddle me this, riddle me that. They're showing it to me as though there have been questions about your life kind of throughout your life. Does that make sense? Like questions about your origination story? Does that make sense?

Steve: Yes, ma'am. [*How/why would she go there so quickly? How did she know that?*]

Maria: I'm asking them, "So what is the story? What does he need to know? What is he experiencing?" They're showing it to me, and the symbol that they're giving me is there's a closet and the door is shut, like the door is sealed or locked. There are things that we have kept in a closet that were purposely kept from you, as a way of, in their mind, keeping you safe. They were not telling you the full story. But as the child, the one who wants to know all these things, it can be very frustrating. Does that make sense?

Steve: Yes, ma'am. [*This was dead-on.*]

Maria: I definitely want to talk about a female force stepping forward. I want to talk about mom who steps forward and is . . . overwhelmingly remorseful. I can, I can feel her tears, I can feel her emotion. She wants to tell you how sorry she is that she didn't come forth with all the information, even though you found ways of asking her—she found ways of not answering. Does that make sense?

Steve: It does. [*Maria's description was exactly how it happened.*]

Maria: She just wants you to know that she's carried that guilt with her over to the other side. She is trying to process, and she shows it to me as though she has found small ways to get an apology to you from other people. Does that make sense?

Steve: Yes, ma'am. [*I have had multiple people address this topic about my mom. Again, an exact match.*]

Maria: I'm going to ask you a question, and this may seem very weird to you or it may not seem very weird to you. Has somebody in your family come to me for a reading with her before? Correct me if I'm wrong. Your wife came to see me, didn't she?

Steve: I'm not sure. I can't answer that. *[Yes, I lied to keep some bit of anonymity. How could she know this? I intentionally used bogus information and IDs on my appointment form to keep her from associating the two of us. I grilled Becky about giving away any information and she said she had no contact with Maria whatsoever.*]

Maria: It's okay. The reason why I asked that is I recognize this woman. I recognize her pain. I know this. I try not to let anything play into it, but I recognize her pain. You don't just forget this kind of guilt and this kind of shame and pain.

She wants me to tell you, "You were my world. I wanted you to have every opportunity, every possibility, and I never wanted you to be . . . I never wanted you to have to partake in my shame and my guilt. I never wanted you to feel any of that. So, I did what I thought was best."

Your mom shows me [an image of] pulling a veil over things and hiding it from you. She wants you to know how sorry she is for all of it. You should have had the right to have spent time and been with the man who helped to create you. She also says that your dad was your dad no matter what. But you have always felt kind of a missing piece through life. Does that make sense?

Steve: Yes, ma'am. *[I have always felt that something was missing. I was missing the genetic mirroring.*]

Maria: And she says, "I should have given you the key. I should have given you the key to unlock the door so that you could find out everything that you needed to find out without finding out accidentally." I don't remember if you knew if it was on purpose or not, but does that "accidentally" part makes sense?

Steve: Yes, ma'am. *[DNA test, by chance/accident.*]

Maria: And I want to talk about Dad, the man who raised you. Dad steps forward. He says, "I need you to know I loved you, no matter what. You are my son." He knew while you were growing up that you were not his. But he didn't allow that to interfere in the relationship.

They both wanted you to have as steady and normal a life as possible without being pulled into any more drama than you needed to. They're basically asking you for forgiveness. They are asking for understanding about why they made the choices they did. For not realizing that this information can affect someone so deeply on a level that nobody understands unless it happens to you. Does that make sense?

Steve: Yes, ma'am.

Maria: They both carry deep regret for this. And they want you to know they made the choices and decisions. This is hard for her to say, but she wants you to know that she made the choices and decisions not to tell you and to keep the other gentleman out of your life.

She says she understands that anger comes with that. She knows there's a lot of processing that you need to do to work through that. She's just hoping at the end of all the processing, all of the guilt, all of the anger, or everything, that you'll be able to forgive her. She really did have your best interest in mind.

She says if you look at the two of them, the man who raised you had a much better background and a much better stability than the man who created you. She says, "That is what I wanted for you. But I had no right to take that away from you—none." She says, "I'm just asking your forgiveness."

Now I want to talk to you about the biological father who is stepping forward. He says to me, that without you even realizing, you carry a lot of his mannerisms. A lot of things about you that are very much like him, even if you don't know it. He says he always carried a missing piece of his heart with him because you were not there and you were not in his life.

He says that he wants to acknowledge being able to see you now as the man that you are, and he says that he wants to acknowledge you leaning toward some OCD and control tendencies. He says this is because you are trying to control the small things that you can control because so much was taken away from you. Does that make sense?

Steve: Yes, ma'am. [*I am mildly OCD. I fight my propensity to be a control freak.*]

Becky: [*He is a control freak.*]

Maria: They're acknowledging some of the choices and decisions you've made in your life have been because of how you felt kind of like an outsider, even in your own home. And not necessarily you know in the house where you've created but growing up. Does that make sense? Knowing that you belong but kind of not belong?

Steve: Yes, ma'am. [*Dead on.*]

Maria: He says you made much better use of your intellect than he did. He talks to me about how smart you are and that you have made such good decisions when it comes to finance and investing and taking care of your family. You have made all things possible for your family because you never wanted any of them to feel the way that you felt. Does that make sense?

Steve: Yes, ma'am.

Maria: He says don't feel like nobody wanted you or "I was this or I was the family secret." It was none of that. "We all did what we thought was best for you." He wants you to know that you turned out to be an amazing man. And he talks to me about you being both a disciplinarian and a loving man at the same time, being able to be both. Does that make sense?

Steve: Yes, ma'am.

Maria: He says that you have found a balance that other people couldn't. He's showing me something that I don't quite understand and maybe you do. I don't know if people have these anymore. I mean, I guess they do. He shows me like a leather briefcase and if I were to open the briefcase, there is something personal related to him [Peter] inside the briefcase, but he's not showing me what it is. Does that make sense to you?

Steve: Yes, yes. I believe it does. [*In my leather briefcase, inside my leather portfolio, I carry a picture of Peter Holmes. It was given to me by my cousin, John Watson. It is the only physical item I have with a connection to Peter.*]

Maria: He says, "That man has one of the neatest closets I have ever seen."

Steve: May I ask a question?

Maria: Absolutely. Please.

Steve: A question for my dad. Not my biological father.

Maria: Yes.

Steve: Is he okay? Is he okay with all that has happened?

Maria: Yes. Yes. He is. He's good. And he is happy. He wants you to know how much he loves you and how proud of you he is. He says, "I know I didn't make all the best decisions. But raising you was one of the best ones." He loves you tremendously. I'm trying to find the word to express this correctly. He wants you to know his love for you and his relationship with you was a reason why he stuck around with your mom.

Steve: That makes sense. Yes.

Maria: Yeah. He shows me that she can be very difficult sometimes.

Steve: He's being kind.

Maria: That's why he wants you to know he stayed for you. She wants you to understand that she was so difficult because she never wanted anybody to know she carried so much guilt and shame that she was angry all the time. She didn't know how to talk about it because we don't talk about those things. She'll have to deal with that and she is.

He was so grateful for the relationship that the two of you had—so grateful. He's glad that everything is out in the open and you know everything, and you can finally feel peace at the end once you're able to find forgiveness for all of them—fully.

Steve: Okay.

Maria: He kind of smiles at you. He says, "You know, he never would have made this appointment voluntarily." But he's glad that you did so that he could speak to you and tell you how much he loves you. Also, this is the closure that you didn't know you needed or wanted? Does that make sense?

Steve: Yes, ma'am. [*How in the hell does she know this?*]

Maria: Do you have other questions you want to ask me? I'm happy to answer them.

Steve: I would just like to hear anything from my mom if she has a message.

Maria: I see her with tears, and she is expressing to me not through words, but through vibration and emotion. That these are all emotions that she wished she could have shown to you while she was here. She hid them all behind a brick wall that was very difficult to penetrate, and she wants to acknowledge making it very difficult at times for her to be loved. She knows that you do love her. And she wants you to know, "I loved you the whole time, and I loved you in the only way that I knew how." Does that make sense?

Steve: Yes, ma'am.

Maria: She truly is hoping for you to be able to find forgiveness in your heart. Because she shows me that there were such times that she could be just cold, more than anything else. Very cold. And that's not what a little boy needs. It's not what a teenager needs. Sometimes they needed to be loved, and she didn't know how to do that.

She's learning how to process her emotions. And she wants to say, "I know that I don't expect you to say, 'Mom, I forgive you. It's all cool right now.'" She goes, "But I just needed you to hear that I am sorry, and that I do love you, and that I am proud of the man that you have become."

She wants to acknowledge how you're a much better parent than she ever was. You have taken lessons from her and said, "That's what I don't want to be," and flipped it around to become someone so much different. She says that you have incorporated the love from your dad into your life and allowed that to be more of a soothing salve than anything else. "Well, at least I had him," and she says that I am grateful that you did that. "I just hope that one day in your heart you'll be able to forgive me and know that I loved you."

"I was just too angry to work through my own stuff, and now I have to work through it." She's going through some of it now, which is why she's able to cry and express her emotions, and she's grateful that she had you in her life. She said, "I know it may not feel that way. But I am grateful that you were there. I'm grateful that I brought you into the world. And I'm grateful that you have beautiful children, and I'm grateful that your family is growing."

Steve: You believe my dad, the man who raised me, knew he was not my biological father?

Maria: Yeah, he did.

Steve: Hmm, well then, he's a hell of a man, isn't he?

Maria: Yes. Yes, he was. He never cared because in his heart, you were his boy. No one was taking that from him. He puffs his chest out. He says, "He is the way he is because of me." He says, "I will take full credit for the man that he's become." Is there anything else I can do for you today?

Steve: I don't believe so.

Maria: Thank you so much for being willing to come on here with me. I appreciate it.

Steve: Thank you very much for your time.

The Zoom call ended with me sitting in astonishment. We spoke for almost forty-five minutes. She did not say one thing that was inaccurate or off. Her words and concepts were extremely specific. Many of the things she said were counterintuitive or the opposite of normal convention. If she had been guessing, or cold reading, she would not have gone to the places she went to. If this was a parlor trick, it was a damn good one.

Genuine, fake, or imagined, it doesn't really matter. It helped me remember and process the things I needed to process. It helped me remember the love that my parents showed to me. It helped me release much of my resentment, my anger, and my guilt. The rationale and comments regarding my origin have all been confirmed through other sources. It did help me heal. I guess the healing is the only thing that needs to be real.

ACKNOWLEDGMENTS

I am eternally grateful to my first cousin, John Watson. By the simple act of taking a DNA test, you set me on a life-changing quest for the truth. Without your responses and assistance, I would still be seeking answers to the most basic of questions. During my NPE journey you offered infinite patience and kindness at the risk of revealing something unpleasant or shocking about your own family. Thank you for being the Rosetta Stone of my DNA search.

To my sisters, Kathy and Laura, for all your love and understanding of our shared past. You alone know how deeply this affected me. Thank you for being there for me.

To my stepmother, Mary Ann Osborne, stepbrother/second cousin* Jerry Osborne, and the whole Osborne clan for not abandoning me when you could have simply walked away. We are "family by choice".

To my in-laws, the Brower Clan, for showing me what a real family can truly be.

To our friends the Throckmortons who lived this story with us as it unfolded and were forced to hear it a dozen times as I worked through the chaos. Other family and dear friends who lent a listening ear: the Kellys, Sadlers, Salzanos, Foxes, Stolls, Snyders, Beshears, LaFleurs, Wilsons, Coopers, Klebenows, Matt Campbell, the late Matt Hakes, and many others whom we encountered through parties, business meetings, and NPE gatherings.

To our beta readers, Jo, Helen, Carolyn, Eric, Michele, Terry, Jon, Lily, Robin, John, and the Lebanon men's book club, thank you for your efforts in turning this therapy project into a publishable product.

To my first comrades in the NPE community, Alexis Hourselt, Jon Baime, Lily Wood, Betsie Norris and many others, thank you for laying the groundwork for sharing my story.

To Kara Rubinstein Deyerin, our incredible publisher, cheerleader, and guide in all things NPE. As an early champion of the misattributed parentage community, you knew and understood only too well this journey and its profound effect on my psyche. That you are also a publisher was a fortuitous stroke of good fortune for us. Your guidance set me on the path to convert what I considered my misfortune into something I can share and hopefully use to help others as you have helped me. We are grateful to the team at Black Sheep Library.

And always, to my wife Becky and daughters Sammie and Jackie. For all the love and support you have provided me. You are the center of my universe. That will never change.

ABOUT THE AUTHORS

J Steven Osborne

Steve is a successful tech entrepreneur, sales trainer, commercial real estate investor, and professional speaker in a career that has spanned over 30 years. His combination of wit, substance, irreverent humor, and exceptional story-telling skills have made him an audience favorite. He graduated with degrees from Miami University and Embry-Riddle University. Steve and his wife Becky are the parents of two grown daughters. He is one of the few people who has produced content which has won an Emmy, and another which was banned on six continents.

Becky Brower Osborne

At 18 months old, Becky contracted spinal meningitis which left her severely hearing impaired. Despite that challenge, she graduated from Miami University and worked several years as a tech analyst for GE and later as a small business executive. While raising two daughters she started a major community service effort in her city. In 2015 she received a Cochlear Implant to restore her hearing and now advocates for and supports the CI community. Married to Steve Osborne since 1993, she currently divides her time between writing, genealogy research, and being present for her family and friends.

J Steven Osborne & Becky Brower Osborne

The End

www.ingramcontent.com/pod-product-compliance
Lightning Source LLC
Chambersburg PA
CBHW072057020426
42334CB00017B/1538